# Pocketguide to

# EASTERN STREAMS



T. TRAVIS AND SHANDA BROWN

STACKPOLE
BOOKS

*To Jolie and Bristol*

You are the loves of our lives and the reason for everything we do. We pray that this book will help to instill in you a love for things that are real and natural, and the knowledge that the most important things in life cannot be bought or sold. It is the realization of a lifelong dream for both of us, and we hope it shows you that, if you work hard, your dreams can come true.

---



Published by
STACKPOLE BOOKS
5067 Ritter Road
Mechanicsburg, PA 17055
www.stackpolebooks.com



Printed in China

10 9 8 7 6 5 4 3 2 1

First edition

Cover design by Wendy A. Reynolds
Photographs by the authors except where otherwise noted

**Library of Congress Cataloging-in-Publication Data**

Brown, T. Travis.
Pocketguide to Eastern streams / T. Travis Brown and Shanda Brown. — 1st ed.
p. cm.
Includes bibliographical references and index.
ISBN 978-0-8117-0640-7
1. Rivers—East (U.S.) 2. Stream ecology—East (U.S.) I. Brown, Shanda. II. Title.
GB1216.B76 2011
577.6'40974—dc22

2010053888

# Contents

# Why and How to Use This Guide

Water has the power to draw all of us. We have a primal, basic need for water, so it's no surprise that our streams, lakes, and oceans draw billions of visitors every year. When we are children we have a natural curiosity for what we see while we play around the water, and if we're lucky, that curiosity continues into adulthood. This book is intended for anyone who spends time around creeks and small rivers. It is dedicated to all those who love to walk or paddle along streams; to the rock flippers, the fishermen and fisherwomen, the naturalists, the educators, the moms and dads, the grandparents, the children, and to all of us who enjoy the amazing things there are to learn, teach, and discover along the arteries of this earth.

## WHY THIS GUIDE?

To look at only the underwater stream environment or only the land next to a river (the riparian zone) would be to get only half the picture. There are excellent guides on each group of plants and animals covered here. We wanted to produce a guide that would help you identify what you see both above and under the water while walking, wading, fishing, or canoeing along some of the most productive and diverse environments in the U.S.

It is our hope that this field guide loses its corners and the pages become rippled with water damage from being used out in the field! There is no substitute for getting into nature and getting your feet wet. We have attempted to include animals and plants that are most commonly encountered along our eastern streams. Most of these streams can be explored by wading, canoeing, or kayaking, and we have elected not to cover species that are mainly found in huge rivers and reservoirs. In some cases we have included relatively rare species because they are such great examples of adaptation to the stream environment (*e.g.*, hellbenders). Some animals included here, such as many of the birds, are not restricted to stream habitats at all but will be seen there quite often because they are common or because, like most animals, they are attracted to water sources. Because there are so many types of streams and so many species, we can't cover everything. After all, there are at least 3,500 species of flies alone that have aquatic larvae! We didn't even scratch the surface for most of the groups. However, this book should help you identify most

things that you see to some level, see a more complete picture of your stream environment, and understand more about how all of the plants and critters in these amazingly diverse habitats interact. If you want to delve further into any of the groups covered here, we have put together a list of excellent resources in a categorized bibliography at the back of the book.

## HOW TO USE THIS GUIDE

Field guides are often organized according to taxonomy. The most primitive groups are usually at the beginning and the most advanced groups are toward the end. This works well if you are very familiar with the particular kind of organism (for instance, birds) but makes little sense if you are a complete novice. In addition, new developments in our understanding of the evolutionary relationships of plants and animals causes frequent reorganization of these evolutionary organization systems. Because few people are likely to be familiar with the taxonomy of so many different groups (and most of us just flip through the pictures anyway), this guide is organized according to the most intuitive methods we could come up with. The organization of the identification sections is as follows:

- Plants are grouped by flower color. Within colors, plants are grouped by family.
- Shrubs and trees are grouped into families. The first trees and shrubs described are those with simple leaves, followed by compound-leaved species, and then conifers.

- Vertebrate animal groups (fish, amphibians, reptiles, mammals, and birds) are organized from smallest to largest in body size as much as possible. However, families are kept together because they share important characteristics that may help you to quickly narrow down the animal you are trying to identify to a few members of a family. For instance, rodents are all together even though they range in size from a mouse to a beaver.
- Invertebrates are grouped loosely from the simplest body form to most complex. This means that worms and invertebrates with wormlike larvae come first and things that always look like "normal" insects come last.

This guide is designed to be page-flipper-friendly. We have attempted to put the taxa that look the most alike together, and in some cases animals are covered at a taxonomic level that includes many species (*i.e.*, at the order, family, and genus levels). Where it is beyond the scope of this book to differentiate the species from all look-alikes, we have attempted to list important anatomical features. These would be good features to photograph or take notes on so that you can confirm the identification later with the help of the internet or specific taxonomic references.

CHAPTER 1

# The Physical Character of Streams

You may live close to a wonderfully clear, small stream that runs into a big, muddy creek. Have you ever wondered why the streams are so different? Each stream has a character all its own that is based on the surrounding geology, elevation change, land cover, and history of human alteration. Some streams are naturally clear, no matter how "messed up" by humans they really are. Some streams are in pristine condition but still have dark, tannin-stained water. The way a creek naturally looks depends a lot on its geology and morphology (the size, shape, elevation gradient, and other characteristics of its channel), and these characteristics vary according to where you are in the world. In the sections that follow we explain how streams are described and what factors influence their characteristics.

## STREAM SIZE

The size of a stream can be measured in many ways. The smallest beginnings of a channel formed by running water are typically called rills or ruts, but the vast number of other names tend to mean different things to different people. After all, it is not uncommon to come across "creeks" or "brooks" in one part of the country that are larger than channels that would be called "rivers" in other parts of the country. One simple, three-level classification system is often used for stream-monitoring purposes: headwater, wadeable, and non-wadeable. Usually headwater streams can be crossed wearing a pair of knee boots, wadeable streams require chest waders, and non-wadeable streams are going to take a canoe.

Another way of measuring streams is by stream "order." Stream order is determined from 1:24,000 scale U.S. Geological Survey topographic maps. On these maps, the smallest recognizable streams (headwater streams) are called first-order streams. When two first-order streams join they become a second-order stream. When two second-order streams join they become a third-order stream and so forth. However, two streams of the same order must join in order to increase the order number. For instance, a third-order stream that is joined by a second-order stream is still a third-order stream.

Another way to measure the size of a stream is by measuring the size of its drainage basin. The drainage basin (also called the watershed or catchment)

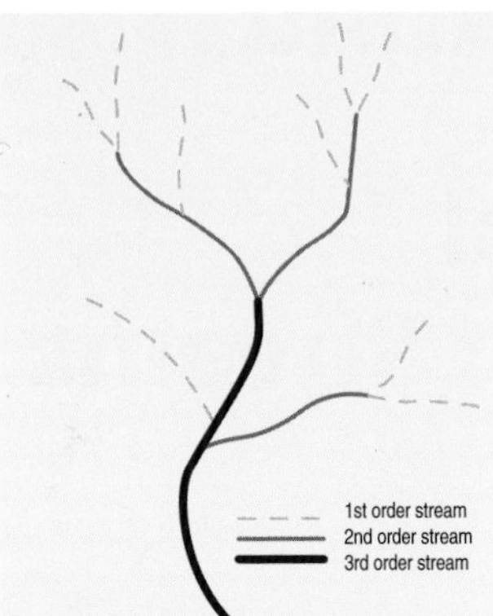


*How streams are classified by stream order.*

includes all the land that is drained by a stream and determines the volume of water that will make it into the stream channel. For instance, the drainage basin of the Mississippi River extends practically from the Rocky Mountains to the Appalachian Mountains, while the drainage basin of the small rivulet of water that runs through your yard when it rains may be only a few acres.

The size of the drainage basin or watershed is linked to a stream's discharge, which is another measure of stream size. Discharge is measured by determining the volume of water that runs down a stream every second and is typically represented by cubic feet per second (abbreviated cfs). The Mississippi River has an average discharge of about 600,000 cfs, while a small stream with a 100-acre watershed may have an average discharge of less than 1 cfs. Streams in the eastern U.S. typically average about 1 cfs of flow for every square mile of drainage area, but many factors can influence this, including local rainfall, contribution from springs, land use, and geology.

Although not exactly a measure of size, streams can also be characterized in terms of the amount of the year that they hold water. This is referred to as their flow regime. Ephemeral streams typically only contain water after precipitation events, intermittent streams contain water seasonally, and perennial streams contain water year-round. Perennial streams typically have some contribution from an underground source and continue to flow even when water from recent rains has passed.

## Stream Morphology

The length of a stream channel can basically be separated into a series of four parts: riffles, runs, pools, and glides. Riffles are the areas where water runs swiftest and shallowest. These areas are often found over a rough bottom of gravel, cobbles, or boulders. Constant splashing at the water's surface makes this the most highly-oxygenated area of the stream, and as a result, riffles can be home to a high diversity of invertebrates and fish. Runs are also areas of fast-moving water but typically occur where the water is not shallow enough to cause a lot of splashing or rippling at the surface. Pools are the ponds of water located in slow-moving portions of the stream. Pools can occur where water piles up before going through a riffle and are often found at the outside of the bend in a meandering stream channel. A glide occurs where the slow-moving water of a pool begins to speed up as it flows out of the pool.

*An ephemeral stream.*

*An intermittent stream.*

*A perennial stream.*

*Riffles and waterfalls are important areas for oxygenation of water.*

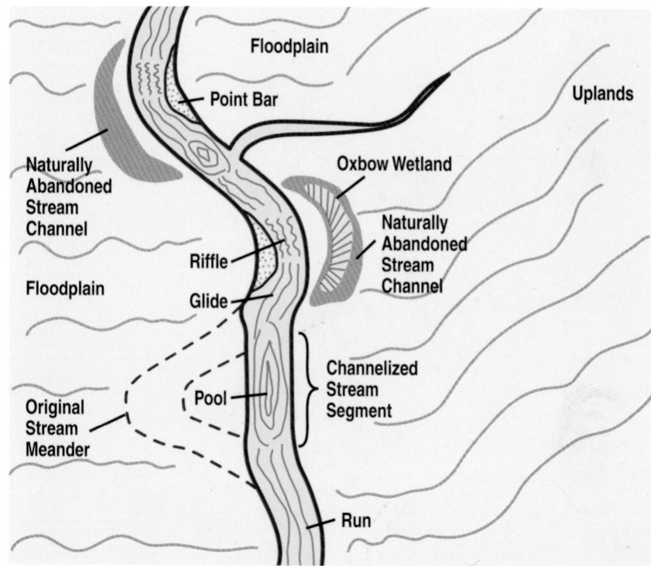


*Basic parts of the stream and floodplain.*

Stable riffle-pool sequences tend to repeat at a rate of one riffle for every five to seven stream widths. However, many coastal plain streams, ditched streams, and slow-flowing bottomland systems don't have riffles. Instead, these streams tend to consist mostly of slowly moving runs and pools, but they can form features that resemble riffles where buried logs or deposits of hard clay perturb the water's surface. In very steep streams, such as those found in mountain areas, streams tend to consist of "step-pool systems." Here, water flows from one plunge pool to another over a series of waterfalls.

Natural streams tend to meander across the landscape. The outsides of bends erode, and sediment gathers on the insides of bends, forming point bars (also known as sand bars or rock bars). The part of the channel where the majority of the current travels is referred to as the thalweg. In natural streams there is typically a "low flow" channel where water is found under normal conditions and a "bankfull" channel that is only full after extensive precipitation. Over time, streams can build extensive floodplains, erode canyons, and leave a complicated pattern of abandoned channels and oxbow wetlands that tell the story of a stream's history.

Elevation change is one of the biggest factors influencing a stream's character. High-gradient streams are those that rapidly change in elevation, and their water flows relatively fast. This type of stream is often found in hilly or mountainous areas. Low-gradient streams are found where there is

*Streams naturally shift over time, leaving behind abandoned channels that often become wetland sloughs.*

little change in elevation along the length of the stream, resulting in slow-moving water. This type of stream consists mostly of a long, slow-moving pool and is typical of flat coastal plains, prairies, and valleys. In much of the eastern United States, a typical pattern is for many small, high-gradient creeks to join into large, low-gradient rivers. Some of our larger rivers begin flowing in cold, turbulent mountain streams but end up as low-gradient, brackish tidal rivers. Where small streams begin on flat land, such as the prairie or coastal plains, they often resemble shallow wetlands. In these situations, creeks may develop small channels for short distances between wetland areas, but often these systems wait until further downstream to form long, continuous channels.

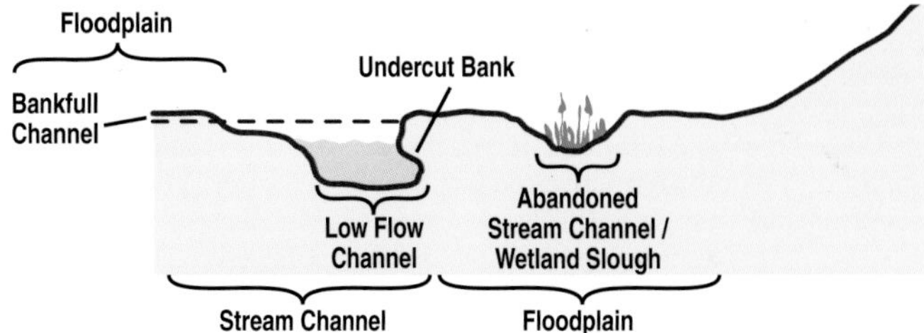


*Basic cross-section of a typical stream.*

## SUBSTRATE

In addition to drainage area and gradient, streams are also shaped by geology. Sandstone, limestone, glaciated soils, granite, or sand from the bottom of an ancient sea all result in different availability of nutrients, water clarity, and sediment sizes. For instance, streams that run on a layer of granite bedrock tend to have very clear water and few nutrients available to algae and other organisms. In contrast, streams running through fertile, glaciated prairies are often relatively turbid and rich in nutrients that feed algae, which can make the water cloudy.

Size is one of the most important characteristics of substrate. Sediment is typically classified according to the Wentworth Scale. For most purposes, the following categories will provide you with the ability to classify a stream's sediment:

- boulder (averaging human head-size or bigger, >256 mm [10 in.])
- cobble (softball-size on average, 64–256 mm [2.5–10 in.])
- pebble (ping pong ball-size on average, 16–64 mm [0.6–2.5 in.])
- gravel (between sand and marble size, 2–16 mm [0.08–0.6 in.])
- sand (0.063–2 mm [0.02–0.08 in.])
- silt (0.0039–0.063 mm [0.001–0.02 in.])
- clay (<0.0039 mm [0.001 in.])

In addition to the above categories, woody debris and decomposing organic matter can also be important components of a stream's substrate.

In streams with cobble or large gravel there are spaces (called "interstices") between the stones where invertebrates such as stoneflies, mayflies, and caddisflies live. Other stream bottoms may consist of silt or thick deposits of organic matter. In this case, woody debris may be the only hard substrate to be found. Mud-bottomed systems are more likely to be inhabited by things like midge larvae and aquatic oligochaetes. There are certain types of mussels, snails, crayfish, fish, and other organisms that tend to live in gravel and cobble substrates and there are other species that tend to be found in silty, organic substrates. Even within a single stream, substrate can vary greatly from area to area. Riffles usually have the largest substrate, while the bottoms of pools tend to be made up of finer sediment particles that can settle out of the water column in the slower current found here.

## STREAM ALTERATION

Humans began changing the courses of streams long ago. Stream alteration most likely began with small ditches dug to drain our habitations and water diversions to irrigate our fields. Eventually, we built larger drainage ditches and canals for transportation of goods and for flood control (although much of our channelization has actually made flooding more frequent and destructive). With the advent of highly effective digging machinery and huge, organized efforts of agencies like the Tennessee Valley Authority and U.S. Army Corps of Engineers, we began to change the riverine landscape on a scale that had only ever been matched by glaciers. Huge dam projects helped dig us out of the Great Depression and brought electricity and income to rural parts of the country. Meandering streams were straightened into drainage ditches in order to increase the speed with which water could be drained from land that we wanted to use for farming, timber harvest, and industry. The height of stream channelization occurred in the mid-1900s, but small efforts to "clean out" streams or "improve" streams still occur today.

Stream channelization is the most common term for straightening and deepening a stream (turning it into a ditch). There are several other landscape changes that generally accompany stream channelization. For instance, parts of the drainage basin are usually converted to row-crop agriculture or pasture that impart fertilizers and other chemicals to the water. In addition, the riparian corridor is diminished or destroyed by clearing or by the trampling and grazing of livestock. As a consequence, the banks erode and then slump into the stream—imparting huge amounts of sediment to the water. This increases a stream's load of suspended sediment (turbidity), which fouls the gills of many aquatic organisms and prevents sunlight from reaching aquatic plants.

Changes in a stream's watershed can change the stream channel, even if the channel itself is not directly excavated. For instance, in much of the world entire watersheds have been clear-cut at least once. When there were no more tree roots to hold the soil and soak up rain, rapid runoff caused the stream channel to cut deeply into the land. Changes in the watershed, such as clear-cutting of forests, virgin grasslands being broken by plowing, stream channelization, installation of field tiles, paving of large areas, and large mining operations, can add up to quite a bit of devastation. The increase in flash flooding associated with watershed changes has caused many streams to erode or "incise" deeply into the ground until they hit bedrock. When the land flattens out downstream, the channels fill with muddy silt. Major landscape changes like this have had huge impacts on the biodiversity of our streams.

Erosion and channelization also have an impact on habitat. Natural streams usually meander through the landscape. The bank on the outside of stream bends erodes, and sediment is deposited on the inside of bends. Erosion and deposition cause the stream to move over time. In the process, diverse habitats are formed that include riffles, undercut banks, sand/rock bars, cliff lines, wetlands, oxbow lakes, logjams, and many other important

*Stream channelization creates low-quality aquatic and terrestrial habitat.*

habitats. When streams are channelized, most of these habitats are lost and the stream becomes a deep, homogeneous ditch. Many aquatic organisms have become imperiled or extinct because they can no longer live in the silt-clogged, low-oxygen, chemical-laced environments that many streams have become. As a result of stream alteration, we will probably never know exactly how many unique species of fishes, amphibians, mussels, crayfishes, and other stream invertebrates disappeared forever before we even knew they existed.

However, animals and plants are not the only ones being negatively affected. Most natural streams flood out of their banks occasionally. Channelized streams are usually too deep and wide to interact with their floodplain. This lack of overbank flooding onto the floodplain prevents many streams from depositing fertile soil on their floodplains. In addition, wetlands next to the stream are no longer provided with the water that once spilled over into them. The water that once slowly soaked back into the ground now runs quickly off the land and no longer recharges our aquifers. Drought becomes increasingly common, and water no longer undergoes the filtering action that once occurred in wetlands. Topsoil, fertilizers, pesticides, and other contaminants are carried downstream—directly contaminating the water and reducing the concentration of dissolved oxygen available to aquatic life. In addition, sediment that would have been deposited on the floodplain during flood events remains in the stream channel and builds up over time. Eventually, the channel may fill with sediment and debris, causing extensive flooding.

For much of human history, stream alteration has been looked upon as a form of landscape improvement, but humans have begun to realize the error of their ways. Today, efforts are under way to restore many of the streams and wetlands that we once altered or drained.

## Identifying Stream Alteration

Identifying stream alteration and prioritizing areas for stream restoration projects have become major undertakings for many state water-quality agencies, fish and wildlife agencies, not-for-profit organizations, and private landowners. Being able to identify which areas have been heavily affected may also help you to find the most diverse and interesting creeks to visit in your area. Identifying stream alterations can give you a richer sense of the history of your local landscape and a better understanding of the forces that shaped it.

U.S. Geological Survey topographic maps can tell you a lot about the landscape. These maps show the location of streams and wetlands. They may identify ponds that have been built by damming small streams, show you very straight sections of stream that have likely been channelized, and help you calculate the size of a stream's drainage basin. Aerial photographs can also help fill in the story of a stream's history—especially if photographs from multiple years are available. In addition, many states host online Geographic Information Systems (GIS) that allow you to overlay layers of maps such as aerial photos, topographic contours, stream channels, roads, land use type, and various other information. U.S. Fish and Wildlife Service National Wetland Inventory (NWI) maps and insurance-related floodplain maps are also extremely useful in understanding the geography and history of streams.

A very straight stream channel shown on topographic maps or aerial photos often indicates channelization. On the ground, one can sometimes see large piles of dirt along the banks of a channelized stream. These are the piles of soil that were removed from the stream when it was being dug out and are referred to as berms, dikes, or levees. Berms are often covered with trees whose age and size can help you identify how long ago the stream was channelized.

The forested land next to a stream may also tell you something about the history of a stream's watershed. For instance, the presence of many small pioneer trees, such as red maple, may indicate that the riparian zone is a second-growth, third-growth, fourth-growth, or so on forest. The presence of many large climax species, such as oaks, may indicate a relatively unaltered stream. A few large trees next to the stream with many smaller trees in adjacent flat land may indicate that the stream once had a narrow riparian corridor in the middle of a farm field. There are an endless number of clues to the history of a watershed, and putting together the history of a stream can be an interesting challenge for those interested in tracking a stream back through time. The effects of glaciers, climate, animals, and humans are all chronicled in the characteristics of a stream channel, and learning to identify them helps us to understand what a stream is like in a natural condition.

CHAPTER 2

# Stream and Riparian Ecology

This chapter is meant only to scratch the surface of stream ecology, cover some of the more interesting and intuitive concepts, and help you to understand a little more about how everything you see around you functions together. This book is primarily a field guide, and there are a huge number of books and scientific publications that cover stream ecology in greater depth. It's also important to note that there is still a lot we don't know about streams and riparian environments. There are many small fish and amphibians whose life history is poorly understood, and some invertebrates that have not even been named. We know a lot about some aquatic insect larvae because they are easy to sample and watch while living in water, but the adults of the same species may be relatively unknown. In addition, we still know much more about the clear riffles of small, fast-flowing streams than we do about places that are harder or less appealing to sample, such as coastal black-water streams and large, deep rivers.

## BIODIVERSITY

If you love biodiversity, there are few better places to be standing than ankle deep in a medium-sized stream. Why is that? For one thing, you are standing in two very different types of habitat: you are double-dipping from both an aquatic environment and a terrestrial environment. There are also many organisms that are specially adapted to exist in the transition zone between the two (the riparian zone).

Streams provide water for animals and plants, so many upland species may spend quite a bit of time at these watering holes. In many parts of the country, streamside corridors are the only remaining natural habitat left on the landscape. They can be important habitat remnants for species that can't live in the adjacent fields and lawns. These riparian strips are also often the only connection left between larger patches of habitat, so they can function as important corridors that allow animals to move between larger forests, meadows, wetlands, and other habitat types.

*Even though the terrestrial environment has shut down for the winter, aquatic organisms are still active under the ice.*

## PATTERNS IN THE DISTRIBUTION OF STREAM LIFE

A big part of ecology is studying where plants and animals are located, why they live there, and why they are not found elsewhere. In a stream ecosystem you can look at the way organisms are distributed in many different ways and on many different scales. For instance, a cobble-sized piece of rock is actually a tiny ecosystem that is divided up into several distinct niches. Heptageniid mayfly larvae and caddisfly larvae may be clinging to the bottom of the rock, while pleurocerid snails graze biofilm from the top, and perlid stonefly larvae prey upon small mayflies living in a leaf pack snagged under the rock. At a slightly larger scale, you might notice a pattern in the distribution of fishes. For instance, rainbow darters will most likely be found on the bottoms of swift riffles, while many shiners cruise the open water of pools, and catfish spend most of their time hanging out under logs and undercut banks. On an even larger scale, it can be easy to see different types of animals using different sizes of streams. For instance, Louisiana waterthrushes are most likely to be found bobbing their tails next to small, forested streams, while egrets and great blue herons are more likely to be stalking the edges of larger creeks, rivers, and nearby wetlands.

One of the best-known attempts to explain the way that streams change along a longitudinal gradient (from small streams to larger streams) is the River Continuum Concept (RCC). We don't have room for a full description here, but the RCC is a theory that basically explains how the physical characteristics of a stream in the eastern U.S. change as the stream gets larger, and how these changing physical characteristics create habitat for different types of organisms in streams of different sizes. For instance, small streams have more canopy coverage, cooler water, and more leaves falling into them, so these streams have many invertebrates that prefer cool water and its high oxygen content (cooler water is better able to hold oxygen than warm water) and many species that are "shredders," eating large, coarse pieces of organic matter (see Functional Feeding Groups). In contrast, larger streams have less canopy cover, warmer water temperatures, and various types and sizes of organic matter, so they have fewer shredders but more "collectors." The full RCC explains these types of relationships for many different taxa. Even without applying a defined theory, it is quite obvious that changes in flow pattern, temperature, water velocity, and substrate along a stream's length create changes in the types of plants and animals that live in or near streams of different sizes.

There are also differences between the riparian zones of small streams and those of larger systems. The riparian zone around a small headwater stream is basically identical to the surrounding uplands. As you move downstream, the riparian landscape becomes increasingly affected by the stream. Flooding builds floodplains, creates wetlands, and provides an important disturbance that allows certain types of plants and animals to thrive. This pattern is perhaps most easily recognized by thinking about the species of trees that live next to streams of different size. Near a small, ephemeral channel the forest often consists mostly of dry land trees such as sugar maple or various upland oak species. In contrast, larger rivers often have an extensive bottomland forest consisting of moist soil trees such as American sycamore and eastern cottonwood.

Stream size is not the only factor affecting the distribution of different types of aquatic and terrestrial organisms. Climate, geology, and geological history are important forces in shaping the character of our entire landscape—including the distribution of plants and animals. The patterns that explain fish distributions can be a useful example of how these forces have shaped our stream fauna. The highest number of freshwater fish species in the U.S. is found in drainages in the southeastern highlands. These areas weren't covered with ice during glaciation (as the prairies and northeastern U.S. were) and they weren't covered by ocean (as the coastal plain was). Therefore, freshwater environments in this area have been around a long time. Consequently, there has been plenty of time for species to evolve or split into new species. Speciation can be caused by adaptation to fill available niches. It can also happen when a subgroup of a species becomes geographically isolated from the rest of the species and is subject to different evolutionary pressures. In many southeastern streams, there are fishes, salamanders, crayfishes, and many other invertebrates that are found only in a single drainage. Over a vast amount of time, the organisms in these drainages remained separate from others of their species long enough to travel down a different evolutionary path.

The distribution of many organisms is broken up into small islands. Some taxa, such as mammals, birds, and plants with airborne seeds, can disperse across areas of poor habitat to islands of good habitat. Strictly aquatic organisms can't do this very well, so their distribution often tells the story of their species through geological history. The range maps of fishes are particularly good for this. Some fishes were probably distributed much more widely in the past, but events such as glaciation left scattered populations only in unglaciated areas or other refuges. Aquatic organisms can also be eliminated or isolated by waterfalls, mountain ranges, reservoirs, and other forms of habitat isolation.

## FUNCTIONAL FEEDING GROUPS

Stream ecologists often separate aquatic invertebrates into four (or more) functional feeding groups, including shredders, grazers, collectors, and predators. These groups typically have specialized mouthparts and other adaptations that allow them to eat in a certain way. Shredders have fairly strong mandibles and are able to chew large, coarse pieces of organic matter. These animals feed on living plants, recently fallen material, and decomposing organic matter (detritus). Examples of shredders include certain stoneflies and caddisflies. Grazers (or scrapers) usually have specially adapted mouthparts that allow them to scrape off the layer of algae, diatoms, and bacteria that grows on hard underwater surfaces. This layer is called biofilm or

*Organic input, such as these leaves from the surrounding forest, provides nutrients for many organisms in small streams.*

*aufwuchs* (a German term). Examples of grazers include snails, water pennies, and certain mayflies. Collectors feed on small particles of organic matter that may be suspended in the water column or lying on the bottom. There are many types of collectors, with various methods of collecting their food. For instance, freshwater mussels siphon water into their bodies to filter out particles of algae and bacteria, while certain caddisflies build elaborate nets to catch particles. Other collectors, such as some mayflies and worms, actively search out particles and pick them up. Predators feed on other animals, but they can do so in a variety of ways. Some predators, such as certain stoneflies, hellgrammites, and dragonfly larvae, swallow their prey whole. Other predators pierce their prey with sharp mouthparts, fill them with digestive enzymes, and suck out the resulting juices. Many stream invertebrates can be put into these categories, and functional feeding groups help explain how a stream processes the organic matter that falls into it. However, it's important to remember that there are numerous other ways in which animals can feed, and some animals may use more than one feeding strategy.

## STREAM/RIPARIAN FOOD CHAIN

Stream and terrestrial environments have a remarkably complex and complementary relationship. In the fall and winter, streams typically receive huge amounts of energy from the terrestrial environment in the form of leaves and other organic detritus. The organic material is broken down and eaten by bacteria and various invertebrates, and many streams are quite biologically active right through the middle of winter. Conversely, in the summer, energy moves from the stream to the terrestrial environment in the form of emerging insects and aquatic organisms that are eaten by various birds, amphibians, reptiles, and mammals. So no matter what season you visit a riparian zone in, it's likely that either the terrestrial or the aquatic environment (or both) will be fairly active.

The following is an example of the path that a single carbon atom might take through a stream/riparian ecosystem. It can be a useful exercise to learn more about how everything is connected. It's also interesting to think about who the specific players might be in your local stream.

Our carbon atom resides in a red maple leaf. The leaf turns crimson, dries, and glides down into the pool of a tiny, intermittent stream. The leaf floats downstream into a perennial part of the stream, tumbles through a riffle, and becomes lodged in the roots of a large sycamore. Eventually, the leaf becomes waterlogged and stays below the water surface. Over time, bacteria infiltrate the leaf's tissue, and it begins to decompose. A giant stonefly larvae shreds part of the leaf and swallows our atom. The next day, the stonefly is eaten by a brook trout, but our atom escapes digestion and is expelled in the fish's feces.

Downstream, a black fly larva catches one of the fecal particles in its brushlike mouthparts. Our atom becomes part of the black fly, which eventually emerges to fly in the terrestrial environment. One day, the fly is hawked out of the air by a bank swallow with a nest full of youngsters. The atom becomes part of the young swallow's breast muscle, but as it is learning to fly, the youngster falls to the water, where it is eaten by a largemouth bass. Our atom becomes part of the bass's skin. One day a lucky fisherman catches our bass and fillets him next to the stream. He buries the remains at the base of a red maple, where invertebrates and bacteria break down the bass into nutrients that are useful to the tree. Our carbon atom travels up the trunk of the tree and becomes part of a leaf. The circle is complete, although the atom is now a mile downstream from where we first met it.

Stories like this one play out in an infinite number of ways, and the species that are involved in such a food web will depend on the type of stream being considered.

CHAPTER 3

# Stream Types

Creek, crick, river, run, gut, coulee, wash, ditch, drain, rivulet, stream, branch, fork . . . The number of names for these water conveyances is a great indicator of the many types of streams that exist. We have developed a few categories of streams, which we will describe in this chapter. However, this is by no means the only attempt to classify or describe streams. Streams are often classified for various purposes according to their physical characteristics (warm-water, cold-water, low-gradient, high-gradient, and so on). In Europe, classifications have been used that relied on the dominant fish species found in certain stretches of river. These zones ranged from headwaters named the "trout zone" to lower reaches named the "bream zone"; similar classifications have been attempted in the U.S. Dave Rosgen, a prominent stream restoration innovator, has developed an elaborate coded system that describes the size and channel type of a stream. State agencies in charge of monitoring stream health also have various categories and descriptive terms that they use to define stream types for comparison and regulation.

The classifications given in this book allow us to talk about the way geology, geography, and climate combine to shape stream ecosystems, but in reality, streams change along their length and respond to very local changes in the environment. A stream may start out as a mountain brook and end up as a sluggish tidal river, but there will be many "gray areas" in-between.

Stream-type classification suffers from the same problems as many other systems of ecological classification. Sometimes the best way to describe a stream is just to use descriptive vocabulary. For instance, the stream that runs through our backyard is a second-order, perennial, mid-gradient, headwater stream with a substrate primarily made up of shale bedrock. The watershed is now used for row crop agriculture but once consisted of temperate deciduous forest, prairie, and wetlands. What we have just described is a typical Midwestern headwater stream. Our creek falls somewhere between the "highland stream" and "central plains stream" categories described here. By trying to describe and categorize streams we can learn a lot about what kind of plants and animals to expect there.

## PHYSIOGRAPHY

In order to understand why streams look different in various parts of the country, one needs to have a sense of the physiography of the eastern U.S. The character of the eastern landscape ranges from the peaks of the Appalachian Mountains to the low, flat coastal plain. Although these areas differ in terms of geologic history, they often share some physical characteristics. For instance, the central plains were most recently flattened by glaciation, which plowed the area flat, while the coastal plain was the bottom of part of the ocean during recent geological history. However, both regions tend to have low-gradient streams with muddy bottom substrate. The flat nature of these landscapes has meant that they have been used for many of the same purposes, such as row crop agriculture. Similarly, the Ozarks and the highlands of Appalachia have comparable land form and land use history. The geology, physiographic characteristics, and history of your area are all important factors to think about and research when trying to answer questions like "Why does my stream look the way it does?" and "What should my stream look like in a natural condition?"

## STREAM-TYPE CLASSIFICATION

### Mountain Brooks

In the eastern U.S. these streams are fed by melting snow, springs, and abundant rain. They are usually clear, nutrient-poor, fairly small, and fast-flowing. The substrate includes a significant amount of rock in the form of bedrock, boulders, and cobbles. In the steepest reaches, mountain brooks consist largely of step-pools and waterfalls.

Because mountains have not been as suitable for agricultural and industrial development, mountain brooks are some of our most pristine streams. However, these streams are still faced with several problems. Prevailing winds carry acid rain and other pollutants produced in the industrialized Midwest to the Appalachian Mountains. Also, the rocky soils often make it difficult to install functional septic tanks for treating human waste, so there are many "straight pipes" that empty sewage into streams' watersheds. One of the most destructive activities facing these streams is mining (usually for coal). Acid mine drainage and coal slurry spills have been extremely devastating to the fauna of many mountain brooks.

The major vegetation changes along the Appalachian Mountains from New England to the southeastern U.S., but several species are typically present, including eastern hemlock and various rhododendron species. In fact, cool temperatures and plenty of moisture allow the ranges of many northern species to extend into the southeastern U.S. along the Appalachian corridor. In the mountains, the streams often start out in small mountain bogs or fens that are home to rare and highly adapted species, including carnivorous plants. Diversity and prevalence of ferns, mosses, and liverworts is high near these streams. Invertebrates that prefer high-gradient streams are found here,

*A representative mountain brook.*

although slow-water species may be found in pools. Mountain brooks have many stoneflies, mayflies, caddisflies, and other insect larvae. Some common and characteristic vertebrates include brook trout, hellbenders, and dusky salamanders.

## Highland Streams

This is a catchall category for the upland streams that aren't really mountain brooks but are located in highlands such as plateaus, foothills, and piedmont areas. Southern highland streams are the most species-diverse systems in the country. The majority of these highlands escaped being covered by glacial ice or coastal plain saltwater in recent geologic time. This long, relatively undisturbed history has allowed more time for speciation to occur as a result of geographic separation and specialization to fill specific niches. Unglaciated upland streams are extremely diverse in terms of geology and morphology. Substrates can include bedrock, boulders, cobble, gravel, and fine particles. The majority of these streams are high-gradient, fast-flowing systems. However, where topography flattens out, such as in floodplains where the streams join larger rivers, these systems may more closely resemble coastal plain or central plains streams. Highland streams tend to have higher water temperatures and lower gradients than mountain brooks, and this class might be considered the intermediate between mountain brooks and more lowland systems.

Highland streams often have more intact watersheds than waterways in flatter parts of the U.S.; they have not been subject to as much row crop agriculture as central plains streams. However, the terrain tends to be steeper—which causes extensive erosion when poor farming practices are employed.

*A representative highland stream.*

Watersheds of these streams have been affected by clear-cutting, coal mining, agriculture, and residential development.

The plant communities adjacent to these streams can be extremely variable depending on the size of the stream and where in the country it is located. Smaller highland streams will be shaded by the canopies of various upland tree species, and there are often many woodland wildflowers found growing on their banks. Larger streams, with their larger floodplains, have more bottomland-adapted species such as American sycamore, eastern cot-

*Highland streams and mountain brooks are typically cold and high in oxygen content.*

tonwood, river birch, wood nettle, and Virginia wild rye. Invertebrate species richness may be very high in highland streams, especially for freshwater mussels, snails, caddisflies, mayflies, and stoneflies. Some common vertebrates include darters, various sunfish, pickerel frogs, map turtles, queen snakes, river otters, muskrats, and great blue herons.

## Central Plains Streams

The defining forces in the recent geological history of central plains streams were glaciers. These ice-block bulldozers crossed much of the Midwest—in some areas multiple times—before retreating only ten to fifteen thousand years ago. Streams in this region are often fairly low-gradient with silty bottoms. Many central plains streams had mud bottoms even before human-induced landscape changes, but the bed and banks were more stable, and less silt would have been suspended in the water prior to European settlement. Woody debris can be important in these systems. It is often embedded in the bottom of the stream, which stabilizes the bottom, simulates riffle habitat, shelters fish, and provides some of the only hard surfaces for certain invertebrates. In many ways, central plains streams are physically similar to coastal plain streams, but they have largely different faunal composition because the central plain occupies the Mississippi River drainage, while much of the coastal plain occupies Atlantic slope drainages. There are pockets in the Midwest that escaped intense glaciations and intense human alteration, and in these areas, streams may more closely resemble the highland brooks already described.

*A representative central plains stream.*

The flat land and deep soils created by thousands of years of prairie grass decomposition created an ideal landscape for row crop agriculture. Much of this area once consisted of huge expanses of marshland, so early farmers began draining the land with ditches. Eventually, more than 90 percent of the wetlands in the Midwest were drained, and the landscape was transformed into a grid of ditches and fields. As a result, water runs off of watersheds very quickly, causing extensive erosion, siltation, and downstream flooding. Soils in this part of the country are some of the most highly erodible in the world, so many of the channelized streams became clogged with silt and muck.

In an undisturbed condition, the headwaters of these streams might have consisted of meandering marshes with species such as grasses, sedges, and rushes. Further downstream, most prairie rivers had a riparian corridor of trees such as cottonwood and American sycamore. Now, ditches often have mowed banks with various exotic plant species and some native grasses, sedges, and rushes. If a riparian corridor of trees is present, it often consists of trees such as box elder, osage orange, eastern cottonwood, and American sycamore. The invertebrate community of most streams and ditches consists largely of low-oxygen adapted taxa such as water boatmen, midge larvae, dragonfly and damselfly larvae, and many true bugs. Common vertebrates include bullhead catfish, various sunfish, largemouth bass, green frogs, leopard frogs, common snapping turtles, northern watersnakes, muskrats, mink, great blue herons, egrets, and various waterfowl.

## Southeastern Coastal Plain Streams

The coastal plain exists as a remnant from a time when a vast portion of the southeastern U.S. was covered by ocean. Streams can be very diverse here

*A representative southeastern coastal plain stream.*

because of the warm climate and productivity that stems from a nutrient-rich environment. Like glaciated areas, the coastal plain was recently (in geologic terms) disturbed, only it was by widespread saltwater coverage instead of ice. Therefore, aquatic taxa have not had as long to evolve and speciate in these streams as they have had in the higher-elevation inland areas. This flat, low area traces the eastern coast but also extends a considerable distance up the Mississippi valley to include parts of states as far inland as southern Illinois. Streams in the coastal plain tend to be low-gradient with substrate made up of sand, mud, and decomposing organic matter. Small coastal plain streams sometimes consist of a series of swamps or sloughs connected by sections of stream channel. Today, many of the streams in this area have been channelized to form straight ditches.

Land in this region has historically been subject to a huge number of human uses, including row crop agriculture, livestock farming, logging, silviculture, and residential development. These land uses lead to elimination of forested watershed area, stream channelization, and the consequent addition of fertilizers, sewage, eroded sediment, and other chemicals to the water. Watershed changes have lead to increased water temperatures, low oxygen, and buildup of toxins in many drainages.

Coastal plain streams display a considerable amount of variation. For instance, black-water rivers often occur along the southeastern coastal plain. The water in these rivers is stained almost black by tannins (tannic acid) leached from leaves and other organic matter. The water can be very acidic, which prohibits bacterial growth, slows decomposition, and often results in a thick layer of organic material in the bottom of the river. At the opposite end of the spectrum are the crystal-clear, spring-fed streams found in much

*A representative black-water stream in the southeastern coastal plain.*

of Florida. In many of these streams, one can see 30 feet or more to the bottom of large pools. The downstream water column may become clouded with algae, tannins, and sediment as in most other coastal plain rivers, but the water issuing forth from the springs is clear.

Many of the species found in coastal plain streams are also typically found in swamps, sloughs, and ponds. Forest canopy near these streams can be highly variable, depending on local topography, and may include baldcypress, red maple, river birch, and various species of pines and bays. Shrub, vine, and herbaceous plant diversity is high near these streams. Some common species include buttonbush, spicebush, fetterbush, river cane, greenbriers, cattails, smartweeds, and many grasses, sedges, and rushes. Invertebrates that can tolerate low oxygen and sluggish water do well in these systems.

Invertebrates that are often found in these streams include many true bugs, predaceous and whirligig beetles, midge larvae, aquatic oligochaetes, physid snails, certain freshwater mussels, fingernail clams, burrowing mayflies, and freshwater shrimp. Common vertebrates include golden shiners, bullhead catfish, largemouth bass, bullfrogs, green frogs, leopard frogs, various pond sliders, plain-bellied watersnakes, cottonmouths, beaver, muskrats, river otters, and wood ducks.

## Tidal Streams

It is fitting that this is the last category because these streams are as far downstream as you can get. They are often very similar to coastal plain streams, but tidal systems have brackish water (a mixture of salt and fresh water). Tidal waters are subject to varying amounts of salinity depending on the tides, direction of the wind, and other factors. Dissolved oxygen in these systems can also range widely and is often quite low due to the extensive amount of organic decomposition that takes place here. Decomposition uses up oxygen and produces other gases such as carbon dioxide and methane. Tidal streams are typically very low-gradient, and water may flow downstream or upstream depending on lunar tides or wind-blown tides. The portions of tidal streams that are furthest downstream look very similar almost everywhere on the Atlantic coast. That's because they typically end in a salt marsh dominated by salt marsh cordgrass *(Spartina alterniflora)*. However, the more upstream habitats will vary quite a bit with latitude.

Tidal creeks have been intensively affected by human activities. Many streams were channelized for agricultural and navigational purposes, and most of the Atlantic coast is connected by a series of channels called the

*A representative tidal stream.*

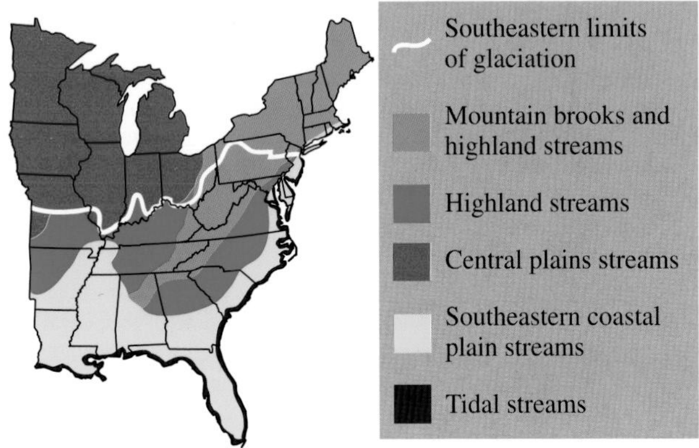


*Generalized map of stream types.*

intracoastal waterway. Humans have dug canals to create travel ways to the ocean, which usually increased the salinity of the fresh waters being connected. This activity sometimes killed off species such as baldcypress and eastern oysters, which have fairly specific salt tolerances. Also, tidal creeks are often heavily crowded by coastal development.

The plant and animal communities that exist at the freshwater/saltwater interface can be quite unique. The upstream reaches are only minorly affected by salt water, so they typically look like whatever the local stream type is. Downstream reaches begin to show signs of salinity as species such as black needlerush and cordgrass show up. Many tidal streams are heavily infiltrated by the exotic common reed *(Phragmites)*. Invertebrates and vertebrates follow a similar pattern of freshwater species in the upper reaches of tidal systems and increasing prevalence of saltwater species downstream.

Tidal streams are important nursery areas for many saltwater animals. Shrimp, blue crabs, pinfish, flounder, menhaden, red drum, Atlantic croaker, spot, American eel, and many other species are born in the open ocean but travel up into tidal creeks to develop into adulthood. Each tidal creek may have its own unique blend of freshwater species, saltwater creatures, and organisms that are specially adapted for the brackish-water environment. Common amphibious and terrestrial species include pond sliders, common snapping turtles, musk turtles, various watersnakes, muskrats, herons, and egrets.

CHAPTER 4

# Studying Streams

There is always something interesting to see in or along a stream. If one thing is failing to show itself, there will be something else to find. The trick is in knowing when to look, where to look, how to look—and how to catch it. Here are a few tips that will help you to enjoy all of the creatures that live in our stream environments.

## BEFORE YOU GO

Whenever we go to a new area one of the first things we do is check out any maps that are available. DeLorme gazetteers are indispensable for finding stream access. Boat launches, fishing access points, and road crossings within publicly owned lands are all excellent places to get your feet wet. We also scout new areas using aerial photography, such as that available through Google Earth; in many cases, you can even tell where sand bars, riffles, and other important features are located through aerial photos. Also, the U.S. Geological Survey provides online data for many of their stream gauges. Stream gauges allow you to see how high the water may be in the stream you plan to visit, and stream gauges for nearby waterways may give you an idea of what's going on in the area.

An excellent way to learn how your local stream behaves is to take a look at it every day as you travel to work or school. How much does the water level rise after an inch of rain? Does it flash flood easily? Do you see any relation between flooding in streams and the amount of pavement or ditches in the watershed? After a while you will get a sense of your stream's behavior.

You may also want to get lists of plants and animals that occur in the county or stream that you are going to be visiting. Often, states keep track of the rare species that have been found in every county in an online natural heritage database. Sometimes, the state division of nature preserves, department of fish and game, or other natural resource agency will have similar databases. They may also have specific lists for each river drainage. State and regional field guides are also great sources for this kind of information. Identifying plants and animals is much easier when you narrow down the most likely species to be seen—or you may record new species for your area!

## TIMING

Certain times of year are better than others to search for particular animals and plants. The great thing about streams is that there is always something going on, no matter what time of year it is. Spring is an excellent time to find the maximum diversity of stream invertebrates or to seine some darters while they are in vibrant spring color. However, at this time of year streams are often flooded. You may arrive at the stream with visions of sparkling, ankle-deep water but end up finding 5 feet of turbid, dangerous flooding. Don't despair; focus your attention on blooming wildflowers or breeding birds that have just returned from winter down south.

Most aquatic insects transform into their winged terrestrial forms in spring and summer, so by late summer and fall many streams are fairly impoverished in terms of aquatic insect diversity. However, this is a great time to look for minnows in breeding color, check out some adult dragonflies, or identify some of those plants that don't bloom until late summer. The low water levels of late summer and fall are an excellent time to find tracks along muddy banks or mammal scats that have had some time to accumulate without being immediately washed away by floodwater. The changing leaf color and moody skies may make for some excellent fall stream photos. As the leaves fall, they feed our streams with organic matter. This gives many stream invertebrates something to eat and cranks up a food chain that should result in an abundant and diverse invertebrate community by late winter. When ice prevents you from sampling inverts, check out mammal tracks or the shells of mussels that raccoons and muskrats have recently eaten.

## EQUIPMENT

It is amazing how much a tiny net can improve your chances of success at catching slippery salamanders and claw-wielding crayfish. We have gotten into the habit of taking a small net everywhere. We cut the handle off an aquarium net or just bend the handle a couple of times until it fits into a pants pocket or the side pouch of a daypack. It will make you much more effective at catching creek creatures. A small, scooplike strainer, which can often be stolen from the kitchen drawer, is also handy for sifting through bottom sediment and scooping up fast-moving creatures.

Fine-mesh dip nets or "D nets" are sold by biological supply companies, and they are particularly well-suited to invertebrate sampling. You can make your own net out of a stout branch, some stiff wire, and fine mesh such as an old window screen, laundry bag, or even a pair of panty hose. You may also want to build a "kick net," which is a piece of mesh fabric or netting attached to a pole on both sides.

If you want to sample deeper habitats or catch faster animals (like fish), you are going to need a larger net. Large-mesh dip nets, seines, and cast nets are excellent tools for sampling fish, and they are available cheaply in most sporting goods stores. Dip nets and seines typically have finer mesh and are better for catching the smallest darters and minnows, while cast nets are great for large fish in snag-free pools. You can carry a seine around already attached to the poles, or you can fold up the seine in a backpack and find the poles after you have hiked to a stream, as we do.

There are a variety of traps available for capturing fish, crayfish, amphibians, reptiles, and other creatures, but be sure to check local fishing regulations. One of the simplest and most effective traps is a funnel trap. Funnel traps come in various designs and sizes in order to target minnows, crayfish, or other animals, but you can also build your own out of wire mesh or even a used plastic drink bottle.

*A tiny net can be carried at all times and substantially increases your ability to catch slippery animals.*

A white tray makes an excellent background for picking invertebrates out of debris with a pair of fine-tipped forceps (tweezers). A couple of clear jars are indispensable for temporarily holding and viewing creatures. An empty peanut butter jar is the perfect size for many animals and is difficult to shatter. Smaller bottles for preserving things in alcohol are available from biological supply companies, but we sometimes use old olive jars and baby food jars to temporarily keep invertebrates in alcohol. Ethanol is the preferred preservative for aquatic invertebrates, but isopropyl alcohol (normal rubbing alcohol) will work if you can get a concentration of 60 percent or higher. Isopropyl alcohol tends to make things brittle, so it may help to add some glycerin and a pinch of crushed antacid tablet to buffer this type of alcohol. Hand sanitizer (which contains ethanol) also makes a serviceable temporary preservative, although it is probably best to kill the animal in liquid alcohol first.

With a camera capable of taking macro photos (many affordable digital cameras now have a mode, denoted with a flower icon, that takes macro photos) and some knowledge of the most important field characteristics of the group of organisms being photographed, there is often no need to preserve animals for later identification. One of the greatest tools for displaying and taking photographs of aquatic creatures is a viewer. Viewers are available from biological supply companies. Small aquariums and other clear containers also work for this purpose, but we enjoy making our own viewers of various shapes and sizes. All that is needed is three rectangular pieces of Plexiglas, a candle, and some clear adhesive. We use the candle to heat and bend the V-shaped middle piece and then glue on the ends.

Aquariums are excellent for learning more about the lives of creatures that are seldom observable otherwise. Aquariums have to be tailored to the oxygen and food requirements of the species you wish to observe. For

*A viewer is easily constructed and is indispensible for viewing, identifying, and photographing aquatic creatures.*

instance, mayflies and stoneflies may live for quite some time if you use a cascading filter to provide current. Other species, such as many dragonfly and damselfly larvae, can be kept in pondlike still water. Crayfish, snails, aquatic plants, true bugs, and aquatic beetles can also make interesting additions to aquariums.

Hand lenses and dissecting microscopes are a necessity for identifying some plants and small animals. Polarized sunglasses and polarized camera lens filters can help you to see past the glare on the water's surface. In clear water, a snorkel and face mask allow you to get remarkably close to small fish and explore a whole other world of aquatic life.

## TECHNIQUES

One of our favorite pastimes is flipping rocks along a streambank or riffle. This is usually an easy way to find salamanders, crayfish, frogs, snakes, and even mice further up the bank. Rocks from riffles may be covered with caddisfly larvae, mayfly larvae, snails, water pennies, stonefly larvae, darter eggs, and many other interesting things. Logs, bark, trash, and old pieces of tin are also great places to find critters along the floodplain or nearby slopes. Two words of caution though: You might want to use a stick, net handle, snake hook, or potato rake to lift objects initially. This will prevent you from being bitten by snakes, black widow spiders, or other creatures that you might encounter occasionally. Also, *please put logs and rocks back exactly where you found them.* It takes a long time to form the microhabitat conditions that salamanders, frogs, and other creatures need to live under a rock or log.

Dip nets and seines are often simply dragged through the water while avoiding snags and trying to corner organisms so that they have to go into the net. Beds of aquatic vegetation are an especially good place to drag a net through. Be sure to keep the lower edge of the net as close to the stream bottom as possible. Another technique is to place the net at the lower end of a riffle and disturb the upstream substrate. This dislodges and spooks fish and invertebrates, which are carried downstream into your net by the current. Where there is little current, invertebrates can be collected by repeatedly jabbing substrate, undercut banks, tree roots, and other habitat with the end of a dip net. The net is then quickly swept over the disturbed habitat, capturing suspended invertebrates, which can then be sorted from debris in a white tray.

Wading small streams at night with a flashlight and dip net is an excellent way to see many creatures that are usually hidden during the day, such as amphibians, various catfish, crayfish, dragonfly larvae, raccoons, mink, owls, and many others. This is also an excellent time to catch sleepy fish that can seem to be mesmerized by the light source. Creek-walking on a summer night generally rewards you with many sightings of previously unseen animals and is often more rewarding than daytime observation. If you want to check out some of the adult versions of stream insects, try leaving a black light shining on a white sheet (or T-shirt) suspended on the streambank at night. You'll be surprised to see how many different kinds of insects are attracted.

There are a huge number of other techniques that you can use to see more of the life inhabiting your creek. We don't have room for all of them, but here are a few more tips. Try sitting in a concealed spot near an animal travelway (such as a deer run) at dawn or dusk. This is the best time of day to catch most animals in action. Hook and line fishing is, of course, a great way to capture aquatic creatures, and there are a huge number of books available on angling. Funnel traps can be placed in natural funnels and hiding places, such as confined channels, parallel to undercut banks, under logs, and in beds of aquatic vegetation. Camera traps are becoming increasingly affordable and can be placed in natural travel areas such as beaver slides and deer runs. A small amount of bait, such as cat food or peanut butter, placed right in front of the camera's trigger area helps slow animals down long enough for the camera to record them.

## REGULATIONS

In most states you can sample the majority of invertebrates without a fishing license, but you usually need a license for fish and crayfish. Fishing license money goes to support conservation, so it's good to buy one anyway. Unless fishing regulations specifically permit it, don't collect live mussels or their shells unless you have a scientific collecting permit. Many mussels are on the federal list of threatened and endangered species, and possession of one of these shells could result in a hefty fine. You should check the hunting and fishing laws in your area before capturing any animal or collecting plants.

## FIELD NOTEBOOK

Throughout the history of ecology, the field notebook has been one of the most powerful tools for learning about the natural world, recording experiences, and providing insights to future naturalists. Field notebooks can be as simple or in-depth as you desire, depending on the purpose of your writing. Below are some useful things to record, but this list could really be endless and depends on what interests you:

- Can you list all of the plants and animals that you saw and heard (or at least the dominant ones)?
- What are the average depth, average width, and most common substrates of the stream?

- What kind of land use is associated with the stream (e.g., row crop agriculture, mining, or undisturbed forest)?
- Why do you think the plants and animals you saw were there? For instance, if you found many mayfly and stonefly larvae, the watershed may be relatively healthy—but what if you caught only leeches?
- Were any insects emerging from the water?
- Did you see a lot of fish? What were they doing—feeding, spawning, sucking air at the surface . . . ?
- What is the weather like?
- When was the last time it rained?
- Do you think the water level was average?
- Are there piles of debris, beaver gnawings, or silt deposits that tell you how high water goes after a big rain?

Hand-drawn maps and sketches of animals, plants, rocks, and so on are essential contributions to a field notebook. Drawing helps you internalize the way things look and will improve your identification skills. *Field notebook drawings do not need to be perfect.* Most of what is important about field sketching is that you take a second to scribble a quick drawing while picturing whatever you are drawing in your mind's eye. This process encourages you to think about the identifying characteristics that you noticed, and the ones that you could notice next time. Drawing a cross-section view of the stream and a top-view map can also help to make important connections between what you saw and why you may have seen it there. (Where was the patch of American water willow in relation to the riffle and the rock bar? Why are there cattails here and not over there?) Field sketches also provide inspiration as you flip back through your notes and can capture information that would have taken much more space to express in words.

CHAPTER 5

# Identification Guide

## TIPS ON IDENTIFYING PLANTS AND ANIMALS

Upon finding an interesting creature, most people will flip through the pages of a field guide in order to see which picture looks the most like what they've found. With that fact in mind, we have endeavored to make this guide as flip-friendly as possible (see the "How to Use this Guide" section). In the descriptions of plants and animals that follow, we have attempted to list some of the most useful distinguishing characteristics. These characteristics should help you make a positive identification, or at least narrow it down to a group of organisms. Range maps and habitat descriptions can provide important clues to what organism you are looking at, but they should not be relied upon entirely because plants and animals can end up in some pretty surprising places. Drawings and photos of the kind of traits mentioned in the distinguishing characteristics sections can become invaluable later if you need to confirm your identification.

Organisms are named according to a taxonomic system that separates them into smaller and smaller groups. Biological taxonomy uses the following categories: Kingdom, Phylum (Division in plants), Class, Order, Family, Genus, Species. These categories are often broken into various subcategories, such as subclass, subspecies, and so on. At the highest level, the organisms covered in this book are organized into the plant and animal kingdoms (Plantae and Animalia). At the lowest taxonomic level covered in this book, organisms are grouped into species. For our purposes, the definition of a species is a group of organisms that are capable of breeding and producing fertile offspring.

## ADDITIONAL RESOURCES

The resources listed in the bibliography are valuable tools. They have been broken up by subject so that you can more easily find detailed references. However, many of the best resources are very region-specific. A few of these regional guides are listed in the bibliography. Often, the best way to find a detailed field guide to species in your area is just to type "the (insert type of plant/animal here) of (insert state or region here)" into an internet search engine. This often yields field guides, scientific publications, publications produced by state natural resource agencies, internet field guides, posters, and other resources.

# Plants

## On Identifying Plants

The plants included here are organized into two major groups: Herbaceous Plants and Trees and Shrubs. Herbaceous (non-woody) plants are organized by flower color proceeding from non-flowering plants to plants with green/brown, white, yellow/orange, red/pink, and purple/blue flowers. In some cases, color grouping will cause plants that are in the same family to be located in different parts of the book, but color is the easiest way for the novice to identify a flower quickly. Trees and shrubs are organized taxonomically, because similar-looking species fall within the same family.

# Herbaceous Plants

## Non-flowering

### Liverworts (Division Hepatophyta)

**Distinguishing Characteristics:** Usually less than a few centimeters tall, but may spread along rocks or other surfaces for a meter or more. Relatively simple, primitive plants that resemble mosses. In contrast to mosses, which usually have leaves spiraled around a central stem, most liverworts consist of a flattened, ribbonlike structure called a thallus. Liverworts are also typically prostrate, while mosses tend to be more erect. The thallus of the green-scented liverwort (*Conocephalum conicum,* pictured) has distinctive hexagonal scales and smells like cinnamon if crushed.

**Habitat and Remarks:** Liverworts love moist habitats. They are often encountered on rocks of headwater streams, on cliff faces with seeping water, or around rotting logs. Like mosses and ferns, liverworts reproduce through spores. These plants are attached to substrate by hairlike structures called rhizoids but lack roots. Liverworts absorb all water and nutrients through their leafy tissue.

## Mosses (Division Bryophyta)

**Distinguishing Characteristics:** Small, simple plants that often resemble a green carpet or growth of algae. Unlike liverworts, which tend to be bilaterally flattened (ribbonlike), mosses have a central stem with leaves spiraled around it. Mosses and liverworts are often referred to collectively as bryophytes.

**Habitat and Remarks:** Mosses are attached to substrate by hairlike structures called rhizoids and, lacking roots, must absorb all water and nutrients through their leafy tissue. For this reason, mosses tend to flourish best in damp habitats, such as streamside rocks, seeps, streambanks, and rotting logs. There are also aquatic mosses, which grow on tree roots or other hard substrates underwater. These mosses provide important habitat for many algae, snails, fish, amphibians, crustaceans, and aquatic insects. Like ferns and liverworts, mosses reproduce through spores.

## Scouringrush Horsetail *(Equisetum hyemale)*

**Distinguishing Characteristics:** Height up to 91 cm (36"). Cylindrical, unbranched plant with sections of stem that are easily pulled apart into short, hollow sections. The tip of the plant ends in a pointed "strobilus" that produces spores. The similar field horsetail *(E. arvense)* is lighter green and produces two types of stems—one type is similar to scouringrush and is fertile, and the other has whorls of thin leaves coming from each node and is sterile. Other species and hybrids exist, but these are the major eastern U.S. species.

**Habitat and Remarks:** Perennial. Native. *Equisetum* is the only surviving genus of a group of plants that once dominated primitive forests. Horsetails are commonly found in moist habitats, including streambanks, wetlands, and fields. They reproduce through spores but also expand the size of their colony by pushing new stems up from underground rhizomes. The stems contain silicates, which give them a sandpapery feel. A handful of these plants can be used as a scouring pad for dishes or they may be dried and used as fine-grain sandpaper.

## Netted Chain Fern *(Woodwardia areolata)*

**Distinguishing Characteristics:** Height up to 46 cm (18"). The leaves of this plant do not resemble what one typically thinks of as a fern frond. Leaves are composed of about ten pairs of pinnae with net venation and finely toothed edges. The netted chain fern is most similar to sensitive fern, which has leaflets with edges that are very wavy but not finely toothed. Sensitive fern leaves are triangular in outline because they lack the reduced lower leaflets that give netted chain fern a more ovular appearance. Sensitive fern also has very distinctive fertile fronds.

**Habitat and Remarks:** Perennial. Native. Netted chain fern is typically found in wetland habitats. Consequently, it can be very common along coastal plain streams, which have lots of associated wetlands. It is not as common along high-gradient, upland creeks but inhabits seeps along sandstone cliffs and other acidic-soil habitats. This species enjoys shade to part-sun. Like other ferns, it reproduces through spores that are held on the fertile fronds. In netted chain fern, the fertile fronds are thinner versions of the other fronds.

## Sensitive Fern *(Onoclea sensibilis)*

**Distinguishing Characteristics:** Height up to 1 m (40"). Light green fern that does not resemble a "typical" fern. The sterile leaves are composed of up to 12 pairs of nearly opposite pinnae with net venation. The edges of pinnae may be very wavy but are not finely toothed, as are the leaves of netted chain fern. Pinnae of the fertile leaves are modified into beaded structures that somewhat resemble rattlesnake rattles.

**Habitat and Remarks:** Perennial. Native. The sensitive fern lives in wet habitats, often along large bottomland swamps or at the headwaters of tiny streams. It is found in both shady and sunny habitats and prefers acidic soils. Like other ferns, this species reproduces through spores that are held in the beaded structures on the fertile fronds. Despite its name, this species is tolerant of a variety of habitat types and even occasional mowing, but it tends to wither and brown at the first hint of frost.

## Maidenhair Fern *(Adiantum pedatum)*

**Distinguishing Characteristics:** Height up to 66 cm (26"). The leaf consists of pinnae arranged in a horizontal half circle. The arc of bright green leaflets, graceful form, and ebony-colored rachis make this elegant fern difficult to mistake.

**Habitat and Remarks:** Perennial. Native. The maidenhair fern is usually encountered in deep, shaded glens with moist soils. It is often associated with small, high-gradient streams in limestone areas and prefers neutral to slightly alkaline soils. It has been used medicinally for a variety of upper respiratory conditions. The stems were once used by Native Americans in a hair wash to make hair shiny (hence the name maidenhair).

## Cinnamon Fern *(Osmunda cinnamomea)*

**Distinguishing Characteristics:** Height up to 1.5 m (60"). Leaves made up of pinnae that are cut deeply into lobes (almost bipinnate). Fertile leaves are modified into a cinnamon-colored "sporophyll" that is usually seen in late spring. Unlike Virginia chain fern *(Woodwardia virginica)*, which has net venation, leaf veins extend straight from mid-vein to the leaf edge. Might also be mistaken for ostrich fern *(Matteuccia struthiopteris)* or interrupted fern *(O. claytoniana)*, but those species lack the light tan tufts of hairs that cinnamon fern have at the base of each pinna.

**Habitat and Remarks:** Perennial. Native. This is a wetland-loving fern often found along low-gradient streams with associated swamps or wet meadows. It is especially common along the coastal plain. Inhabits sunny and shady areas. Like other ferns, it reproduces from spores and by pushing up stems from underground rhizomes. The furled sprouts or "fiddleheads" from this fern and some others may be eaten raw in moderation or boiled briefly like spinach (just make sure it's not another plant, such as poison hemlock). Deer and other animals also feed on fiddleheads.

## Christmas Fern *(Polystichum acrostichoides)*

**Distinguishing Characteristics:** Height up to 81 cm (32"). Evergreen fern with leathery dark green leaves. The fronds are made up of 20 to 40 pairs of pinnae, each with a distinctive tab or ear at its base that points toward the tip of the frond. Tiny bristles line the edges of the pinnae, and the lower stem (stipe) is covered in light brown scales. Similar species lack the distinctive ears at the base of each pinna.

**Habitat and Remarks:** Perennial. Native. Christmas ferns are common on shady slopes and cliff sides. They often line the hillsides associated with tiny streams but can also be found in upland forests and many other habitats. It is one of the few evergreen herbaceous plants in eastern deciduous forests. This is a common fern that is often sold as a houseplant. Like other ferns, it reproduces from spores and by pushing up stems from underground rhizomes. Unlike some other ferns with edible fiddleheads, the wooly shoots of Christmas fern are best left alone.

## Mosquito Fern *(Azolla caroliniana)*

**Distinguishing Characteristics:** Length up to 25 mm (1"). Red or green fern that floats on the surface of the water with a small root hanging down from each stem. The fronds appear to be made up of small, overlapping scales and resemble a small piece of cedar leaf. In shade these plants are green, but they turn red in sun. Duckweeds (*Lemna* spp. [see photo]) and watermeal (*Wolfia* spp. [see photo]) only have one to three leaves, instead of many overlapping scalelike leaves.

**Habitat and Remarks:** Annual. Native. Mosquito fern is the only free-floating aquatic fern typically found in the eastern U.S. It is found in the backwaters of sluggish streams and swamps, often where duckweed and watermeal grow—most commonly in the coastal plain. This plant may form thick mats that can reduce light penetration into the water below it, but it is native to the U.S. and not typically considered to be invasive. Like other ferns, it reproduces by spores, but plants also break apart to reproduce asexually. *Anabaena azollae,* a blue-green algae, is almost always found growing on this species. These two species have a mutualistic relationship in which the algae lives on some byproducts of photosynthesis produced by the mosquito fern, and the fern receives nitrogen fixed by the algae (somewhat like the way nitrogen is fixed by symbiotic bacteria of legumes).

# Green, Brownish, or Indistinct Flowers (Including Grasses)

## Virginia Wild Rye *(Elymus virginicus)*

**Distinguishing Characteristics:** Height up to 76 cm (30"). Superficially resembles wheat but usually grows in much different habitat. This species has an erect seedhead with stiff bristles. Similar species of *Elymus* tend to have more curving bristles. Bottlebrush grass *(E. hystrix)* is another common streamside member of this genus. It has distinctive, radiating flower clusters, with long bristles that give the seedhead the appearance of a bottle brush.

**Habitat and Remarks:** Perennial. Native. Often grows in large stands in the moist soils and shade of floodplain forests. However, it can also grow in more upland forests. The seed of this species is easy to collect and makes an excellent addition to stream restoration seed mixes. The seeds are a food source for birds and small mammals, and the leaves are eaten by various herbivores, including livestock.

## Barnyard Grass *(Echinochloa crus-galli)*

**Distinguishing Characteristics:** Height up to 152 cm (60"). A robust grass with large, hairy seedheads, often with a reddish tinge. Leaves usually glabrous. The native species in this genus *(E. muricata)* is extremely difficult to distinguish from the introduced plant and can be found in similar habitats.

**Habitat and Remarks:** Annual. Introduced exotic. Barnyard grass is common in many kinds of disturbed habitats, including streambanks and wetlands. There is fairly little difference between *E. crus-galli* and native *Echinochloa*, so this species is usually not a major target of exotic invasive species control measures. However, any habitat restorations should use native species. Barnyard grass provides seeds and structural habitat for many birds and small mammals and is highly valued as a waterfowl food.

## Japanese Stiltgrass *(Microstegium vimineum)*

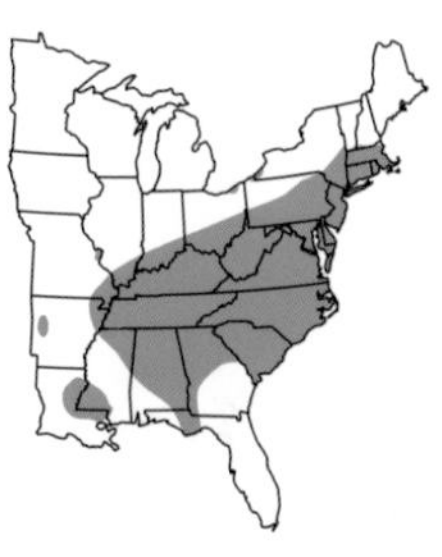

**Distinguishing Characteristics:** Height up to 102 cm (40"). Semi-prostrate. Lance-shaped leaves with a distinctive shiny mid-vein. If not in flower (which it often isn't), this plant might be mistaken for rice cutgrass *(Leersia oryzoides)*, but stiltgrass lacks the clinging, cutting leaves of cutgrass. Seedheads mostly consist of single thin spikes.

**Habitat and Remarks:** Annual. Introduced exotic noxious weed. Japanese stiltgrass, also called Nepalese browntop, was introduced from Asia in the early 1900s. It quickly spreads to fill the understory of forests, crowding out native species. It may often be seen near small, forested streams or, very often, along floodplain trails. This species is favored by periodic disturbance, such as mowing and flooding. Exotic species control measures include pulling or aggressive mowing prior to seed production in late summer. Herbicides are used on large infestations.

## Deertongue *(Dichanthelium clandestinum)*

**Distinguishing Characteristics:** Height up to 61 cm (24"). Deertongue, along with other panic grass species, was formerly classified in the genus *Panicum*. There are several hundred species of panic grasses, but this is one of the most distinctive. The seedhead is a pyramid-shaped panicle, and the seeds are suspended on relatively long stalks. These long-stalked seeds look similar among many of the switchgrass species. The leaves are long and tapering (supposedly like a deer tongue), clasp the stem at the base, and are quite pubescent.

**Habitat and Remarks:** Perennial. Native. Deertongue loves to grow in sunny, moist meadows. It's often found near floodplain trails and sunlit stream banks. Young sprouts are eaten by many herbivores and some waterfowl. The seeds are eaten by many songbirds and small mammals. This species and switchgrass *(P. virgatum)* are fairly aggressive and are useful for native vegetation restoration along streambanks and floodplain grasslands because they can compete with exotic invasive plants.

## Indian Woodoats *(Chasmanthium latifolium)*

**Distinguishing Characteristics:** Height up to 144 cm (55"). This grass has a distinctive seedhead that is difficult to mistake for anything else. Highly flattened spikelets dangle from a bowing seedhead.

**Habitat and Remarks:** Perennial. Native. Also known as northern sea oats or wild oats. This is a common grass of shady bottomlands and may be found near streams of many sizes. It has become fairly popular in landscaping, especially because it does so well in the shade, where many other grass species do not thrive. The dried stalks have been used in flower arranging, and the seeds are eaten by birds and small mammals.

## Reed Canarygrass *(Phalaris arundinacea)*

**Distinguishing Characteristics:** Height up to 2.75 m (9'). Usually a fleshy, coarse grass forming monospecific stands in wet spots. Stem hairless. Leaves rough on top and bottom. Ligule is highly transparent.

**Habitat and Remarks:** Perennial. Native to the U.S. (sort of). This plant was probably native to the U.S. but, as with common reed, cultivars from other continents have been introduced. The non-native cultivars have become quite invasive. Large monocultures of canarygrass engulf and strangle native streamside and wetland plants, especially in disturbed areas. This grass has been used extensively to produce hay in lowland fields and for erosion control. It also provides habitat and food for some native animals, but there are many non-invasive grasses and sedges that provide far better habitat.

## Common Reed *(Phragmites australis)*

**Distinguishing Characteristics:** Height up to 4 m (13'). Seedhead is a large, distinctive plume. In summer these plumes are purple but turn grayish in fall/winter. Hollow stem. Native and introduced forms are difficult to differentiate.

**Habitat and Remarks:** Perennial. Native to the U.S. (sort of). Often simply called *Phragmites*. Forms monospecific stands in damp areas. Most commonly encountered near tidal streams, roadside ditches, and disturbed wetlands throughout the world. Common reed is native to the U.S., but a highly aggressive variety has been introduced (most likely from Eurasia). Eradication efforts are being undertaken in some areas because this species crowds out many native wetland plants—including the native form of common reed. Increased salinity, due to road salt runoff, has been cited as one reason for the explosion of this salt-tolerant species into freshwater areas. Common reed is extremely useful. It can be used to make baskets, sleeping pads, straws, arrows, boats, thatching, paper, and many other items. All parts of the plant are edible, although new shoots are the most palatable. A variety of small mammals and birds feed on reeds, and many more inhabit the cover provided by this plant.

## Giant River Cane *(Arundinaria gigantea)*

**Distinguishing Characteristics:** Height up to 6.1 m (20'). A woody, evergreen plant with a tall, straight, hollow stem. Leaves are 5 to 12 inches long, dark green, and sharply pointed at the tip. They occur in groups of three or five at the ends of short branches. The leaf sheath is rounded and overlapping and is attached to the stem by a row of short hairs.

**Habitat and Remarks:** Perennial. Native. Grows in large thickets along streambanks, bottomlands, and some uplands. These thickets were once a dominant part of the southeastern U.S. landscape; however, it is believed that less than 2 percent of these remain today. The biggest reasons for their decline are fire suppression and farmland clearing. River cane sends out underground rhizomes from which new shoots sprout. The plants rarely produce fruit, and usually the colony dies after seeds are produced. It is the only member of the bamboo family that is native to the United States. It was used by Native Americans as food and fuel, in weapons, and for making baskets and flutes. Rivercane thickets (called canebreaks) make excellent wildlife habitat and were once used as year-round grazing for livestock. They are also important for erosion control and have been found very effective at filtering agricultural runoff.

## Broadleaf Cattail *(Typha latifolia)*

**Distinguishing Characteristics:** Height up to 1.5 m (5'). Leaves are flat and lack a midrib. The seedhead is large, distinctive, sausage-shaped, and brown when mature. In summer the seedhead is green with a spike extending above it, which is covered in yellow or green pollen. Might be mistaken for an iris *(Iris* spp.*)* or sweetflag *(Acorus calamus)* if the seedhead is not present, but those species have a midrib in each leaf, at least near the leaf base. There is no bare space between the seedhead and the pollen of broadleaf cattail, as is the case in narrowleaf cattail *(T. angustifolia)*.

**Habitat and Remarks:** Perennial. Native. Usually found in sluggish or standing waters such as low-gradient streams, beaver ponds, and ditches. Narrowleaf cattail is not native to the eastern U.S. but has been widely introduced. Cattail species spread rapidly through wind-blown distribution of their downy seeds and by rhizomes. They are used by a huge number of invertebrates, amphibians, fish, mammals, and birds for food and structural habitat. Cattails are also useful to humans. The young shoots may be eaten raw (in clean water). The roots may be roasted and peeled for a potatolike vegetable. Flour may be produced from the peeled roots by crushing them in cold water. The starchy flour eventually settles to the bottom of the container, and water can be poured off. The pollen may be used as flour, and the green seedheads make a decent green vegetable. The leaves are useful for weaving baskets, thatching shelters, and producing cordage.

## Common Rush *(Juncus effusus)*

**Distinguishing Characteristics:** Height up to 2 m (6.6'). Round, smooth, dark green stem. The inflorescence extends from the side of the stem and consists of a panicle of flowers that become oblong capsules. Can be mistaken for softstem bulrush *(Schoenoplectus tabernaemontani)* but *Juncus* has capsules while *Schoenoplectus* species have cone-shaped clusters of seeds.

**Habitat and Remarks:** Perennial. Native. This species is found in very wet soils from full sun to part shade. It can often be found in ditches, backwaters, and along streambanks. The seeds of *Juncus* species are eaten by birds and small mammals, and the shoots and roots are eaten by muskrats. Rushes provide soil stabilization and structural habitat for a huge variety of riparian wildlife.

## Softstem Bulrush *(Schoenoplectus tabernaemontani)*

**Distinguishing Characteristics:** Height up to 2.75 m (9'). Unlike most other members of the sedge family, which have triangular stems, softstem bulrush has a rounded, spongy stem. The seedhead is a compound umbel of spikelets, with a bract (0.5 to 3 inches long) that looks like a continuation of the stem. Might be mistaken for a *Juncus*, such as common rush *(J. effusus)*, but *Schoenoplectus* species have cone-shaped clusters of seeds instead of the capsules found in *Juncus*.

**Habitat and Remarks:** Perennial. Native. Also known as great bulrush, this species is found on streambanks and in ditches, beaver ponds, and wetlands. It typically grows in full sun. The seeds are eaten by a variety of birds, and muskrats dine on the rhizomes and stems. The young shoots are excellent eaten raw or cooked. The roots can be roasted and eaten, and the ground seeds and pollen can be used as flour. The stems are useful for weaving mats and baskets.

## Sawgrass *(Cladium mariscus ssp. jamaiciense)*

**Distinguishing Characteristics:** Height up to 3 m (118"). Like other members of the sedge family, this species has a triangular stem (species in the grass and rush families have round stems). Sawgrass has small, sharp teeth on the edges and midrib of the leaves that slice skin readily. Forms dense, monospecific stands. There are several inflorescences spaced along the upper stem.

**Habitat and Remarks:** Perennial. Native. Sawgrass grows along coastal streams and is often found toward the upper reaches of brackish, tidal streams. Many people know that the Everglades of Florida are composed largely of dense stands of sawgrass, but this species actually has an extensive range outside of the Everglades. The seeds are eaten by some waterfowl and wading birds, and the roots are used by muskrats. The foliage provides food for insects and structural habitat for many other species.

## Woolgrass *(Scirpus cyperinus)*

**Distinguishing Characteristics:** Height up to 150 cm (4.9'). Like other members of the sedge family, this species has a semi-triangular stem (species in the grass and rush families have round stems), although the stem is not as sharply triangular as those of some sedges. Has drooping clusters of spikelets with woolly bristles that give the seedhead a woolly appearance.

**Habitat and Remarks:** Perennial. Native. Commonly found near low-gradient streams and wetlands. The seeds are eaten by a variety of birds, and the roots and shoots are eaten by muskrats and some waterfowl. This is an excellent species to plant for soil stabilization in wet areas and to provide wildlife habitat.

## Fox Sedge *(Carex vulpinoidea)*

**Distinguishing Characteristics:** Height up to 98 cm (3.2'). Like other members of the sedge family, this species has a triangular stem (species in the grass and rush families have round stems). Many of the small grasslike plants with triangular stems that are encountered along streams and wetlands are in the genus *Carex*. The shapes of the seedhead and seeds are very important for identification of sedges. Fox sedge has dense seedheads that somewhat resemble a disheveled fox's tail.

**Habitat and Remarks:** Perennial. Native. Common in mostly sunny, wet areas, such as streambanks, ditches, and wetlands. This is an excellent choice for planting at stream and wetland restoration sites. The seeds and shoots are eaten by a variety of birds and mammals.

## Yellow Nutsedge *(Cyperus esculentus)*

**Distinguishing Characteristics:** Height up to 76 cm (2.5'). The triangular stem, which is typical of members of the sedge family (species in the grass and rush families have round stems), is very pronounced in this species and other members of this genus. Single nutlets or tubers are found attached to the roots of this species (not chains of nutlets). The seedhead is an umbel—made up of several stalks that extend from a single point. The spikelets occur at the end of these stalks and are mostly two-ranked (occurring in rows along two planes, so they form an X when viewed from the end of the stalk. There are many species of *Cyperus,* and they are difficult to distinguish from each other, but most have this sort of seedhead.

**Habitat and Remarks:** Perennial. Native. Also known as chufa. This species is commonly found along streams and wetlands. It can tolerate a fair bit of disturbance, and some consider it a nuisance because it can survive in moist areas of manicured lawns. The nutlets or tubers found attached to the roots are sweet and can be eaten raw or cooked. The nutlets of some other *Cyperus* are bitter. Nutsedge seeds and tubers are eaten by rodents, waterfowl, and a variety of other birds.

## Dark Green Bulrush *(Scirpus atrovirens)*

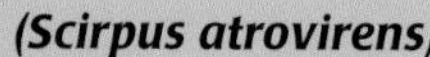

**Distinguishing Characteristics:** Height up to 1.8 m (5.9'). Like other members of the sedge family, this species has a triangular stem (species in the grass and rush families have round stems), although it is somewhat more rounded than the stems of other sedges. The stem and leaves are fairly dark green and glabrous. The seedhead consists of a compound umbel. Each branch of the umbel terminates in a small cluster of 6 to 26 short, ovate spikelets.

**Habitat and Remarks:** Perennial. Native. This is a very common plant that is found in a variety of wet habitats, including streambanks, ditches, and sunny gaps in forested wetlands. This species is very hardy, which makes it a good choice for wetland/stream restoration projects. The seeds of this species are eaten by a variety of songbirds, waterfowl, and small mammals. The shoots are grazed by some waterfowl, and muskrats eat the roots and shoots.

## American Eelgrass *(Vallisneria americana)*

**Distinguishing Characteristics:** Height up to 1.5 m (5'). Leaves are submerged, unbranched, straplike, and about 1 inch wide. They have rounded tips and parallel raised veins. The small, white flowers become small, bananalike seedpods. Tends to have wider leaves than other types of submerged aquatic vegetation such as eelgrass *(Zostera marina)*.

**Habitat and Remarks:** Perennial. Native. Also known as wild celery, eelgrass inhabits a variety of stream types and still waters. This plant prefers sandy or silty substrate. American eelgrass provides food and habitat for a variety of algae, invertebrates, fish, and amphibians. The leaves and roots are a famously important food for waterfowl, such as the canvasback *(Aythya valisineria)*, whose scientific name is actually derived from that of this favorite food plant. Besides providing important habitat for animals, eelgrass and other species of submerged aquatic vegetation (often called SAV for short) stabilize bottom sediment and oxygenate water through photosynthesis.

## Jack-in-the-Pulpit *(Arisaema triphyllum)*

**Distinguishing Characteristics:** Height up to about 47 cm (18"). Typically has three leaves, each composed of three smooth-edged leaflets. Fleshy stem and leaves. Flowers are located at the base of the cylindrical structure (spadix) inside of a distinctive hooded "pulpit" (spathe). Root is very round. In the fall, the flower structure becomes an egg-size clump of shiny red berries as the leaves brown and wither away.

**Habitat and Remarks:** Perennial. Native. Found in moist, shady areas, including stream bottoms associated with medium-sized streams to large rivers. *If eaten fresh, calcium oxylate crystals in the root of this plant cause an extremely intense burning inside the mouth and may lead to breathing difficulty.* However, if the root is thinly sliced and dried until crispy, this plant can be eaten like potato chips or ground into flour.

## Green Dragon *(Arisaema dracontium)*

**Distinguishing Characteristics:** Height up to about 47 cm (18"). Leaves cut into seven or more leaflets arranged in a rough half circle. With a little imagination, some of these leaves resemble a dragon's face. The flower is composed of a long, thin, cylindrical green structure (spadix) partially contained by a thin sheath (spathe). The flower becomes a clump of red berries in late summer.

**Habitat and Remarks:** Perennial. Native. Inhabits moist, shady bottomland areas often located in the floodplains of streams and rivers. *If eaten fresh, calcium oxylate crystals in the root of this plant cause an extremely intense burning inside the mouth and may lead to breathing difficulty.* Varieties of this plant, and its close relative jack-in-the-pulpit, are sometimes used in ornamental landscaping for shady areas.

## Skunk Cabbage *(Symplocarpus foetidus)*

**Distinguishing Characteristics:** Leaves up to 55 cm (21.6") long. The flowers are contained in a mottled, purple, hoodlike structure (spadix) that comes out before the leaves in spring. Leaves are large, ovular, fleshy, and smooth. Leaves have branched venation. Leaves superficially resemble those of young false hellebore *(Veratrum viride)*, but that plant has parallel leaf venation and a much different flower. This plant smells like a skunk if bruised or broken.

**Habitat and Remarks:** Perennial. Native. This plant loves forested wetlands, which are often found at the headwaters or in the floodplains of eastern streams. The leaves are edible if dried for a long period of time, but *if eaten green, calcium oxylate crystals in this plant cause an extremely intense burning inside the mouth and may lead to breathing difficulty. The superficially similar false hellebore is toxic.* The flowers are very attractive to early spring insects.

## Giant Ragweed *(Ambrosia trifida)*

**Distinguishing Characteristics:** Height up to 3.7 m (12'). Leaves usually three- or five-lobed and arranged oppositely. Stem is hairy, and leaves have a very rough surface with moderately toothed edges. Flowers are small, nondescript, and arranged on a spike. Seeds are large and tough.

**Habitat and Remarks:** Annual. Native. This huge plant is often found on riverbanks and field edges. It can grow in sunny uplands but prefers the rich soils and slight shade afforded by bottomland openings such as streams. Giant ragweed often shades out competing vegetation, so it can be considered a nuisance, but this species is native to the U.S. A variety of insects feed on the nectar of this species and on the aphids that often inhabit it. Giant ragweed is often cut down, and probably eaten as well, by beavers. The tough seeds are eaten by birds, but not as often as those of annual ragweed. Ragweed pollen is a potent allergen.

## Annual Ragweed *(Ambrosia artemisiifolia)*

**Distinguishing Characteristics:** Height up to 1.2 m (48"). The leaves are highly dissected and lacey in appearance because they are nearly bipinnately compound (actually twice pinnatifid). Ragweed has racemes (unbranched stems with flowers along its length, with each flower borne on a separate stalk) of nondescript flowers that become abundant seeds in late summer.

**Habitat and Remarks:** Annual. Native. Although this plant is considered to be an agricultural weed, it is native to the U.S., and the seeds provide an excellent wildlife food. Ragweed does well in frequently disturbed habitats, such as sand bars and rock bars, and is a fast colonizer of recently cleared areas. In fact, researchers who study how vegetation has changed through time use ragweed pollen. When analyzing layers of pollen deposited in the bottoms of natural lakes, they often use the first thick layer of ragweed pollen to identify when Europeans colonized North America and began farming. From pollen layers below the ragweed pollen reference layer, they can often determine what the previous, natural vegetation types were. Ragweed pollen is a potent allergen.

## Canadian Clearweed *(Pilea pumila)*

**Distinguishing Characteristics:** Height up to 61 cm (24"). A succulent, translucent-stemmed plant with opposite leaves. Clearweed leaves are usually elliptical with rounded teeth and fine white lines on the bottom side. Flowers are a panicle of tiny greenish white flowers. Might be mistaken for false nettle *(Boehmeria cylindrica)*, but that plant is at least a little bit pubescent and the stem isn't translucent. The succulent stem of clearweed is superficially similar to those of the jewelweeds *(Impatiens)*, but the flowers are very different, and jewelweeds have alternate leaves.

**Habitat and Remarks:** Annual. Native. Clearweed is usually found in moist soils of shaded areas. It is particularly fond of bottomlands and areas around small streams. Like other members of the nettle family, this species provides food for several kinds of caterpillars.

## False Nettle *(Boehmeria cylindrica)*

**Distinguishing Characteristics:** Height up to 1.2 m (48"). An erect plant with opposite leaves. The leaves are finely toothed and the small greenish white flowers are in small, spikelike clusters. Somewhat resembles clearweed, but unlike that species, false nettle is slightly pubescent and lacks a transparent stem. The "true" nettles (*Laportea* [see below] and *Urtica* spp.) have alternate leaves and stinging hairs.

**Habitat and Remarks:** Perennial. Native. False nettle can often be found growing with the stinging nettle species, but it is harmless. This species likes moist, shaded areas such as floodplains, wetland fringes, and the banks of streams. Like other members of the nettle family, this species provides food for several kinds of caterpillars.

## Wood Nettle *(Laportea canadensis)*

**Distinguishing Characteristics:** Height up to 1.2 m (48"). Alternate leaves. Large, pubescent leaves with a toothed edge. Wood nettle has large panicles of greenish white flowers. *Parts of this plant (especially the upper stem) are covered with stiff hairs that can cause an intense burning sensation if they come in contact with skin.* It is somewhat similar to false nettle, but that plant has opposite leaves and lacks burning hairs.

**Habitat and Remarks:** Perennial. Native. If you have ever tried to walk in a bottomland forest during mid-summer, then you probably already know about this "itchweed." The itch/burn of the spines can cause large welts, but this sensation subsides after a few minutes. Wood nettle is a surprisingly useful plant. The top leaves can be boiled and eaten as fresh spring greens. The fibrous inner bark layer of the stem can be twisted into strong cordage. If you learn to recognize this plant in winter, then you can gather the stems without fear of stinging.

# White Flowers (at Least Primarily White)

## American Water Willow *(Justicia americana)*

**Distinguishing Characteristics:** Height up to 92 cm (3'). Long, linear, opposite leaves with entire (smooth) edges and indistinct venation. The bicolored (white and purple) flowers are irregular in shape and rise on stalks that come from the leaf axils. Flowers form a dense cluster at the tips of these peduncles. Looseflower water willow *(J. ovata)* is similar but has flowers scattered along the peduncle, and its leaf veins are distinct.

**Habitat and Remarks:** Perennial. Native. This is one of the most important plants in many streams in terms of animal habitat and stream stability. Large beds of *Justicia* often occur near riffles. These plants provide perches for many insects, such as damselflies, and hiding places for aquatic invertebrates, fish, amphibians, and reptiles. Water willow beds also provide stable substrate for freshwater mussels and refuges from high flows that become increasingly intense as watersheds are cleared, ditched, and paved.

## Aniseroot *(Osmorhiza longistylis)*

**Distinguishing Characteristics:** Height up to 91 cm (36"). Palmate leaf with three leaflets, each of which are divided again into three leaflets with toothed edges. Has heads composed of small white flowers. Styles (the tubes extending out of the flower from the ovary) are longer than petals of flowers. Relatively hairless stem. Strong licorice scent comes from crushed roots, and from the stem, leaves, and seeds to a lesser degree. Sweet cicely *(O. claytonia)* is similar but has a very hairy stem. It is not as sweet and aromatic as aniseroot.

**Habitat and Remarks:** Perennial. Native. Also known as sweet aniseroot. This plant most often inhabits the moist, fertile soils of bottomlands next to medium to large streams and rivers. The dried and ground root has been used as a substitute for fennel, and the green seeds can be used similarly. A pleasant tea can be steeped from the dried root of this plant (using 1 teaspoon per cup of water). The tea has been used as a stomach tonic, astringent wash for wounds, and various other medicinal purposes. If you plan on using this plant, *make sure the plant you have is not one of aniseroot's extremely toxic look-alikes, such as poison hemlock and water hemlock.* In years gone by, aniseroot was chewed and spit onto fishing bait to increase fishing success. It must work, because many fishing stores now carry anise-flavored bait sprays.

## Water Hemlock *(Cicuta maculata)*

**Distinguishing Characteristics:** Height up to 2 m (6.7'). Flower is made up of a bractless, loose umbel of white flowers (unlike Queen Anne's lace *[Daucus carota]*, which has bracts under the umbel). Leaves are bi- or tripinnately compound. Leaflets are lance-shaped with toothed margins.

**Habitat and Remarks:** Biennial/Perennial. Native. Also known as beaver poison, this plant is often found in bottomlands and wetlands in shade or partial sun. *Water hemlock is lethal if ingested. Don't even touch it without gloves!* This plant superficially resembles several edible plants. Symptoms of poisoning include dilated pupils, muscle spasms, dizziness, convulsions, diarrhea, and stomach pain.

## Poison Hemlock *(Conium maculatum)*

**Distinguishing Characteristics:** Height up to 2.5 m (8.2'). Flowers are bractless umbels of white flowers (unlike Queen Anne's lace *[Daucus*

*carota]*, which has bracts under the umbel). Leaves are finely dissected, like those of a carrot. Stem is hollow, hairless, and purple-spotted. The plant gives off a foul odor when bruised.

**Habitat and Remarks:** Biennial. Introduced exotic invasive species. Poison hemlock is often found in sunny bottomlands and on streambanks and can grow to form almost monospecific stands that force out native species. *Poison hemlock is lethal if ingested. Don't even touch it without gloves!* This plant superficially resembles several edible plants. Symptoms of poisoning include vomiting and intense salivation. Poison causes muscle weakness and paralysis, which results in respiratory failure.

## American Water Plantain *(Alisma subcordatum)*

**Distinguishing Characteristics:** Height up to 92 cm (36"). Leaves are oval shaped with parallel venation. Flower petals (less than 5 mm in length) are smaller than those of the arrowheads (*Sagittaria* spp.), which are usually more than 10 millimeters long. There are about six species in this genus, but this is the most common one throughout our area.

**Habitat and Remarks:** Perennial. Native. Also called mud plantain. Found mainly along very sluggish streams, backwaters, and wetlands. This is an obligate wetland plant, meaning that it prefers to grow in places where its roots will be underwater for most of the year. Roots are edible, and the roots and seeds are eaten by wildlife such as muskrats and ducks.

## Lizard's Tail *(Saururus cernuus)*

**Distinguishing Characteristics:** Height up to 76 cm (30"). Heart-shaped leaves. Very distinctive white, nodding spike of flowers. It's hard to mistake this plant for anything else if it is blooming.

**Habitat and Remarks:** Perennial. Native. Found mainly along very sluggish streams, backwaters, and wetlands. Often grows in the shade of forested wetlands and in overflow channels but will also grow right in the channels of low-gradient creeks. For this reason, it can be very useful in preventing erosion along streams. This plant is also thought to have some medicinal potential as an anti-inflammatory.

## Smartweed *(Polygonum spp.)*

**Distinguishing Characteristics:** Plants in this genus vary from small, erect herbs to 3-meter-tall weeds. There are also vining *Polygonum,* such as tearthumb *(P. sagittatum).* Members of this genus usually have alternate, simple, entire (smooth-edged) leaves. However, the leaves can be various shapes, including elliptical, linear, hastate (arrowhead-shaped), cordate, and obovate. A tubular sheath that encircles the stem at the base of each leaf (called an "ocrea") is usually present in members of this family. Flowers of many of the species look like the one pictured. Stems of many species are reddish.

**Habitat and Remarks:** Some species are annual and some are perennial. Some smartweeds are native and some are not native to the U.S. Many members of this genus are found along streams, and many species prefer to have their roots in water. Smartweed seeds are an extremely important food source for wildlife such as small mammals, waterfowl, and many other birds. Smartweeds are quick colonizers, and some introduced *Polygonum,* such as Japanese knotweed *(P. cuspidatum),* are extremely invasive and are pushing out native species. Fortunately, some of the invasive species are edible (such as Japanese knotweed), so we can help out native plants and fill our refrigerators at the same time by adding them to the menu.

## American Hogpeanut *(Amphicarpaea bracteata)*

**Distinguishing Characteristics:** Length up to 1.5 m (5'). Vine with leaves made up of three palmately-arranged leaflets, each less than 4 centimeters in length and with smooth margins. The vine lacks tendrils. There are two types of flowers—conspicuous white or lavender flowers like those of pea plants, and inconspicuous flowers that lack petals and grow near the ground. Seedpods produced by upper flowers contain three to four mottled seeds, and lower flowers produce single underground seeds.

**Habitat and Remarks:** Annual or Perennial. Native. Hogpeanut is most often found in the rich soils of shaded bottomland forests. The underground seeds can be boiled for 15 to 20 minutes and eaten, but the upper seeds are relatively inedible. The underground roots are eaten by hogs (hence the common name), and the upper and lower seeds are eaten by birds and small mammals.

## Garlic Mustard *(Alliaria petiolata)*

**Distinguishing Characteristics:** Height up to 1.2 m (4'). Plant consists of a basal rosette of heart-shaped, large-toothed leaves during the first year. Second-year plants send up a flower stalk with clusters of white, four-petaled flowers. Leaves give a very strong scent of garlic when crushed.

**Habitat and Remarks:** Biennial. Invasive, exotic, noxious weed introduced from Europe. Inhabits stream bottoms and disturbed woodland edges. Garlic mustard forms thick stands and chokes out native species. This plant should be removed any time it is found by pulling plants or cutting them to the ground before mature seeds are formed. Extreme cases may require herbicide, and all removal efforts should continue for multiple years, as seed remains viable for five years. Garlic mustard is edible; the leaves can be used to add flavor to raw salads or made into pesto.

## White Snakeroot *(Ageratina altissima)*

**Distinguishing Characteristics:** Height up to 1.5 m (5'). Summer blooming. The white flowerheads (compound corymbs) at the top of the plant are made up of many tiny, tubular florets. The leaves are mostly hairless and oppositely arranged. Leaves at the top of the plant are lance-shaped, while those toward the bottom are larger, more cordate, and occur on a long petiole (1.9 cm [0.75"] long or more). Leaf margins are serrate.

**Habitat and Remarks:** Perennial. Native. This plant is commonly found in shady bottomlands and dislikes too much sun. It can tolerate a good deal of disturbance and can usually even be found in areas degraded by overgrazing and invasion by exotic species. The flowers provide food for a great variety of insects, but *the foliage and roots are bitter and toxic.*

## Common Boneset *(Eupatorium perfoliatum)*

**Distinguishing Characteristics:** Height up to 1.2 m (4'). Flowerheads consist of broad, branching, flat-topped clusters (corymbs) of tiny grayish white flowers. The stem is covered with hairs, and the leaves have a rough texture. The leaves serve to readily separate this species from similar-looking members of this genus. They are oppositely arranged and broadly joined at the base (especially the large lower leaves). This gives the appearance that the stem is growing through the middle of a single leaf (perfoliate).

**Habitat and Remarks:** Perennial. Native. Usually found in very wet soils in full to partial sun. Boneset often grows in sunny openings of forested wetlands, wet meadows, and headwater streams. Boneset is a widely used remedy for the common cold and influenza. Scientific research suggests that this plant has immune system–stimulating properties. However, if taken in large or concentrated doses, it has strong laxative and vomit-inducing properties. A tea made by steeping a handful of the leaves in a cup of water for about thirty minutes serves as a good cold remedy.

# Yellow/Orange Flowers

## Buttercups and Crowfoots (*Ranunculus* spp.)

**Distinguishing Characteristics:** Height up to 1 m (3.3'). Yellow, five-petaled flowers of most species bloom in spring and early summer. Petals of some species (especially those with the common name crowfoot) are greatly reduced. Leaves are often divided into three parts, and the margins are toothed, cleft, and lobed in various ways.

**Habitat and Remarks:** Annual, biennial, and perennial species. Many native and some introduced species. Buttercups can be found in a variety of habitats but are most common in moist soils. Several species are found in the partial shade of bottomland forests, and some can be found in sunny meadows. Buttercups have been used medicinally in the past, but most species are considered to be poisonous. *These plants contain a poison that severely irritates mucous membranes, the digestive tract, and even the skin if handled.* Be careful not to mistake a *Ranunculus* for the edible marsh marigold (*Caltha palustris*).

## Jewelweed *(Impatiens spp.)*

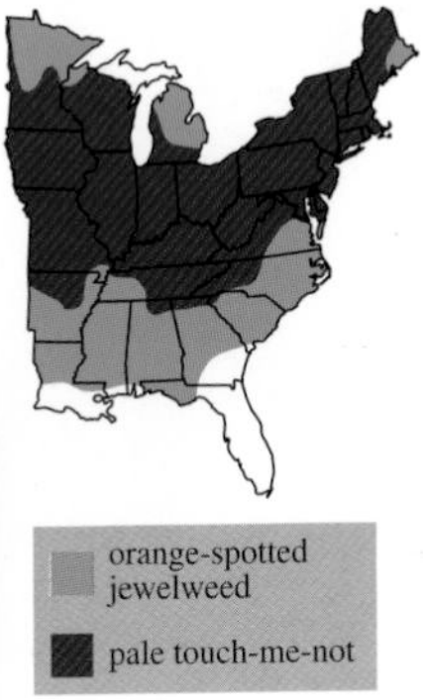

orange-spotted jewelweed

pale touch-me-not

**Distinguishing Characteristics:** Height up to 1.5 m (5'). Juicy, translucent green stem. Oval leaves with wavy margins. Leaves appear silver when submerged in clear water. Ripe seeds shoot off of plant when disturbed. There are two native jewelweeds in the eastern U.S. Orange-spotted jewelweed *(I. capensis)* has orange flowers with black spots and pale touch-me-not *(I. pallida)* has pale yellow flowers.

**Habitat and Remarks:** Annual. Native. Both jewelweeds are commonly found in shady, moist soils—often growing side-by-side in bottomland forests. Orange-spotted jewelweed is widespread in a variety of geography types, while pale touch-me-not prefers calcareous soils often found around streams of our mountains and other highlands. The shoots of both species may be eaten after boiling in two changes of water to remove some of the bitterness (don't drink the water). Crushed leaves and juice from the stem are well-known and effective remedies for poison ivy rash, nettle stings, and many other skin maladies. Hummingbirds love to feed from the flowers, and other birds eat the seeds.

## Beggar's Ticks *(Bidens spp.)*

**Distinguishing Characteristics:** Height up to 1.5 m (5'). This genus of yellow asters is often collectively referred to as beggar's ticks or bidens. Most species have conspicuous, symmetrical, many-rayed yellow flowers, but in some species the rays are greatly reduced. The leaves are arranged oppositely and often have serrate margins. Leaves may be simple or compound. In winter, *Bidens* species are most readily noticed by the small, two-pronged "beggar's ticks" that stick to clothing and animal fur.

**Habitat and Remarks:** Annual/Perennial. Many are native. Many of the approximately two hundred species of *Bidens* love to grow in moist ground in full sun, but some prefer shade. *Bidens* are often encountered along streambanks, and many species do well in disturbed habitats. Waterfowl, game birds, and songbirds feed on the seeds, and cottontail rabbits (*Sylvilagus* spp.) feed on the foliage. Several species are important host plants for caterpillars.

## Wingstem *(Verbesina alternifolia)*

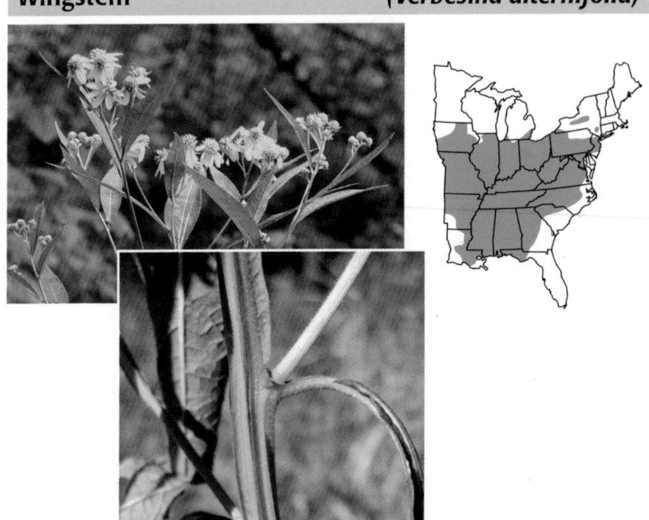

**Distinguishing Characteristics:** Height up to 2.4 m (8'). A late summer- or fall-blooming yellow flower with two to ten drooping or recurved petals and a greenish center. The leaves are alternately-arranged, lance-shaped, smooth or slightly serrate, and hairy or coarse feeling. The stem has prominent wings running longitudinally.

**Habitat and Remarks:** Perennial. Native. Wingstem grows in full sun to partial shade and is often found in moist soil along streambanks and openings in bottomland forests. Plants send up shoots from long rhizomes, and often produce large colonies. This property, and wingstem's love of sun, makes it an excellent candidate for streambank restoration. Wingstem flowers are visited by insects such as bees, and the foliage serves as larval food for butterflies, but the leaves are left alone by most vertebrate herbivores.

# Pink/Red Flowers

## Cardinal Flower *(Lobelia cardinalis)*

**Distinguishing Characteristics:** Height up to 1.5 m (5'). Summer blooming. This plant has bright red, asymmetrical flowers consisting of three petals at the bottom and two petals at the top united into a long tube at the base. Alternate leaves. Leaves are lanceolate, with small teeth along the margin. They are glabrous to slightly hirsute.

**Habitat and Remarks:** Perennial. Native. This plant can grow under a variety of conditions from sun to shade. However, it does require moist soil and is often found along streambanks or near the edge of bottomland forests. This plant is poisonous to humans if eaten in large quantities, but it is an excellent choice for showy streambank restorations. Hummingbirds are highly attracted to the flowers of this plant.

## Beefsteak Plant *(Perilla frutescens)*

**Distinguishing Characteristics:** Height up to 1.5 m (5'). Square stem and opposite leaves, like other members of the mint family. Leaves and stem are often purple, although there are many color variations. Leaves are hairless, wrinkled, and oval-shaped with a pinched tip and large-toothed margins. The plant has a somewhat foul, minty odor when crushed.

**Habitat and Remarks:** Annual. Introduced from Asia. This is a highly invasive plant that spreads quickly in disturbed, sunny areas, such as roadsides, gravel bars, and streambanks. Beefsteak plant can be used as a spice or made into teas, but avoid ingesting large concentrations (in fact, *Perilla* has been used as a fish poison). This plant is used in herbal medicine for a variety of ailments, and the seeds are made into perilla oil, which is used in inks and waterproof coatings. The winter seedheads make a high-pitched rattling noise as they scuff clothing, which may explain another common name of this plant, rattlesnake weed.

## Swamp Milkweed *(Asclepias incarnata)*

**Distinguishing Characteristics:** Height up to 1.5 m (5'). Summer blooming. Inflorescence consists of umbels of small, pink or purple flowers.

Each flower consists of five erect hoods and drooping petal-like parts. Leaves are oppositely arranged, lance-shaped, and pubescent on the underside, and have smooth margins. Unlike in similar-looking milkweeds, the leaf veins form an acute angle with the midrib (in other species they form a right angle).

**Habitat and Remarks:** Perennial. Native. Swamp milkweed inhabits sunny areas with moist soils. It can often be found on rock bars, in sunny side channels, or along the banks of many types of streams. The flowers are highly sought after by butterflies and hummingbirds. *Mature parts of this plant are toxic to humans in large quantities.* The young seedpods and very small shoots (less than 6 inches tall) can be eaten if boiled for about 15 minutes in several changes of water, and the flowers can be boiled briefly, battered, and fried as fritters. Fibers from the stem make excellent string, but it rots quickly if left outside.

## Trumpetweed *(Eupatorium fistulosum)*

**Distinguishing Characteristics:** Height up to 1.8 m (6'). Summer blooming. Flowers consist of a large pink/purple convex-topped cluster. The leaves are 1.5 cm wide or more, whorled, serrate, and lance-shaped. The stem is glabrous below the flower and purple, and nodes in the upper and mid-sections of the stem are hollow (hence another common name, "hollow-stemmed joe-pye weed"). Purple-node joe-pye weed *(E. purpureum)* is similar and widespread, but its nodes are not hollow and its stem is darkest purple at the nodes.

**Habitat and Remarks:** Perennial. Native. This plant loves full sun to partial shade in moist soils. It is often encountered along streambanks and sunny edges of riparian corridors. The flowers are visited by a great variety of butterflies and bees, and the foliage is a food plant for several moth caterpillars. Rhizomes send up shoots, which can form large, soil-stabilizing colonies along streambanks.

# Blue/Purple Flowers

## Great Blue Lobelia *(Lobelia siphilitica)*

**Distinguishing Characteristics:** Height up to 1.5 m (5'). Summer blooming. This plant has blue, asymmetrical flowers consisting of three petals at the bottom and two petals at the top united into a long tube at the base. Unlike most other blue *Lobelia,* the flower tubes have a slit in each side at the base. The flower tube has small, dark stripes. Alternate leaves. Leaves are lanceolate with small teeth along the margin. The stem and leaves are mostly smooth. Downy lobelia *(L. puberula)* also has slits in the flower tube, but its leaves are downy and its flowers have whitish centers.

**Habitat and Remarks:** Perennial. Native. Great blue lobelia is often found growing along streambanks and gravel bars. It prefers full sun to part shade and requires moist soil. This plant is poisonous to humans if eaten in large quantities, but it is an excellent choice for showy stream restorations. Hummingbirds feed from the flowers, and the foliage is occasionally browsed by deer.

## American Bellflower (*Campanulastrum americanum*)

**Distinguishing Characteristics:** Height up to 1.8 m (6'). A summer-blooming flower with symmetrical, five-petaled, light blue flowers lining the upper stem. The alternately-arranged leaves are lance-shaped with serrate margins. Unlike most other members of the bellflower family, the flowers of this species are flattened rather than bell-shaped.

**Habitat and Remarks:** Annual. Native. Also known as tall bellflower, this species loves moist soils and part shade. This perfectly describes the habitat found along streambanks and bottomland forest openings. The flowers are visited by hummingbirds and a variety of butterflies. The leaves and roots were used by Native Americans to treat coughs and tuberculosis.

## Virginia Iris *(Iris virginica)*

**Distinguishing Characteristics:** Height up to 0.9 m (3'). The flower is made up of three horizontal sepals and three vertical petals. These are usually purple or lavender, and the sepals each have a spot of yellow or orange at their midpoint. The leaves are sword-shaped blades that might be mistaken for cattail if not for the midrib usually present at least at the base of iris leaves. The leaves of sweetflag *(Acorus calamus)* are similar, but the roots of that plant have a sweet smell. There are other iris species and various domesticated varieties, but Virginia iris is one of the most common.

**Habitat and Remarks:** Perennial. Native. Also known as blue flag, this plant usually grows in moist soils. It is often found near backwaters, wetlands, coastal plain streams, and even tidal streams. Iris is an excellent native plant for adding color to streambank restoration projects and is visited by hummingbirds. However, iris is not edible for humans.

# Trees and Shrubs

## Fetterbush *(Lyonia lucida)*

**Distinguishing Characteristics:** Height up to 2.7 m (9'). Diameter up to 0.6 cm (0.25"). A sprawling evergreen shrub with arching branches. Leaves are alternate, leathery, elliptical, shiny green above, and dull green with black spots below. The leaf edges are smooth, and there are parallel veins along the outside edge of the leaves. Twigs are red or green, turning brown with age. Bark is covered with black scales. Flowers are pinkish white, urn-shaped, and occur in clusters. The fruit is an ovular capsule with five chambers that occurs in clusters surrounding the stem. Hobblebush *(Leucothoe fontanesiana)* is a very similar species found near mountain streams. Maleberry *(L. ligustrina)* is similar and widespread, but that species is deciduous, and the flowers are pure white instead of pinkish. There are several other less-common *Lyonia* species, but separation of all species is beyond the scope of this book.

**Habitat and Remarks:** Native. Occurs in a variety of habitats but prefers moist, well-drained soils. It thrives in the acidic sandy soils of coastal plain streambanks and floodplains. The flowers are an important source of nectar for bees, and deer occasionally browse on the foliage.

## Spicebush *(Lindera benzoin)*

**Distinguishing Characteristics:** Height up to 3.7 m (12'). Diameter up to 5.1 cm (2"). Leaves are alternate, elliptical, and hairless, and have smooth edges. They are dark glossy green above and lighter below. Twigs are light green, and the leaf buds are distinctly spherical and resemble a BB. Flowers are tiny and pale yellow, forming in clusters in early spring before the leaves appear. Fruit is a small red berry. The leaves, twigs, flowers, and berries of this plant are very aromatic, especially when crushed.

**Habitat and Remarks:** Native. Found in moist, rich soils in shady woods and along stream edges. This plant is very attractive to birds and butterflies and serves as a host for butterflies such as the spicebush swallowtail *(Papilio troilus)*. Native Americans used teas steeped from the berries, twigs, and bark of this plant for a multitude of ailments such as fever, colic, croup, and measles. They also pressed oil from the berries to apply to bruises or as a treatment for rheumatism. The berries can be dried and crushed and used as an alternative to allspice.

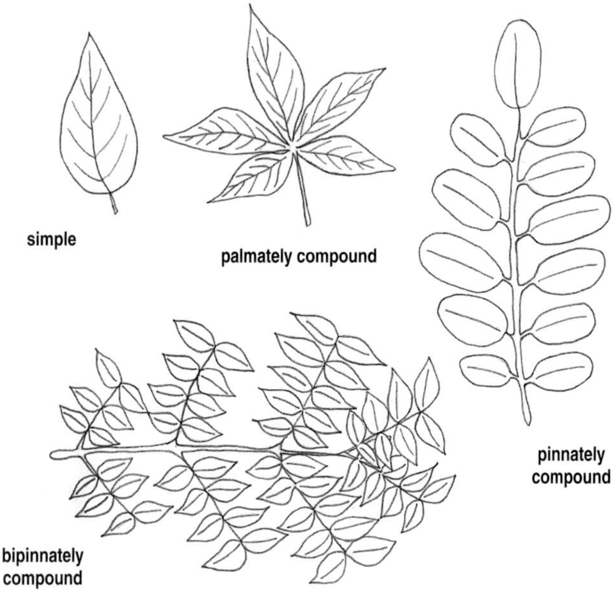

simple
palmately compound
pinnately compound
bipinnately compound

*Common types of leaf arrangement.*

palmately lobed
pinnately lobed

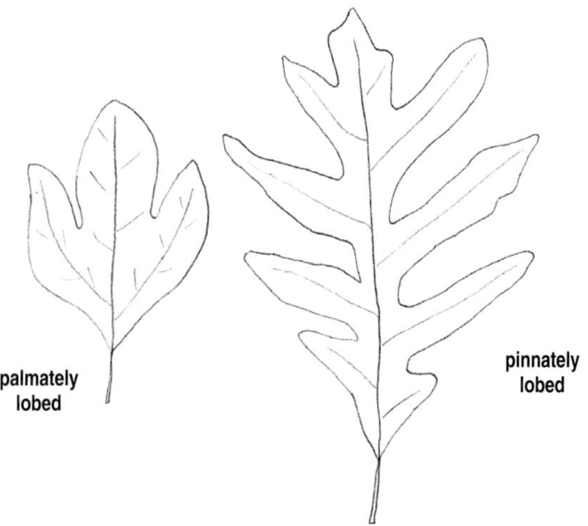

*Common types of leaf margins.*

## Buttonbush *(Cephalanthus occidentalis)*

**Distinguishing Characteristics:** Height up to 15 m (50'). Diameter up to 10.2 cm (4"). A shrub or, rarely, small tree with many crooked branches, often leaning. Leaves are opposite or whorled with three at a node, and ovate or elliptical with pointed tips. They have round bases and smooth edges. They are smooth, shiny green above, and paler below, sometimes with hairs. Leaves are very late to fall. Twigs are reddish brown, usually smooth, and marked with large lenticels. Bark is very dark brown or gray and is deeply furrowed with broad, flat, scaly ridges. Flowers are small, white, and tubular, and form into dense, round clusters with many flowers each. Fruit is a rough brown ball consisting of many nuts.

**Habitat and Remarks:** Native. Buttonbush thrives in the wettest places that a shrub will grow. It is often found in wetlands, low-gradient streams, and along the fringes of reservoirs, and often forms dense thickets. Leaf tea from this shrub has been used as a home remedy for such things as fever and cough; however, *its foliage is poisonous and has been known to be toxic to grazing animals.* The bark has been used as treatment for toothache and eye inflammation. Ducks and other water and shorebirds eat the seeds.

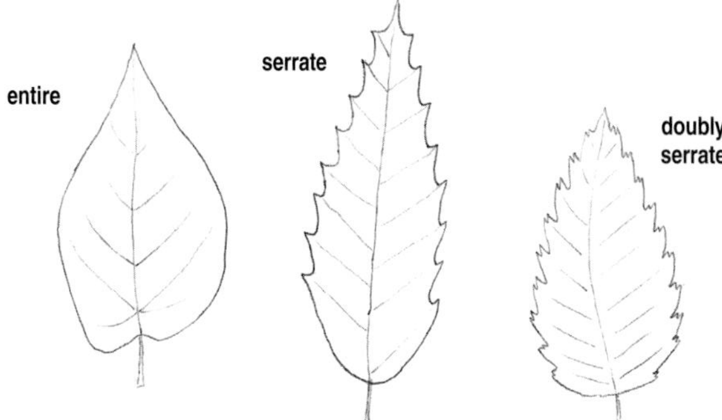

## Pawpaw *(Asimina triloba)*

**Distinguishing Characteristics:** Height up to 11 m (35'). Diameter up to 38 cm (15"). Shrub or small tree with straight trunks and spreading branches. Leaves are alternate, simple, elongate, and obovate with the broadest point beyond the middle. They have a short pointed tip and taper to a wedge-shaped base with a short petiole that has rust-colored hairs when young. Leaves have a very unpleasant odor when crushed. Bark is dark brown or gray with gray patches and is warty. Fruit is up to 12.7 cm (5") long, slightly curved, green, and turns brown upon ripening, with sweet, yellow edible pulp and several shiny, dark brown seeds.

**Habitat and Remarks:** Native. Prefers moist soils, especially in floodplains and along stream edges. The pawpaw belongs to a family chiefly made up of tropical species and is the northernmost occurring species of this family in the New World. Pawpaw fruit was once harvested on a broad scale, but clearing of forests has greatly reduced the supply now. It is still a food source for wildlife, including birds, raccoons, and squirrels. The seeds are toxic and have insecticidal properties. They were once powdered and applied to the heads of children to control lice. Although the fruit is delicious, it has also been used as a laxative.

## Rosebay Rhododendron *(Rhododendron maximum)*

**Distinguishing Characteristics:** Height up to 6.1 m (20'). Diameter up to 15 cm (6"). An evergreen shrub or small tree with rounded crown made up of many thick, crooked branches. Leaves are alternate, simple, oblong, and more than 10 cm (3.9") long. Leaves are leathery, glossy green above and light-colored and fuzzy below (but they lack brown scales on the underside). Twigs are green when young, with red hairs on the glands, and become scaly red-brown with age. Bark is thin, scaly, and reddish brown. Flowers are 3.8 cm (1.5") wide and bell-shaped with five rounded petals. They have a waxy texture and are white or sometimes light pink. The largest petal has many green spots, and the flowers occur in clusters in summer. Fruit is a woody, oblong capsule that is red-brown, sticky, and contains many small seeds. It splits apart in five parts.

**Habitat and Remarks:** Native. Forms extensive thickets (often called "rhodos" or "rhodohells" by those that have to hike through them). Prefers to grow in moist soils along streams in mountain forests of the Appalachians. It is one of the largest of the evergreen rhododendrons. The wood is sometimes used for tool handles, and Native Americans once used poultices of the leaves as a remedy for headaches and arthritis. They also ingested controlled doses for heart ailments, although *the leaves have been found to be toxic and should not be eaten, as consumption can cause a coma.*

## Elderberry *(Sambucus nigra ssp. canadensis)*

**Distinguishing Characteristics:** Height up to 5 m (16'). Diameter up to 15 cm (6"). Multistemmed shrub with an irregular spreading crown. Leaves are opposite and pinnately compound with three to seven leaflets. Twigs are green and angular with homogeneous white pith and node rings. Bark is brown or gray with raised dotlike growths (lenticels). Flowers form in flat-topped clusters up to 20 cm (8") wide late in the spring and are very fragrant. Fruit is a small, purple or black berry that is juicy and somewhat sweet.

**Habitat and Remarks:** Native. Also called American elder. Prefers wet soils in open areas, such as near stream edges. It is a common, tough, and widespread species that does well in disturbed areas and is an excellent choice for riparian buffer plantings. The berries are only mildly sweet and are actually a little unpleasant when raw, but if prepared correctly, can make delicious jellies and pies. Drying the fruit will also remove the unpleasant smell and taste, and it can be stored for later use in muffins or pies. Many species of birds and mammals also feed on the fruit. The flower clusters can be battered and deep fried. *The plant's greenery, roots, and unripe fruit, however, are toxic* and cause severe stomach upset. By removing the pith from a stem, one can also make whistles, flutes, and blowguns.

## Wax myrtle *(Morella cerifera)*

**Distinguishing Characteristics:** Height up to 9 m (30'). Diameter up to 15 cm (6"). An evergreen shrub with a narrow, rounded crown. Leaves are oblanceolate and coarsely sawtoothed, especially from the middle of the leaf to the tip. They are thick and aromatic with short stalks; shiny yellow-green above and paler and often hairy below with conspicuous orange gland dots. Young twigs are "waxy." Bark is smooth, whitish gray with darker gray patches. Flowers are tiny and occur in round clusters at the base of the leaf. Fruit is a small, round, warty cone that looks like a berry coated in thick blue wax. The fruits remain attached to the tree in winter.

**Habitat and Remarks:** Native. Prefers moist, sandy soil in a variety of habitats such as along banks of freshwater and slightly brackish streams and in swamps. Colonists boiled the fruit to separate the wax, which they used for candles and scenting soaps. In some countries, this is still practiced today, though it has been reported that some components of the wax may be carcinogenic. Many types of birds eat the fruits, but usually in small quantities because they can interfere with digestion and become fatal.

## Witch Hazel *(Hamamelis virginiana)*

**Distinguishing Characteristics:** Height up to 9 m (30'). Diameter up to 20.3 cm (8"). Leaves are alternate, oblong, and uneven at the base with rounded teeth or wavy lobes especially beyond the middle. They are dark green above and paler below. Twigs are slim, zigzag-shaped, and coated with hairs. Flowers are 2.5 cm (1") wide, yellow with four twisted petals and appear in fall or winter. Fruit is a hard capsule that ends in four sharply curved points. It opens in two parts, each containing one or two shiny seeds that are forcibly ejected as the walls of the capsule contract.

**Habitat and Remarks:** Native. An understory tree that prefers moist soils in hardwood forests. It often grows along the banks of small upland streams. The leaves, twigs, and bark are used in ointments, eyewashes, and lotions as a mild astringent to treat acne, eye ailments, and piles. Witch hazel is commercially used as an ingredient in medications to treat itching and minor pain. A forked branch of witch hazel was believed to be useful for dowsing or "water witching"—a method used to find underground water. The fruit capsules are capable of ejecting their seed as far as 9 meters.

## Sweetgum *(Liquidambar styraciflua)*

**Distinguishing Characteristics:** Height up to 36 m (120'). Diameter up to 1.2 m (4'). A tall tree with a small crown. Leaves are alternate and distinctively star-shaped. They have five to seven deep lobes with five main veins, finely toothed margins, shiny bright green above and paler below. Twigs are round or slightly angled and commonly develop corklike wings during the second year. Bark is gray-brown, thick, and deeply furrowed with rounded scaly ridges. Flowers are very small and occur in round green clusters. Fruit is a brown ball that droops down from a long stem and consists of several individual fruits that end in two long prickly points.

**Habitat and Remarks:** Native. Prefers moist soils in bottomland, along streams, and on low slopes. It is often one of the first trees to appear after clear-cutting occurs, or in abandoned fields. The wood of this tree is very important in the timber industry, with oak being the only hardwood of which more is harvested. Pioneers once made gum out of resin that they scraped from behind the bark of these trees. It was used for chewing and as a remedy for multiple ailments such as cough and sore throat. It is currently an ingredient in "compound tincture of benzoin," which is available in pharmacies and has a variety of respiratory- and skin-related uses.

## Smooth Alder/Common Alder *(Alnus serrulata)*

**Distinguishing Characteristics:** Height up to 6.1 m (20'). Diameter up to 10.2 cm (4"). A large, spreading shrub or occasionally small tree with many trunks. Leaves are alternate, occurring in three rows, obovate or elliptical, finely toothed, sometimes with wavy edges. They are dark green above and lighter below and have nine to twelve parallel straight veins on each side. The undersides of the leaves often have hair on the veins. Young twigs are covered with rust-colored hairs. The bark is smooth and dark gray or brown. Flowers are tiny and form yellowish drooping catkins in males and reddish cones in females.

**Habitat and Remarks:** Native. Forms thickets in wet soils in swamps, and bordering streams and lakes. This is the only alder indigenous to the southeastern U.S. Native Americans used bark tea for a number of ailments, including as a remedy for childbirth pain. It was also used in the 1800s as a treatment for malaria.

## Paper Birch *(Betula papyrifera)*

**Distinguishing Characteristics:** Height up to 21.3 m (70'). Diameter up to 0.9 m (3'). A small to medium tree (sometimes a shrub) with a narrow crown and slightly drooping branches. Leaves are alternate, ovate, and coarsely double-toothed. They are dull dark green above and yellowish green below, with five to nine pairs of veins. Twigs are green at first and marked with orange lenticels; they become dark shiny orange-brown by late summer. Bark is creamy white and smooth, separating into thin strips, revealing the inner bark; the bark becomes scaly, furrowed, and brown, bronze, or purplish at the base. Inner bark is orange. Fruit is a cylindrical cone with many two-winged nuts that mature in the fall.

**Habitat and Remarks:** Native. Found in moist upland soils near streams, floodplains, and clear-cut lands, often in pure stands. It is one of the most beautiful native trees. This tree is used for specialty products such as popsicle sticks and toothpicks. It was used by Native Americans for birch-bark canoes, which were made by stretching the bark over wooden frames. The bark can also be folded into waterproof containers and used as paper.

## River Birch *(Betula nigra)*

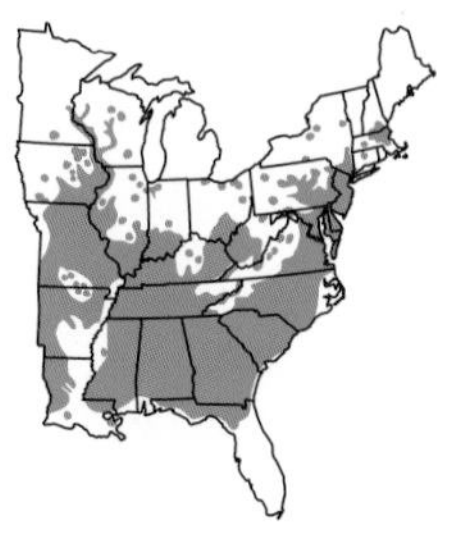

**Distinguishing Characteristics:** Height up to 24 m (80'). Diameter up to 0.6 m (2'). Usually a small tree with multiple, leaning trunks. Leaves are alternate, sharply double-serrate, shiny dark green above, and whitish and hairy below, with seven to nine pairs of veins. Twigs are reddish brown and hairy, with buds that are hairy through the summer. Bark is thin and yellowish, silver, or bronze, and separates into long, curled, papery strips. Fruit matures in May or June and takes the shape of a cone with hairy scales and two-winged nuts.

**Habitat and Remarks:** Native. Characteristic of moist sites along streambanks. It is useful for erosion control. This is the southernmost birch in the United States and the only one that exists at low altitudes in the Southeast. The sap of all birches is edible and can be made into a syrup similar to molasses. The inner bark can be dried and made into flour, and the twigs can be boiled to make tea.

## American Hornbeam *(Carpinus caroliniana)*

**Distinguishing Characteristics:** Height up to 21 m (70'). Diameter up to 0.3 m (1'). The trunk and larger limbs are distinctively ridged in a manner that resembles flexed muscles of a human arm or leg. Bark is smooth and deep gray in color. Leaves are elliptical and doubly serrate along the margin. Fruit is a hoplike cluster of three-lobed samaras.

**Habitat and Remarks:** Native. Also known as musclewood, ironwood, and blue beech. American hornbeam is most often found in the understory of bottomland forests. The seeds are eaten by songbirds, and the twigs are browsed by rabbits and deer. This tree is also used quite often by beaver. The wood is dense, hard, and heavy and has been used for tool handles, mallets, wedges, and bowls because it does not split or crack easily.

## Slippery Elm *(Ulmus rubra)*

**Distinguishing Characteristics:** Height up to 21 m (70'). Diameter up to 0.9 m (3'). Broad, flat-topped crown. Leaves are large and elliptical, with an abruptly long, pointed tip and a rounded base with very uneven sides. Leaves are thick, rough, dark green above, and covered with soft hairs below and have double-toothed margins. Twigs are thick, brown or ash gray, and hairy, with large, rust-colored, hairy buds. Bark is thick, dark reddish brown, and deeply furrowed. Fruit is a key up to 1.9 cm (0.75") long and almost round with a broad, light green, hairless wing. Each contains one seed.

**Habitat and Remarks:** Native. Can be found in upland forests but prefers wet soils, especially in floodplains. The common name comes from the gluelike inner bark, which can be dried and then moistened to use as a cough medicine. Inner bark can also be dried and then ground into a nutritious flour. A number of slippery elm supplements are available over the counter today, including lozenges for cough and dry mouth and powders and tinctures for things such as digestive health. The newly peeled bark can be fashioned into a variety of waterproof containers.

## Hackberry *(Celtis occidentalis)*

**Distinguishing Characteristics:** Height up to 37 m (120'). Diameter up to 0.9 m (3'). Occasionally shrubby but usually a large tree with a large spreading crown and slightly drooping branches. Leaves are alternate, asymmetrically ovate, sharply-toothed, shiny green above, and paler below, often with hairy veins and an acuminate tip. Twigs are slim, light brown, and ridged. Bark is thick, gray or brown, and distinctly marked by wartlike growths and long ridges. Fruit is a one-seeded, red or dark purple berry that matures in the fall. The more southern sugarberry *(C. laevigata)* is extremely similar but has narrower leaves and smoother bark.

**Habitat and Remarks:** Native. Hackberry thrives in moist, rich soils in valleys near rivers and streams. This species is also drought resistant and will grow in drier areas, but tends to be scraggly in these sites. The common name for this species was derived from "hagberry," which means "marsh berry" and in Scotland is the name for a cherry. The berries of this tree are an important food for many birds, including pheasant and quail. The branches often become deformed with bushy growths caused by mites and fungus. These growths are called witches' brooms.

## Black Willow *(Salix nigra)*

**Distinguishing Characteristics:** Height up to 36 m (120'). Diameter up to 0.76 m (2.5'). Tree, usually with a divided trunk. Trunks are straight and usually leaning. Leaves are alternate, narrowly lanceolate, and usually curved to one side. They are finely toothed and smooth, shiny green above and paler below. Twigs are brownish, slender, and delicate. The bark is very dark brown to black and deeply furrowed into scaly ridges. Flowers form in catkins with hairy yellow scales. Fruit is a reddish brown capsule that matures late in the spring.

**Habitat and Remarks:** Native. Found in wet soils along streams and lakes. It grows very fast and sometimes occurs in stands but also occurs with other mixed hardwoods. This is the largest American willow, and the only one important for wood products. Native Americans used the young branches and twigs in basketmaking. The dried inner bark can be steeped in hot water (1 or 2 teaspoons per cup of water) for about 30 minutes to produce an aspirinlike pain reliever. Green stakes of this species are often used in stream restoration projects (see chapter 6).

## Swamp Bay *(Persea palustris)*

**Distinguishing Characteristics:** Height up to 25 m (83'), but usually only around 9 m (30'). Diameter up to 0.6 m (2'). Small tree with a compact, rounded crown and thick, upright branches. Leaves are alternate, elliptical or lanceolate, thick, bright shiny green above, and pale and hairy below, with smooth margins that are curled slightly under. Leaves are pungently aromatic if crushed. Twigs are slender, fuzzy, and dark green. Hairs on twigs and leaves are often rust-colored. Bark is dark reddish brown with broad, scaly ridges. Flowers are yellow and appear in many clusters at the leaf base in early spring. Fruit is up to 1.5 cm (0.6") long, oblong, shiny dark blue with a six-lobed cup at the base. The red bay *(P. borbonia)* is very similar except the twigs are smooth.

**Habitat and Remarks:** Native. Found in moist soils of stream valleys and swamps and in sandy soils. The wood is handsome and used for cabinetry as well as for lumber. The leaves can be dried or used fresh in place of commercial bay leaves for seasoning soups and other foods. The berries are also a food source for many types of birds.

## Sweetbay *(Magnolia virginiana)*

**Distinguishing Characteristics:** Height up to 18 m (60'). Diameter up to 0.5 m (1.5'). A small tree with a slim, rounded crown. It is almost evergreen in the southern part of its range. Leaves are alternate and oblong with a blunt tip. They are leathery, sweetly aromatic, shiny green above, and whitish and finely hairy below Twigs have ring scars at the nodes and buds covered with white hairs at the tips. Bark is smooth, thin, and gray. Flowers are white, up to 6.4 cm (2.5") wide, and are cup-shaped, with nine to twelve petals. They appear in late spring and early summer and are very fragrant. Fruit is dark red and conelike and is made up of many fruits that each contain two red seeds.

**Habitat and Remarks:** Native. Prefers wet soils near streams and in swamps. Early settlers used the roots of this tree to bait beaver traps and called the tree "beavertree." Native Americans used leaf tea as a cure for colds. The bark was used as a source of quinine as a treatment for diseases such as malaria and typhoid fever.

## Tulip Poplar *(Liriodendron tulipifera)*

**Distinguishing Characteristics:** Height up to 37 m (120'). Diameter up to 1.8 m (6'). Deciduous tree with a long, straight trunk and narrow crown. Leaves are alternate, four-lobed, and hairless, with smooth margins. They are shiny dark green above and paler below. Twigs are stout and reddish brown. Bark is smooth and dark green on young trees, becoming dark gray and deeply furrowed with age. Flowers are cup-shaped, around 5 cm (2") long and wide, and have six rounded, green petals that are orange at the base. Fruit is about 7.6 cm (3") long and conelike, consisting of many overlapping narrow-winged nutlets.

**Habitat and Remarks:** Native. Prefers moist, well-drained soils, and is often found on the banks of small streams and in relatively dry bottomland forests. Tulip poplar is an important commercial hardwood. These trees are fast growing and reach a massive size. Early settlers made canoes by hollowing out a single trunk of one of these trees. Native Americans used bark tea as a cough syrup and for ailments such as indigestion and rheumatism.

## Black Tupelo *(Nyssa sylvatica)*

**Distinguishing Characteristics:** Height up to 30 m (100'). Diameter up to 0.9 m (3'). Mid-size tree with a dense rounded or sometimes flat-topped crown and nearly horizontal branches. Leaves are alternate, widest near the middle, and elliptical or obovate. They have smooth edges and often an acuminate "drip tip." Leaves turn scarlet in the fall and are some of the first to begin changing. This tree can be very nondescript, but the presence of three dots within the leaf scar separates this one from other genera of trees. Bark is dark brown or gray, rough, and deeply furrowed into rectangular ridges, resembling the hide of an alligator. Fruit is a dark bluish black fruit. Unlike those of the water tupelo *(N. aquatica),* black tupelo petioles are less than 3 millimeters long. Swamp tupelo *(N. biflora)* has leaves that are widest toward the ends, and the bases of these trees are often swollen (which tends not to happen to black tupelo). Ogeechee tupelo *(N. ogeche)* of the extreme Southeast has red fruits.

**Habitat and Remarks:** Native. Also called black gum. Prefers moist soils in valleys or upland areas near stream edges and swamps. The scientific name actually means "water nymph of the woods" in Latin. It is also often planted as a shade tree or ornamental. The fruit is an important food supply for many species of birds and mammals. Black gums can live for more than four hundred years. The wood is very strong, resistant to splitting, and was once used to make ox yokes.

## Water Oak *(Quercus nigra)*

**Distinguishing Characteristics:** Height up to 30 m (100'). Diameter up to 0.76 m (2.5'). Semi-evergreen oak with a rounded crown and slim branches. Leaves are small, long, and wedge-shaped; the tips are bristled and are shallowly three-lobed. Twigs are slender, reddish brown, and smooth. Bark is dark gray and smooth, becoming black and furrowed with age. Acorns are up to 1.5 cm (0.6") long and are nearly round. They have a shallow saucer-shaped cap and almost no stalk.

**Habitat and Remarks:** Native. As the name implies, this tree prefers wet soils in floodplains bordering streams and swamps. It is a fast-growing tree, although fairly short lived. Because they are often found near bodies of water, the acorns of this tree are an important food staple for waterfowl, especially wood ducks and mallards. Water oak is in the red oak group, so the acorn contains high amounts of tannin and is very bitter. Early settlers and Indians preferred acorns from trees in the white oak group to eat as nuts or grind into flour for bread; however, repeated boiling of red oak acorns until the water no longer turns brown removes the tannin and makes them as palatable as their white oak counterparts.

## Pin Oak *(Quercus palustris)*

**Distinguishing Characteristics:** Height up to 27 m (90'). Diameter up to 0.9 m (3'). A sturdy tree with a long, straight trunk and nearly horizontal branches. Leaves are alternate with five to seven bristle-tipped lobes and deep, rounded sinuses. They are shiny, dark green above, and lighter green below, with hair tufts along the vein angles. Twigs are very thin and smooth. Winter buds are shiny reddish brown, sharp pointed, and fringed with hairy margins. Bark is dark gray, thick, and smooth, with broad, scaly ridges. Acorns are nearly round and light brown with thin, reddish brown, saucer-shaped caps. Pin oak often hybridizes with many other species.

**Habitat and Remarks:** Native. Prefers poorly drained soils in wet sites, usually in pure stands in bottomland forests and swamps. It is named for its many short, pinlike branches and spurs. It is a popular yard tree and transplants easily because of its shallow root system. The relatively small acorns are eaten by a variety of animals, such as waterfowl, turkeys, deer, and squirrels.

## Swamp Chestnut Oak *(Quercus michauxii)*

**Distinguishing Characteristics:** Height up to 24 m (80'). Diameter up to 0.9 m (3'). A thick-branched tree, with a narrow, rounded crown. Leaves are alternate, obovate, and similar to chestnut leaves, with rounded teeth that abruptly come to a point, sometimes with glands at the tip. They are dark green and shiny above, and paler and hairy below. Twigs are thick and green to reddish brown. Bark is thick, gray, and scaly. Acorns are about 2.5 cm (1") long with a third or less of the acorn encased in a thick cap composed of many hairy, wedge-shaped scales.

**Habitat and Remarks:** Native. Prefers moist, well-drained sandy or silty soils in floodplains along streams. This tree is also called "basket oak" because its fibers were once used to make baskets. Its acorns are sweet and can be eaten raw. Cows commonly eat them, which is why it is also sometimes called "cow oak."

## Eastern Cottonwood *(Populus deltoides)*

**Distinguishing Characteristics:** Height up to 31 m (100'). Diameter up to 1.5 m (5'). A large-branched tree with broad, open crown. Leaves are triangularly shaped with long points and coarse, curved teeth. Leaves are shiny green and have long, flattened leaf stalks that allow them to flutter in the slightest wind. Twigs are thick, yellow-brown, and angular. Bark is yellow-green and smooth in young trees, becoming ash gray and thickly furrowed in old ones. The fruits, which are produced in early summer, consist of small seeds attached to cottonlike fibers.

**Habitat and Remarks:** Found near streams and in moist valleys in pure stands, or often with willows. This was likely the most common tree found growing next to our midwestern prairie streams prior to conversion to farmland, and they often dominate bottomlands adjacent to larger rivers throughout the U.S. Cottonwood is one of the first trees to appear on sand bars and in floodplains. It is one of the fastest-growing native trees and can grow up to 1.5 m (5') per year in prime habitats. It is possible for this tree to grow up to 4 m (13') tall in the first year of life. Cottonwood is a favorite beaver food, and the buds are eaten by many mammals and birds. These trees are relatively short lived, but this characteristic makes the cottonwood an excellent home for snag-loving species such as wood ducks, woodpeckers, and various bats.

## American Sycamore *(Platanus occidentalis)*

**Distinguishing Characteristics:** Height up to 30 m (100'). Diameter up to 2.4 m (8'). A large, strikingly colored tree, with a massive straight trunk and crooked, spreading branches. Leaves are alternate and very shallowly three- or five-lobed with three to five main veins and coarsely toothed margins. Twigs are slender and green and grow in zigzag patterns. Bark is smooth and flakes off in large patches, exposing the inner bark and giving the upper trunk a very mottled appearance of white, green, brown, and gray. The base of the tree is dark reddish brown and deeply furrowed. Fruit is a brown ball 2.5 cm (1") in diameter on a long stalk and is made up of many tiny nutlets, each with a hair tuft.

**Habitat and Remarks:** Native. The white upper branches of sycamore are visible from far away and can often be used to locate rivers and streams in the distance. This tree inhabits wet soils along streambanks, floodplains, and the edges of swamps and lakes. Sycamore is one of the first trees to inhabit abandoned farmland and is among the largest of the eastern hardwoods. The largest American sycamore on record had a trunk diameter of almost 4.6 m (15'). American sycamore can be tapped like a maple and the sap can be boiled down to make sugar or syrup, although it takes huge amounts of sap to do this. However, the sap is an excellent source of pure drinking water where water is contaminated. Chimney swifts once used the large hollow trunks of old sycamores as homes.

## Silver Maple *(Acer saccharinum)*

**Distinguishing Characteristics:** Height up to 24.4 m (80'). Diameter up to 0.9 m (3'). A large tree with a short, thick trunk, and a few spreading forks. Branches are long and curving. Leaves are opposite and deeply five-lobed. The middle lobe is often three-lobed with the margins spreading apart toward the long pointed tip. Leaves are sharply double-toothed with five main veins, and are dull green above and silvery white below. Twigs are slim and long, range from light green to dark red, and have an unpleasant odor when crushed. Bark is gray and smooth in young trees but becomes furrowed into scaly, shaggy plates with age. Flowers are small reddish clusters that turn greenish yellow before leaves appear. Fruit is a paired, widely forked key.

**Habitat and Remarks:** Native. Grows in wet soils such as swamps, floodplains, and the banks of rivers and streams. It is very fast growing but has brittle limbs that are easily broken in high winds. Sugar and syrup can be made from the sap; however, silver maple sap is lower in sugar content than sugar maple *(Acer saccharum)*, so more sap is needed.

## Red Maple *(Acer rubrum)*

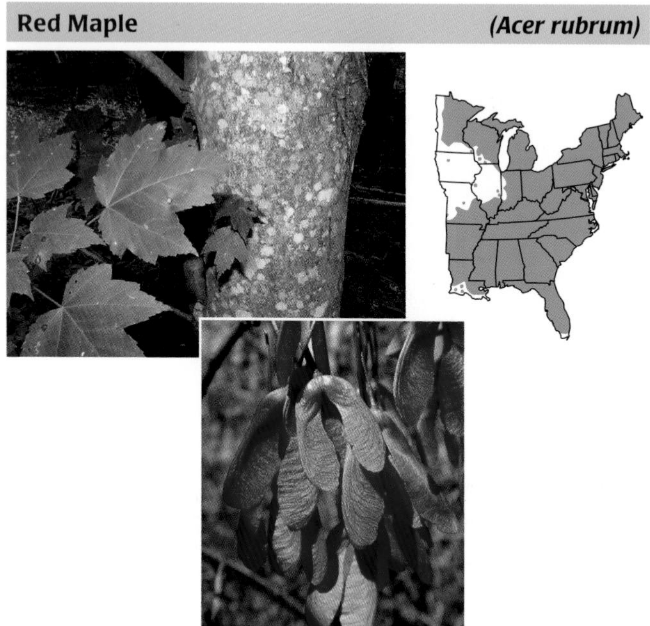

**Distinguishing Characteristics:** Height up to 27.4 m (90'). Diameter up to 0.9 m (3'). A large tree with a rounded crown. Leaves are opposite, and shallowly three-lobed. The margins of the terminal lobe converge toward the point. Leaves are dull green above and lighter and hairy below, with five main veins. Twigs are slim and dark red and do not have an unpleasant odor when crushed, unlike those of the silver maple. Bark is gray, thin, and smooth in younger trees and becomes separated into long scaly plates as the tree ages. Flowers are reddish and crowded into clusters, appearing in late winter or very early spring before the leaves appear. Fruit appears in reddish, paired, forking keys. The foliage turns bright red in the fall.

**Habitat and Remarks:** Native. Occurs most often in moist soils along stream and riverbanks, and in swamps and valleys. It has the largest distribution north to south of any tree on the east coast. Early settlers used the bark to make ink and dye. Red maple sap can also be harvested to produce syrup.

## Boxelder *(Acer negundo)*

**Distinguishing Characteristics:** Height up to 18 m (60'). Diameter up to 0.8 m (2.5') Short trunk and a large round crown of spreading branches. Leaves are opposite and pinnately compound, with three to seven leaflets on a long, slender petiole. Leaves with three leaflets closely resemble poison ivy. Leaflets are ovate or lanceolate, with long pointed tips and coarsely serrated edges. Twigs are green, smooth, and slender with rings at the nodes. Bark is thin and light gray or brown and fissured into many narrow ridges, becoming deeply furrowed with age. Fruit are paired keys up to 3.8 cm (1.5") long with a long, curved wing. They are pale yellow, contain one seed each, and occur in drooping clusters that mature in summer and remain attached in winter.

**Habitat and Remarks:** Native. Prefers wet or moist soils in valleys and along the banks of various types of streams. Also grows along roadsides and waste places and tolerates disturbance well. Boxelder is a fast-growing species and is planted to protect soil from erosion but is easily damaged in storms. The sap was used by Native Americans to make sugar, and inner bark tea was used to induce vomiting.

## Chinese Privet *(Ligustrum sinense)*

**Distinguishing Characteristics:** Height up to 6.1 m (20'). Diameter up to 15 cm (6"). A semi-evergreen shrub or small tree with multiple stems and long, leafy branches. Leaves are opposite and elliptical. They are shiny dark green above and paler with a hairy mid-vein below. Trunk is often covered with oppositely arranged, thornlike twigs. Flowers are white and tubular, have four petals, and occur in clusters. Fruit is an ovate drupe containing up to four seeds that is green in the summer and ripens to dark purple or black in the fall. Berries often last well into winter. There are several nonnative species of privet in the eastern U.S. that closely resemble this species; however, *L. sinense* is distinguished by having fine hairs on the twigs and the undersides of the leaves.

**Habitat and Remarks:** Nonnative, very invasive plant that was first introduced to the U.S. in the 1800s. Thrives in moist soils of bottomland forests. It reproduces by seed distribution, and also by underground rhizomes. It is very detrimental to the environment because of its ability to reproduce and spread so quickly, displacing native plants, sometimes to the point of extinction. Soil disruptions such as forest clearing, animal activity, or fallen trees provide opportunity for colonies of this plant to form. It also readily takes over abandoned farmland. *The berries of Chinese privet are toxic and cause severe stomach upset if ingested.*

## Green Ash *(Fraxinus pennsylvanica)*

**Distinguishing Characteristics:** Height up to 18 m (60'). Diameter up to 0.6 m (2'). Medium-size tree with a thick, rounded, or irregular crown. Leaves are opposite and pinnately compound with seven to nine oblong or lance-shaped leaflets that are finely toothed. Leaflets are paired (except at the tip), shiny yellow-green above, and paler and slightly hairy below. Twigs are rounded, green when young, and then gray with age, and have semi-orbicular (shield-shaped) leaf scars below the buds. The similar white ash *(F. americana)* has U-shaped leaf scars that partially enclose the bud. Fruits are a yellowish narrow-winged key up to 5.8 cm (2.3") long that hang in clusters and mature early in the fall.

**Habitat and Remarks:** Native. Prefers loose, moist soils in floodplains and along streams. This species is the most widespread native ash as it extends from the east coast nearly to the Rocky Mountains. It is hardy and fast growing. Unfortunately, all ash species are susceptible to damage and eventual death from the emerald ash borer *(Agrilus planipennis)*, an exotic beetle introduced to this country accidentally (probably in wood packing material) from Asia. Adult beetles eat leaves and cause little harm, but the larvae live and feed on the inner bark and disrupt the tree's ability to transport food and water from the leaves to the roots. In many states, quarantine is in effect and it is illegal to move firewood to prevent the spread of the pest. It is a particular concern because green ash was planted in many suburban areas after Dutch elm disease all but eradicated the American elm (*Ulmus americana*).

## Bitternut Hickory *(Carya cordiformis)*

**Distinguishing Characteristics:** Height up to 24 m (80'). Diameter up to 0.6 m (2'). Tall trunk and a broad, rounded crown. Leaves are alternate, pinnately compound, with seven to eleven leaflets and a hairy rachis. Leaflets are lanceolate, stalkless, and finely toothed. The bright yellow buds at the tip of the twig easily separate this species from other hickories. Bark is thick and gray with shallow furrows and narrow, forking ridges. Fruit splits into quarters halfway to the base. The nut has a thin husk with tiny yellow scales.

**Habitat and Remarks:** Native. Prefers moist soils of stream valleys but is also found on drier upland in the northern part of its range. It is easily adaptable, making it one of the most abundant species of hickory in the United States. The fruit of the bitternut hickory is definitely true to its name, although rabbits have been observed eating it. Pioneers used oil extracted from the nuts to fuel lamps.

## Honeylocust *(Gleditsia triacanthos)*

**Distinguishing Characteristics:** Height up to 24 m (80'). Diameter up to 0.9 m (3'). Large thorny tree with spreading branches and a flattened crown. Leaves are alternate, pinnately or bipinnately compound, with paired, finely wavy-edged leaflets. They are thin, smooth, shiny dark green above, and duller yellowish green below. Twigs are thick, shiny, and brown and grow in a zigzag pattern with many sharp spines. Bark is dark brown or black and is fissured into thin, scaly ridges. There are huge, often branching, thorns up to 20 cm (8") long. Fruit forms in a flat, dark brown pod up to 45 cm (18") long and 2.5 cm (1") wide, each containing 12 to 14 dark brown, beanlike seeds. Pods are slightly curved and twisted and fall from the tree late in the fall.

**Habitat and Remarks:** Native. Found in moist soils in floodplains near rivers and streams and also in dry upland in sandy soils. It is fast growing, hardy, and good for shade; a thornless variety is usually used in landscaping. This variety can also occasionally be found in the wild. The pulp that surrounds the seeds is edible and sugary sweet; however, this tree should not be confused with the Kentucky coffee-tree *(Gymnocladus dioica)*, which has poisonous seeds and pulp. Honeylocust pulp is consumed by wildlife and livestock. The juice of the seedpods is antiseptic, and leaf compounds have been studied as treatments for certain cancers.

## Eastern Hemlock *(Tsuga canadensis)*

**Distinguishing Characteristics:** Height up to 21 m (70'). Diameter up to 0.9 m (3'). Evergreen tree with a conical crown and horizontal branches extending down to the ground, typically with a drooping leader (the highest terminal shoot of the plant). Needles are flat and rounded at the tip. They are shiny dark green above and have two thin white lines below. Bark is reddish brown and becomes deeply furrowed into scaly ridges as the tree ages. Cones are about 2 cm (0.75") long, brown with rounded scales, and hang down at the ends of the twigs.

**Habitat and Remarks:** Native. Can be found in moist, cool sites with acidic soil. Very common in valleys, ravines, and north-facing rock outcrops of the Appalachian Mountains but also occurs in scattered refuges throughout the Midwest. Occurs in pure stands or in mixed groves with pine and hardwoods. The bark of this tree was once a very important source of tannin for the leather-making industry. Native Americans made tea from leafy twigs as a treatment for kidney ailments and used it in steam baths for cough and rheumatism. The bark was once used as a salve for bleeding wounds. Early settlers made brooms out of the branches.

## Loblolly Pine *(Pinus taeda)*

**Distinguishing Characteristics:** Height up to 33.5 m (110'). Diameter up to 0.9 m (3'). Evergreen conifer with a long, straight trunk and a rounded crown. Needles are fragrant, resinous, stiff, often twisted, and occur in bundles of three. Twigs are slightly rough, slender, and yellow or reddish brown. Bark is dark gray or black, very thick, and deeply furrowed into scaly ridges. The brown inner bark is revealed by these ridges. Cones are up to 12.7 cm (5") long with very short stalks. Cone scales are keeled with a short spine at the tip.

**Habitat and Remarks:** Native. Loblolly pine can be found in a variety of habitats but often occurs near streams and rivers in poorly drained floodplains. Often forms pure stands, especially in abandoned farm fields. It is the principal commercial pine in the Southeast, being one of the fastest-growing pines. In the South, the word "loblolly" is used to mean "mud puddle," which is where these trees often grow.

## Bald Cypress *(Taxodium distichum)*

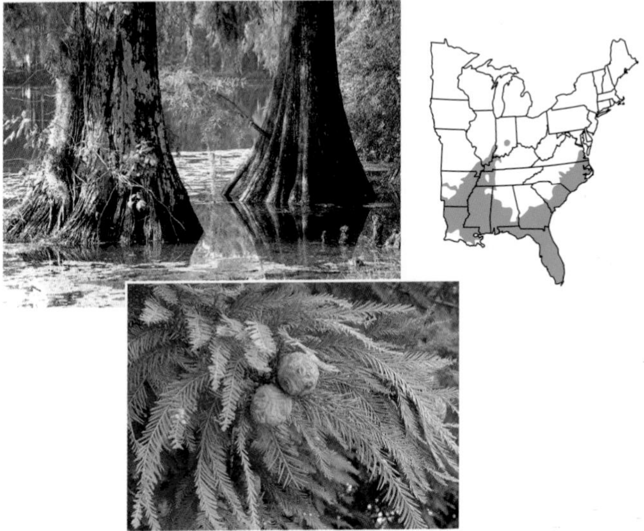

**Distinguishing Characteristics:** Height up to 37 m (120'). Diameter up to 1.5 m (5'). A large aquatic conifer with spreading branches, a flat-topped crown, enlarged trunk base, and cone-shaped "knees" growing from the submerged roots. Though it is deciduous, it has needles that grow in two rows on flattened or four-angled green twigs. They are light green above and white below, feathery, and soft. Bark is brown or gray and fibrous, with scaly ridges that peel off in horizontal strips. Cones are round and gray and 2.5 cm (1") in diameter. They grow either singly or in pairs at the end of the twig and contain several hard, quadrangular cone scales that are shed in the fall.

**Habitat and Remarks:** Native. Prefers very wet soils along lowland river banks and swamps and thrives in areas where flooding is common. Cypress can often be seen growing in the middle of a shallow body of water; however, this species does not sprout and grow underwater and therefore requires periodic drying in order to become established. The heartwood is resistant to decay, giving it the nickname "wood eternal." The lumber is used for docks and boats.

# Invertebrates

Freshwater invertebrates are widely studied, and with good reason. Macroinvertebrates (the ones you can see without a microscope) are some of the most useful indicators of stream health. They lead extremely interesting and varied lives, and they make excellent subjects for ecological research. There is an endless number of mysteries out there, ready to be uncovered by lifting up a rock or shaking some roots into a net. In order to cover as many plants and critters as possible, we are only able to skim through invertebrates at the order level. Where possible we've included some details on some of the more interesting or recognizable families.

## On Identifying Invertebrates

Most of the invertebrates we've covered are found throughout the eastern U.S., so we have elected to save a little space here by skipping range maps. The information provided should help you identify macroinvertebrates at some taxonomic level, but there are other resources that cover each of these groups in great detail and will allow you to identify species. Many nonprofit foundations and state stream-monitoring agencies provide simple taxonomic keys that allow you to systematically identify aquatic invertebrates at some level. These are good resources to supplement the photos and descriptions found here. A quick flip through this guide and a little reading about some of the likely candidates should allow you to identify what you have found at some level. This section is organized with the simplest larval body forms (wormlike) toward the beginning and more complex (insectlike) larval forms toward the end.

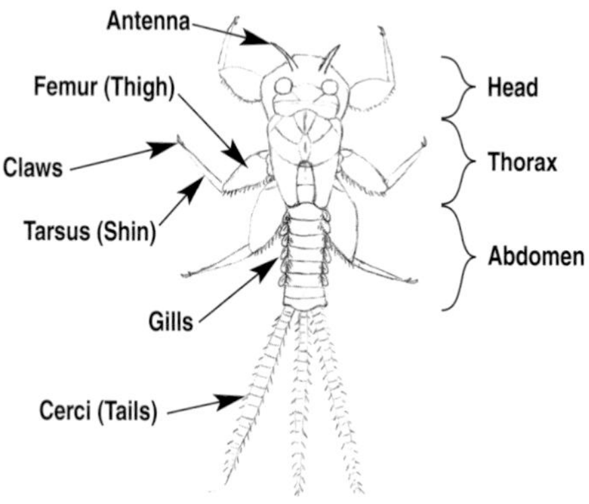


*Anatomy terms useful in identifying insects.*

*Above: A trail left by a freshwater mussel.*

*Above: Exuviae (larval exoskeletons) are sometimes used to identify what insects are emerging.*

*Right: A chimney created by a burrowing crayfish.*

## Signs of Invertebrates

Macroinvertebrates leave behind a variety of signs of their presence. Even the simplest worm may build burrows or leave behind droppings. Snails often leave conspicuous, wandering trails where they graze algae from rocks or sand. Some mussels slowly travel through sand, leaving behind a trail, and their shells can be found on sand bars and muskrat middens. Some crayfish build chimneys above the entrances to their burrows, and caddisflies build many types of elaborate homes (called cases) out of rocks, twigs, and silk. Aquatic insects that have a terrestrial adult form often leave their old skins (called exuviae) floating on the water surface or attached to plants or rocks when they emerge from the water.

## Flatworms (Class Turbellaria)

**Distinguishing Characteristics:** Length up to 32 mm (1.25"). Many species are less than 1.5 mm (0.06") long. These are flat, wormlike creatures but often appear to be amorphous blobs, especially after being preserved. If you watch them move for a while, you will probably see that the head region is arrowhead-shaped. Some have two eyespots. Unlike the tube-shaped aquatic earthworms, flatworms are flattened on top and bottom. Flatworms lack the suckers found on each end of leeches. Flatworms lack legs, jointed mouthparts, and segmented bodies, which separates them from other wormlike stream creatures. Identification of individual species usually requires dissection and mounting on a slide for investigation through a microscope.

**Habitat and Remarks:** There are about 200 freshwater species of flatworms in North America. Many of the worms in this phylum (Platyhelminthes) are parasites of larger animals. The free-living flatworms are also called "planarians." Flatworms feed largely on other invertebrates, detritus, diatoms, and other microscopic organisms. Some types engulf their prey whole, and some types use piercing mouthparts to suck out their prey's body fluids. Some flatworms extrude a thread or layer of sticky material, which is used to gather protozoa, bacteria, diatoms, and other material. They then eat the net and its contents. These worms are typically photonegative, meaning that they try to avoid sunlight and are often found on the underside of rocks. Flatworms are famous for their ability to reproduce asexually (basically cloning themselves). If you cut a flatworm into several pieces, many of them will produce complete new worms. Many types of flatworms are tolerant of low oxygen, and a high proportion of these worms in stream samples may indicate organic pollution such as sewage.

## Aquatic Earthworms (Class Oligochaeta)

**Distinguishing Characteristics:** Length up to 152 mm (6"). Similar in appearance to night crawlers and red worms used for fishing but usually much longer and thinner. Aquatic earthworms are round in cross section, have many body segments, lack suckers, lack eyespots, and have microscopic clumps of bristles on their body.

**Habitat and Remarks:** There are about 170 species of freshwater oligochaetes in the U.S. Many of them are found in sediment or organic matter of pools, but some species may also be abundant in riffles. These animals are capable of reproducing sexually or asexually. The majority of oligochaetes feed on fine-grained organic matter and small organisms found in the mud they eat as they burrow. Freshwater earthworms are extremely important in the diet of other invertebrates and vertebrates such as fish and salamanders.

## Leeches (Class Hirudinea)

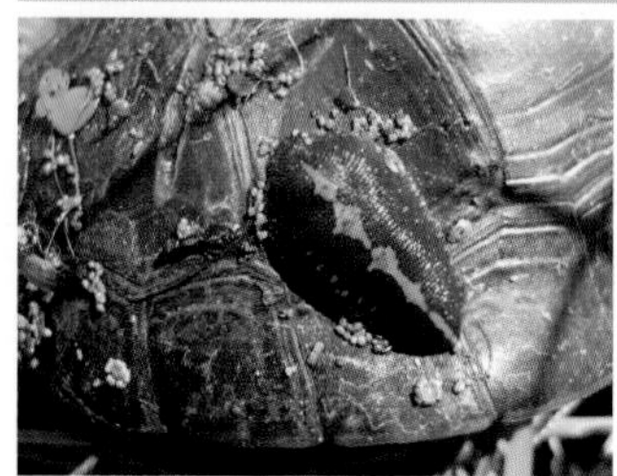

**Distinguishing Characteristics:** Length up to 457 mm (18"). Worm-like creatures that are flattened from top to bottom. Unlike flatworms, leeches have segmented bodies, but they lack the bundles of bristles present on aquatic earthworms. Leeches also have a sucker at each end of the body that is used in locomotion and for attachment to prey or host animals. They have eyespots on the first few body segments. Many leech species are brilliantly colored with green, orange, red, and yellow.

**Habitat and Remarks:** There are about 69 species of freshwater leeches in North America. Unlike many other types of animals, there are more species of leeches in the northern U.S. than in the South. Leeches are often found in the still waters of pools or other parts of streams where organic matter tends to build up. However, you may also see them swimming fluidly in the waters of pristine plunge pools. Some kinds are parasitic, using rows of small teeth to make a puncture in the host. Their saliva contains an anticoagulant, which makes feeding on the fluids much easier. Leeches are quite often found attached to turtles but also feed on fish, frogs, birds, and occasionally mammals. Most leeches that are captured with a net are not parasitic. Instead, these species engulf smaller invertebrates whole or pierce them and drain their body fluids. Some leech species are tolerant of low oxygen, and a high proportion of leeches in stream samples may indicate organic pollution.

## Aquatic Snails (Class Gastropoda)

**Distinguishing Characteristics:** Length up to 69 mm (2.75"). Aquatic gastropods are mostly spiral-shelled, but limpets (such as members of the family Ancylidae) are flat, cone-shaped animals that are attached to rocks and other hard substrate. Aquatic snails can be divided into two groups: Operculates (gilled snails, previously called prosobranchs) and Pulmonata (lunged snails). Operculate snails have a hard structure, called an operculum, attached to the end of the foot (the soft part of the body that extends out of the shell), which can be used to close the shell's opening. Lunged snails lack this structure. Body shape in the spiral-shelled families found in streams can vary from the extremely large, inflated Viviparidae (mystery snails) to the often small and elongated families such as Pleuroceridae (peri-

*Pleuroceridae.*

*Lymnaeidae.*

*Viviparidae.*

*Planorbidae.*

*Physidae.*

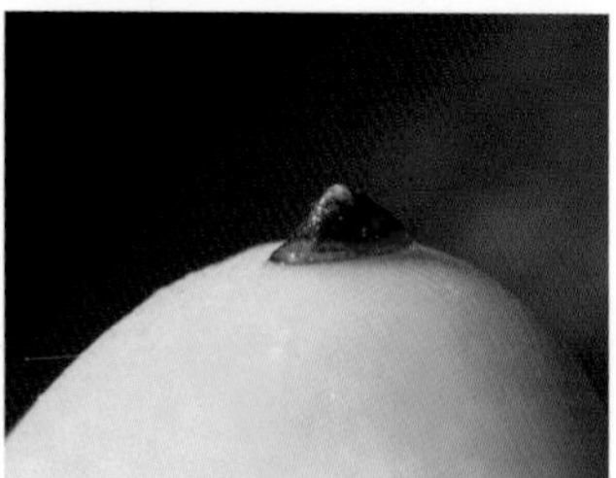

*Ancylidae.*

winkle snails). Only members of the family Physidae have shells that open to the left when viewed with the tip of the spiral pointed up.

**Habitat and Remarks:** There are about 500 species of freshwater gastropods in North America. Aquatic snails inhabit most kinds of streams (except for highly ephemeral channels) and most habitats in streams. Periwinkle snails are often found on rocks in riffles, while other families, such as Physidae, tend to inhabit pools and other still water. Most snails feed on biofilm that is scraped from surfaces with their radula (sort of like a tooth-covered tongue), but some kinds collect bits of detritus or feed on living plants. Snail egg masses often consist of a clear gelatinous or mucousy mass attached to rocks and logs and are often found when collecting invertebrates from the undersides of rocks. Snails are an extremely important food source for aquatic predators. Many kinds of snails are sensitive to pollution, but the presence of a very high proportion of lunged snails (such as the family Physidae) in invertebrate samples may indicate low-oxygen conditions often caused by organic enrichment (sewage or fertilizer).

## Freshwater Mussels and Clams (Class Bivalvia)

**Distinguishing Characteristics:** Length up to 250 mm (9.8"). These mollusks have two shells connected on one side by a hinge ligament. There are two major groups of native bivalves in our streams: the native mussels (superfamily Unionoidea) and the pea clams (family Pisidiidae). Freshwater mussels attain much larger sizes than pea clams (which are usually less than 25 mm [1"] long). Also, the shells of pea clams have a long, linear "lateral tooth" on both sides of the umbo. Mussels have only one of these lateral teeth or lack teeth altogether (see page 120). Native mussels come in a wonderful variety of shapes, colors, and sizes. The common names of mussels, often given to them by old-time musselers, are some of the most descriptive and interesting names given to any group of animals. We've included some pictures of several of the most common and easily recognized species. There are also two major species of introduced, exotic bivalves—Asiatic clams *(Corbicula fluminea)* and zebra mussels *(Dreissena polymorpha)*. Asiatic clams are relatively small and have two lateral teeth (like pea clams) but, unlike pea clams, Asiatic clams have sharp, concentric ridges that are easily seen or felt by running a fingernail down the shell. Native freshwater bivalves are easily distinguished from zebra mussels (see photo), which are typically attached to hard substrate by several bissal threads.

*Two pea clams (left) and one Asian clam (right).*

*Mucket* (Actinonaias ligamentina).

*Threeridge* (Amblema plicata).

*A zebra mussel on a native mussel.*

*Wabash pigtoe* (Fusconaia flava).

*Spike* (Elliptio dilatata).

*Fatmucket* (Lampsilis siliquoidea).

*Eastern elliptio* (Elliptio complanata).

*White heelsplitter* (Lasmigona complanata).

**Habitat and Remarks:** There are about 300 species of native mussels and 36 species of pea clams in North America. The vast majority of these are found in the eastern United States, which is home to the greatest mussel diversity in the world. Many mussel species have become extinct in the last century because of dams, stream channelization, wetland drainage, chemical pollution, exotic species introduction, and siltation. About 60 percent of the remaining mussel species are considered to be threatened, endangered, or of conservation concern, making them one of the most imperiled groups of animals in North America (if not the world). Non-native, invasive mollusks are causing havoc in North American streams. Asiatic clams compete heavily with native filter feeders, as do zebra mussels, which also suffocate native mussels, snails, and other creatures by attaching themselves, in massive amounts, to the shells and exoskeletons of native animals.

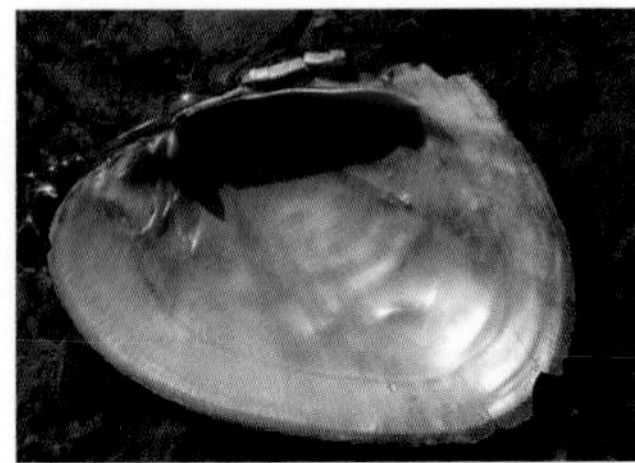
*Pink heelsplitter* (Potamilus alatus).

*Mapleleaf* (Quadrula quadrula).

*Giant floater* (Pyganodon grandis).

*Pistolgrip* (Tritogonia verrucosa).

Many freshwater mussel species have very specific habitat requirements. Most mussels prefer runs of streams with gravel substrate, but some species are more adapted to live in pools, silt-bottomed streams, among submerged vegetation, or jammed into the cracks in rock slabs. Pea clams are most often found in pools or other still waters where they may attain great densities. Muskrats, raccoons, river otters, and freshwater drum are some major predators of freshwater mussels. Pea clams are important in the diets of fishes and many aquatic amphibians.

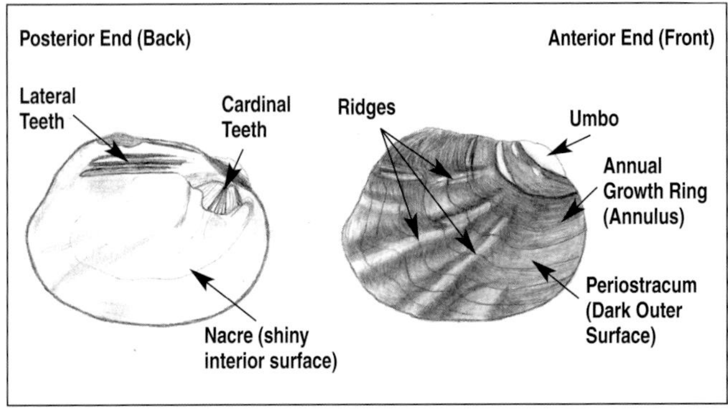


*Anatomy terms useful in identifying mussels.*

Bivalves are filter feeders. They feed primarily on plankton and algae and absorb oxygen out of the water that they draw through their bodies. Consequently, bivalves can contribute significantly to water clarity. The majority of mussels are intolerant of low-oxygen conditions, but pea clams and Asiatic clams can often be found in the tiniest streams where low oxygen often becomes a problem during low water. Most native bivalves are sensitive to many kinds of pollution, and their benthic, filter-feeding lifestyle makes them prone to accumulating pollutants such as heavy metals.

## Dobsonfly/Fishfly/Alderfly Order (Order Megaloptera)

**Distinguishing Characteristics:** Larvae length up to 90 mm (3.6"); adult length up to 127 mm (5"). Larvae of dobsonflies and fishflies (family Corydalidae) are so distinctive that they have their own common name, "hellgrammite." These ugly creatures are hard to mistake for anything else. They have a large set of pinchers on the fronts of their faces and three pairs of jointed legs on their thoraxs, each with one claw at the tip. They also have a small pair of prolegs on the end of the tail, each with two claws. If not for these distinctively clawed prolegs, smaller stages might be mistaken for beetle larvae or caddisfly larvae. Adult corydalids are quite impressive. Adult males are often adorned with huge pincherlike face ornaments, but these are harmless. Larvae of the other megalopteran family, the alderflies (family Sialidae), are similar to hellgrammites except they have a long single tail filament extending from the end of the tail (similar beetle larvae have two long tails).

*Dobsonfly (Corydalidae).*

*Hellgrammite larva (Corydalidae).*

*Alderfly larva (Sialidae).*

**Habitat and Remarks:** There are two families containing 46 total species in this order. Hellgrammites are a popular fishing bait, but watch out, because they can pinch pretty hard. As larvae, they inhabit a wide variety of habitats, from the silty bottoms of pools to cobble riffles where almost no detritus builds up. Some species can commonly be found under rocks in very little water even in the middle of summer. Megalopterans actively search for smaller animals to capture and swallow whole. Species vary widely in their tolerance for low-oxygen conditions and pollution.

## Caddisflies (Order Trichoptera)

**Distinguishing Characteristics:** Body length of larvae up to 43 mm (1.7"), but case length up to 76 mm (3"). Adult length up to 25 mm (1"). Most kinds of caddisfly larvae build elaborate cases or nets which they live in or use to collect food, or both. However, the cases or nets are often destroyed while collecting, and some caddisflies (Ryacophilidae) only inhabit a case briefly during pupation. If cases aren't present, caddisfly larvae can be distinguished from other small, wormlike invertebrates (such as worms, fly larvae, and beetle larvae) by these characteristics: they have an obvious head region, at least the first segment of the thorax is covered with a hard plate on top, three pairs of segmented legs come from the thorax, the end of the abdomen has a pair of claws that may or may not be on two prolegs, and the abdomen

*Common netspinner (Hydropsychidae).*

*Saddlecase maker (Glossosomatidae).*

*Left: A representative adult caddisfly.*

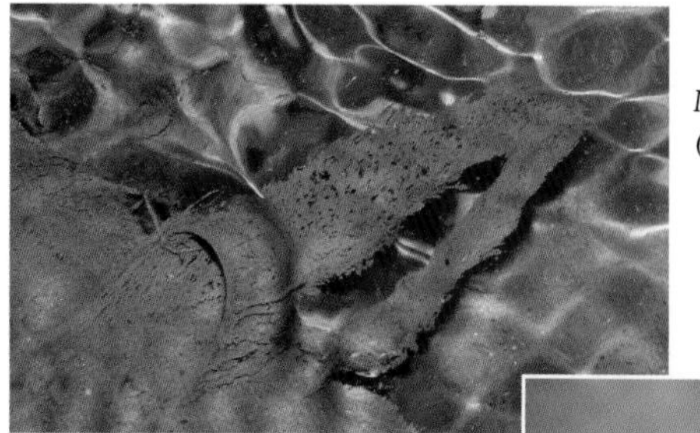

*Netspinner (Polycentropodidae).*

*Rock encrusted with caddisfly cases.*

*Northern casemaker (Limnephilidae).*

lacks other leglike appendages—although there may be single or branched gills. Caddisfly cases, constructed of silk and debris, are highly variable. For instance, Helicopsychidae cases look exactly like spiraled snail shells constructed of tiny rocks. Many caddisfly families, such as Limnephilidae and Hydroptilidae, construct variable cases made of leaves, sticks, stones, and sand grains. Others, such as Hydropsychidae, Philopotamidae, and Polycentropodidae, build nets from vegetative debris and silk. The somewhat mothlike adults have the following characteristics: hairy wings held together to form a peaked roof over the body, two sets of wings that are similar in length extending past the end of the body, thin antennae projecting in front of the body, and two hairy appendages extending down from the head. We still do not know what many adult caddisflies look like as larvae.

**Habitat and Remarks:** There are about 1,400 known species and 21 families of caddisflies in North America. The majority of these species inhabit streams as larvae, and they are adapted to many different types of stream habitats, from the most sluggish backwaters to the fastest riffles. Larvae of most trichopteran families take full advantage of the silk they produce to provide themselves with food and shelter. They often collect detritus, algae, and small invertebrates with their nets, but some varieties, such as the free-living caddisflies (Rhyacophilidae), are active predators. All caddisflies pupate into adults inside a silk cocoon similar to those of moths and butterflies. These insects are extremely important prey items as larva (for other invertebrates and for fish) and as adults (for amphibians, fish, birds, and bats).

## True Flies (Class Diptera)

**Distinguishing Characteristics:** Length of larvae up to 35 mm (1.5"); length of adults up to 60 mm (2.4"). This order of invertebrates includes some of the ugliest aquatic larvae you will ever encounter. Larvae vary in appearance from tiny, blood-red midge larvae (Chironomidae) to huge, turgid cranefly larvae (Tipulidae). Larvae are usually somewhat wormlike and can be distinguished from other invertebrates by the combination of the following characteristics: no segmented legs (but there may be some fleshy appendages), no wing pads, and two opposing jaws or two fanglike mouthparts (which may not be evident to the naked eye). Adults vary in appearance from microscopic biters like no-see-ums (Ceratopogonidae) to relatively huge crane flies. Adults can be identified by the combination of the following characteristics: only one pair of wings is obvious, the pair of hindwings is reduced to two small stalks with knobs on the ends, and the mouthparts are modified for piercing or sucking.

**Habitat and Remarks:** There are more species of Diptera than in any other insect order besides beetles (Coleoptera), and Diptera has more species with an aquatic stage than any other order of insects. Twenty-nine of the 108 dipteran families (about 3,500 species) have an aquatic larval stage. Larvae live in a wide variety of habitats where they may feed on particles of detritus, scrape organic matter from surfaces, or act as predators of smaller organisms. Adults feed on a wide variety of things, including plant nectar and blood, but many do not feed at all as adults—instead, these species live most of their

*Deer fly larva (Tabanidae).*

*Adult deer fly.*

*Adult crane fly (Tipulidae).*

*Crane fly larva.*

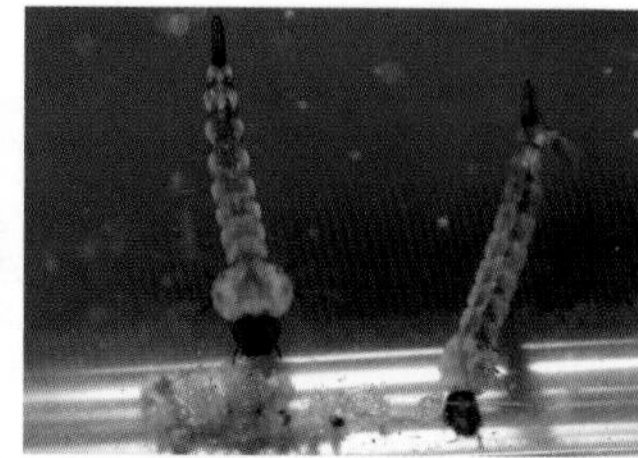

*Mosquito larvae (Culicidae).*

*Midge larva (Chironomidae).*

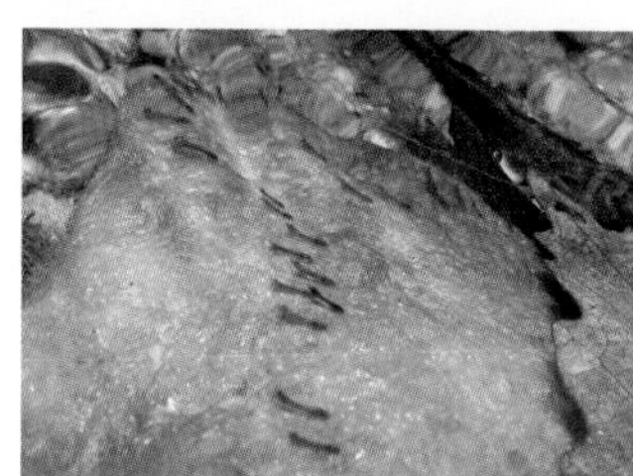

*Black fly larvae (Simuliidae).*

lives in the larval form and transform into adults only to breed quickly before dying. One of the most important roles of true flies may be as prey for thousands of aquatic and terrestrial species. Dipterans exhibit a wide range of tolerance for pollution. Some taxa, such as midge larvae and rat-tailed maggots (Syrphidae), can live under very low-oxygen conditions, while others, such as black fly larvae (Simulidae) are fairly intolerant of low oxygen.

## Beetles (Order Coleoptera)

**Distinguishing Characteristics:** Larval length up to 83 mm (3.25"); adult length up to 41 mm (1.6") (both lengths exclude antennae and tails). The front wings of beetles are modified into a hard, smooth carapace and meet in the middle to form a straight line. Most beetle larvae (except for the very distinctive water pennies [Psephenidae]) are wormlike and may be distinguished from other larvae by these characteristics: distinguishable head with a tough covering, three pairs of jointed legs coming from the thorax, no wing pads, back surface usually somewhat hardened, and no hooks or prolegs on the end of the abdomen (although there may be two tails).

**Habitat and Remarks:** There are more species in the order Coleoptera than in any other order of insects in the world. There are 113 families and approximately 24,000 species in North America, but only about 1,000 species within 20 families are found in aquatic environments. Several of the families, such as predaceous diving beetles (Dytiscidae), water scavenger beetles (Hydrophilidae), riffle beetles (Elmidae), and whirligig beetles (Gyrinidae),

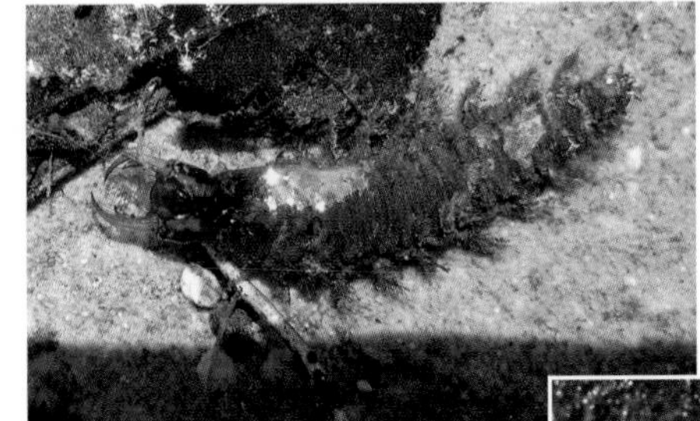

*Water scavenger beetle larva (Hydrophilidae).*

*Water penny (larval Psephenidae).*

*Puedaceous diving beetle (Dytiscidae).*

*Whirligig beetle (Gyrinidae).*

*Typical beetle larva.*

are aquatic both as larvae and adults. Other families, such as the water pennies, are only aquatic in the larval stage. Beetles vary widely in life history and are able to fill many different kinds of niches. For instance, water pennies scrape biofilm (algae, diatoms, and bacteria) that accumulates on stones in swift current while predaceous diving beetles, whirligig beetles, and several other families prey mostly on smaller invertebrates. Beetles have quite a few excellent defense mechanisms, which are perhaps best exemplified by adult whirligig beetles. These invulnerable little creatures' defenses include a hard carapace, eyes that are specially divided to see below and above water at the same time, foul-tasting secretions, an unpredictable swimming pattern, and a tendency to swim in groups (which confuses predators).

## Sow Bugs and Scuds (Orders Isopoda and Amphipoda)

*Isopod.*

*Amphipod.*

**Distinguishing Characteristics:** Length up to 22 mm (0.9"). Seven pairs of legs. Two pairs of antennae. In sow bugs (isopods), one pair of antennae is much longer than the other. In scuds (amphipods), both pairs are about the same length. The familiar "roly-polies" that are often found under logs and other areas of damp soil are isopods and have typically segmented and flattened body forms (though not all isopods can roll into balls like roly-polies). Isopod bodies are flattened horizontally (like a pancake), while amphipod bodies are flattened vertically.

**Habitat and Remarks:** There are approximately 130 species of freshwater isopods, but many new species (especially cave-dwelling species) are still to be described. There are approximately 150 to 175 species of freshwater amphipods in North America. In small streams these are often the most commonly captured orders. They are often found in leaf packs or living among underwater roots and vegetation. Isopods tend to crawl more, while scuds swim around rapidly when disturbed. Both types of animals feed on a variety of food sources, from detritus and biofilm to smaller invertebrates. These animals are extremely important for breaking down organic matter and as prey items for larger invertebrates, fishes, amphibians, and birds. Most isopods are fairly tolerant of pollution, and amphipod species vary widely in their pollution tolerance.

## Crayfish (Family Cambaridae, order Decapoda)

*Genus* Cambarus.

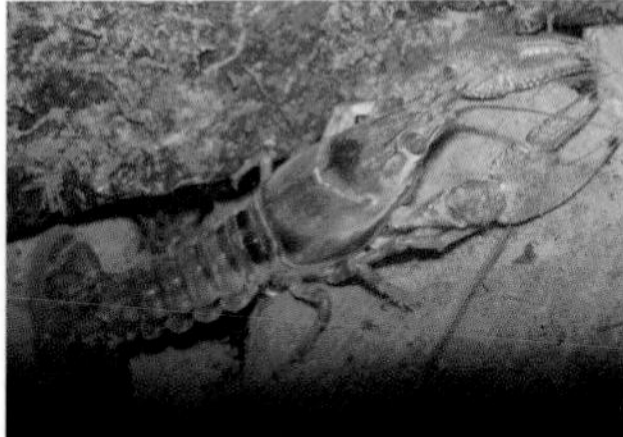

*Genus* Orconectes.

**Distinguishing Characteristics:** Length up to 200 mm (8") (not including antennae). Lobsterlike creatures with five pairs of walking legs coming from the thorax and five additional pairs of tiny legs coming from the abdomen (called "swimmerets" or "pleopods"). The first three pairs of walking legs have claws, but the first pair of claws is greatly enlarged. Crayfish often have one claw that is larger than the other, which usually means that one claw is regenerating after being torn off—some unlucky individuals may be missing both large claws. Shrimp of eastern North America (Palaemonidae) lack the two large claws but they still have five pairs of walking legs. The two major genera of stream crayfishes are *Orconectes* and *Cambarus*. *Orconectes* tend to have rostrums that end in a pinched point, more slender claws, and straight, slender male gonopods (the first pair of swimmerets, which is modified for mating). *Cambarus* have more rounded rostrums, more robust claws, and male gonopods that are usually short, rounded, and curved. Male crayfish in breeding condition (called form I males) are usually needed in order to make identification to the species level, and characteristics of the gonopods are very important.

**Habitat and Remarks:** There are two families of crayfish, but only Cambaridae is naturally found in the eastern U.S. There are about 315 species of crayfish in North America. Many species are found in streams, but some live in more upland areas where they burrow deeply into the ground to reach the water table, leaving a characteristic "chimney." Many species live in streams part of the time and burrow part of the time. Crayfish eat a variety of things, including living and dead plant matter, carrion, biofilm, and smaller invertebrates. Soft-shelled, helpless crayfish are sometimes found hiding under rocks or debris. These are individuals that have freshly molted, and their new exoskeletons have not fully hardened. Females carry eggs and hatched larvae attached to the underside of their tails with a sticky substance in what seems like an amazingly precarious cluster. Many crayfish species are tolerant of organic pollution and siltation, but they can be sensitive to pollution by heavy metals, insecticides, and other chemicals.

## True Bugs (Order Hemiptera, suborder Heteroptera)

*Water scorpion (Nepidae).*

*Water striders (Gerridae).*

*Giant water bug (Belostomatidae).*

**Distinguishing Characteristics:** Length up to 66 mm (2.6"). Adults and larvae are very similar, except that larvae lack developed wings. This order includes many common but different-looking families, including water striders (Gerridae), water boatmen (Corixidae), backswimmers (Notonectidae), water scorpions (Nepidae), and giant water bugs (Belostomatidae). Adults typically have a triangle-shaped area in the center of the back created by the folded wings. Adults and larvae both have mouthparts that have been modified into a cone or tube (called a "rostrum"), which is excellent for piercing and sucking juices out of prey.

**Habitat and Remarks:** There are about 15 families and 400 species of hemipterans that inhabit North America's fresh waters. They tend to inhabit still waters, such as the edges of pools, springs, and backwaters. *Many of the true bugs are capable of delivering a painful bite.* Their saliva contains poisons that are used to immobilize prey but usually only cause a painful welt in humans. The saliva contains enzymes that dissolve internal parts of the prey, which are sucked out using the strawlike rostrum. Except for water boatmen, which engulf very small prey like protozoans and algae, all true bugs are predators of other small animals. Some, such as the water scorpions and especially the giant water bugs, have been known to eat tadpoles and even fish up to 89 mm (3.5") long! Many species are capable of flying, although they seldom do. Most lay eggs on aquatic plants or moist soil. Certain giant water bugs probably have the most interesting egg-laying strategy: the eggs are laid on the male's back where he can protect them and maintain flowing water over them. Hemipterans breathe air and lack gills. Many species are naturally found in slow-moving water with lots of organic material. They can live in water that is very polluted, so a large proportion of true bugs in invertebrate samples may indicate pollution.

## Dragonflies and Damselflies (Order Odonata)

**Distinguishing Characteristics:** Length of larvae up to 64 mm (2.5"); length of adults up to 109 mm (4.3"). Damselfly larvae (suborder Zygoptera) have three paddle-shaped tails (which are actually gills). Mayflies typically also have three tails, but theirs are long and thin, like whiskers. Dragonfly larvae (suborder Anisoptera) are broader than damselfly larvae and lack gills on the end of the tail; however, they have three short, pointed structures that form a pyramid-shaped valve there. All odonates have a large, hinged lower lip (called a "labium") that can be extended to catch prey in both the larval and adult stages. The characteristics of this structure are very important for identifying both damselfly and dragonfly larvae species. Most adult damselflies hold their two sets of wings together vertically when perched, and dragonflies spread the wings flat when perched. Adult dragonflies can be identified to species quite reliably using coloration, but some groups of damselflies are significantly more challenging to identify this way.

*Ebony jewelwing* (Calopteryx maculata), *one of the most common streamside damselflies.*

*Below: Adult damselflies mating.*

*Adult dragonfly.*

*American rubyspot* (Hetaerina americana), *one of the most common streamside damselflies.*

*Clubtail dragonfly (Gomphidae).*

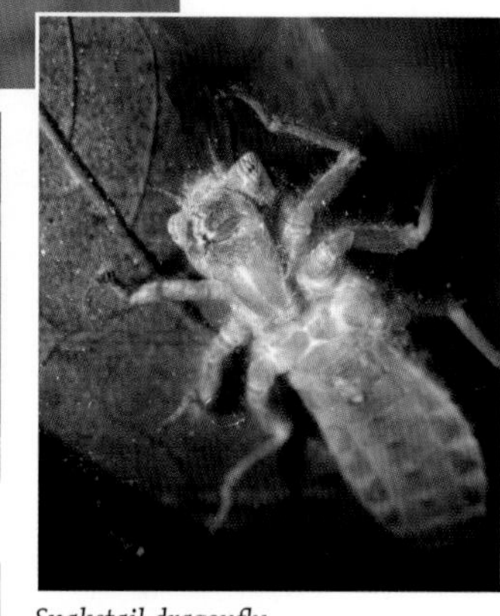

*Snaketail dragonfly (Cordulegastridae).*

*Darner dragonfly (Aeshnidae).*

*Narrow-winged damselfly (Coenagrionidae).*

*Broad-winged damselfly (Calopterygidae).*

**Habitat and Remarks:** There are 5 families and about 130 species of damselflies in North America. There are 6 families and about 320 species of dragonflies in North America. Some female odonates inject their eggs into underwater live plant tissue, while others may be seen depositing them on the water's surface. Larvae of most odonates live among underwater root wads and vegetation, but some species live in silty pools or in rocky riffles. They largely rely on their camouflaged appearance to ambush passing prey. Dragonfly larvae are fierce predators of invertebrates but will also eat small fish and tadpoles. Dragonflies can remain in the larval form for up to six years before emerging to fly the skies. Adult odonates feed mostly on small insects, especially flies. Male and female odonate adults are often different, with bright colors, adding to the beauty that these creatures provide to their growing following of "dragonfly watchers." Most odonates are moderately tolerant of pollution, but this varies by group.

## Stoneflies (Order Plecoptera)

**Distinguishing Characteristics:** Length of larvae up to 70 mm (2.75"); length of adults up to 66 mm (2.6") (both lengths exclude antennae and tails). Larvae are most similar in appearance to larval mayflies, except stonefly larvae always have two tails and two claws on the end of each leg. Adults look fairly similar to the larvae. They have two thin antennae that extend in front of the face, and clear, veined wings that fold to lie flat on top of the back. The front wings extend past the abdomen. The rear wings are wider than the front wings and have pleats to allow folding.

*A representative adult stonefly.*

*Small winter stonefly (Capniidae).*

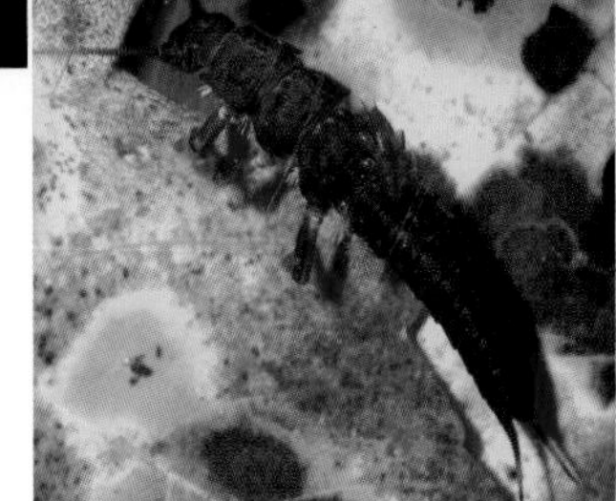

*Giant stonefly (Pteronarcyidae).*

*Winter stonefly (Taeniopterygidae).*

*Common stonefly (Perlidae).*

**Habitat and Remarks:** There are 9 families and 626 species of stoneflies in North America. Chances are, if you have found some stonefly larvae, then you enjoyed a wonderful day in a clear, clean stream. For the most part, stoneflies are highly sensitive to pollution. They prefer cool, clear streams, so their absence from low-gradient streams and large rivers does not necessarily mean that those streams are polluted; they may just not be stonefly habitat. One of the best places to look for many of the stonefly families is in leaf-packs that accumulate behind rocks or logs in riffles. Stonefly larvae are mostly shredders or predators. Some kinds, such as the rolled-winged stoneflies (Leuctridae), feed on detritus, while others, such as the common stoneflies (Perlidae), eat smaller invertebrates—including other stonefly larvae. Unlike mayflies, stoneflies usually feed as adults (mostly on plant matter) and may live for several weeks after emergence. Stoneflies may emerge during any month of the year. Some families (such as the winter stoneflies, Capniidae and Taeniopterygidae) are known for their tendency to emerge during the snowy winter months.

## Mayflies (Order Ephemeroptera)

**Distinguishing Characteristics:** Length of larvae up to 32 mm (1.26"); length of adults up to 38 mm (1.5") (both lengths exclude antennae and tails). Unlike stonefly larvae, mayflies most often have three tails, but some species have only two. In addition, mayflies have only one claw on the tip of each leg, whereas stoneflies have two. The tails are hairlike, in contrast to those of damselflies, which are flattened. Mayfly larvae have gills on at least some of the abdominal segments. Adult mayflies have clear wings held together over the back. The front set is much larger than the rear wings. They may have two or three long tails.

**Habitat and Remarks:** There are 676 known mayfly species in North America, which are organized into about 21 families. All members of this order are aquatic as larvae, and they live in habitats that vary from rocky riffles to burrows in the muddy bottoms of reservoirs. Larval mayflies are mostly collectors or scrapers that feed on organic matter, although a few filter feed or engulf small prey animals. Many adults are very short lived. They emerge from the water only to breed and then die. Many do not feed as adults, and some don't even have mouthparts.

*Pronggilled mayfly (Leptophlebiidae).*

*Adult mayfly.*

*Flathead mayfly (Heptageniidae).*

## Fishing Spiders (*Dolomedes* spp.)
## Fishing and Nursery Web Spiders (Pisauridae)

**Distinguishing Characteristics:** Length (including legs) up to 76 mm (3"). Like all spiders, they have eight legs. Some fishing spider species are extremely large and may superficially resemble a slender tarantula or a large wolf spider. Fishing spiders are hairy and mottled with white, gray, black, or brown. They are the largest spiders to be encountered in most of the eastern U.S. and the most likely to be found in or near a stream. Water striders (Order Hemiptera) also move around on top of the water surface, but they have six very thin legs.

**Habitat and Remarks:** There are nine species of fishing spiders in North America, although only half of them are typically found near streams. Fishing spiders inhabit a variety of stream types, but are often found in the sluggish water of pools, near beds of aquatic vegetation, on cliff faces, or on nearby tree trunks. It is easiest to find these spiders at night when they are more active. Their eyeshine can be surprisingly intense in the beam of a flashlight. Adult females of this family carry the egg sac around with their chelicerae (tiny arms that bear the fangs). They build a silken tent for the young, which they guard until the young leave the nest. Fishing spiders typically perch head-down near the water and wait for prey that include various swimming invertebrates and even small fish. Fishing spiders will actually dive underwater in pursuit of prey or to avoid predators.

# Fish

The eastern U.S. is home to a great diversity of fishes. Ample rainfall, relatively warm temperatures, and variable geographical characteristics have provided an excellent platform for fish speciation. Not only are there many species, but fish can look very different depending on what time of year you find them. In breeding season (spring or summer for most species) males of many fishes become brilliantly colored. Some also develop warty projections called breeding tubercles, mostly on the face and head. This is often in response to environmental cues, such as water temperature, day length, and water pH. These facts may make some fish (such as the shiners) quite difficult to identify, but it also makes them a fascinating group to learn about. The species accounts that follow are grouped into families. The families described here are loosely organized by increasing body size, but some families (such as minnows) have species that range greatly in size.

In order to tell fish apart, it is necessary to learn a little anatomy. The illustration below gives a crash course in fish anatomy. In addition to the major anatomical characteristics mentioned here, ichthyologists use characteristics that are almost microscopic to positively identify some species (such as counts of fin rays and spines, scale counts, and characteristics of pores and canals).

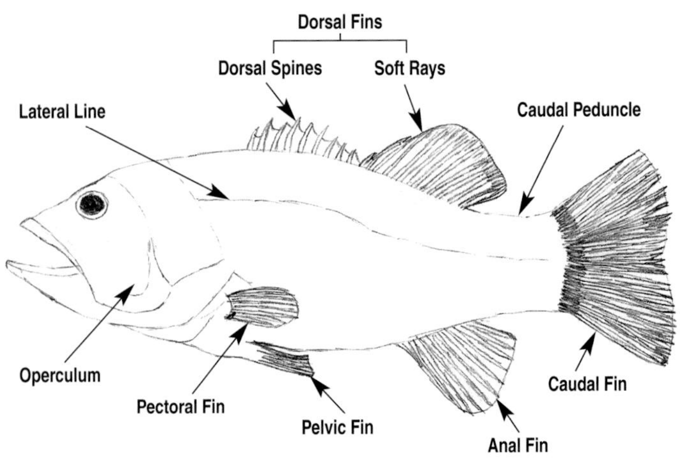


*Anatomy terms useful in identifying fish.*

There are some fish species that can be found very reliably. For instance, creek chubs are in virtually every headwater stream outside of the coastal plain, and mosquitofish may be found in almost any intermittent puddle in the coastal plain. Other species have very specific habitat requirements. There are many fish species (particularly among darters and minnows) that are only found in a single river. We only have room to cover wide-ranging species but have mentioned some of their restricted-range counterparts.

## Mosquitofish *(Gambusia affinis)*

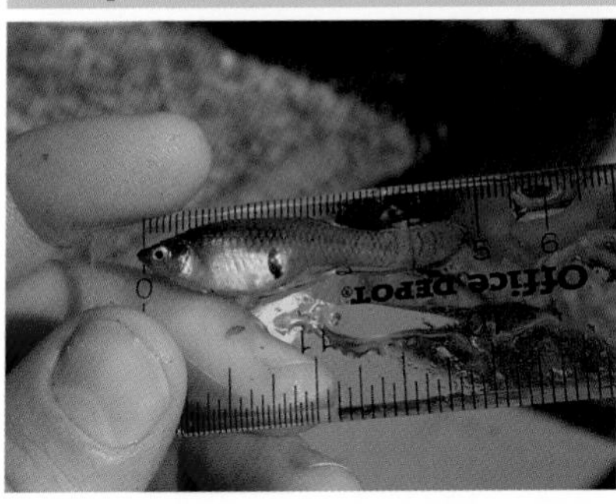

**Distinguishing Characteristics:** Length up to 6.5 cm (2.5"). One of the tiniest fish you are likely to encounter in the eastern U.S. Mosquitofish have upturned mouths designed for eating top-water invertebrates, such as mosquito larvae. They have a large, blackish teardrop marking under each eye and lack the horizontal lines present on many topminnows. Males have a long gonopodium (modified and elongated anal ray used for reproduction) extending from the front of the anal fin. Females are typically larger than males and have a black abdominal spot.

**Habitat and Remarks:** The mosquitofish is the only *Gambusia* in the eastern U.S., although Atlantic slope and central U.S. forms were once considered to be separate species. Mosquitofish were originally native to coastal plain streams but have been introduced very widely for mosquito control. They feed on a variety of aquatic insects, microscopic crustaceans, snails, and small fish. Mosquitofish are very tolerant of warm water and low-oxygen conditions that would kill most other fish. Three or four broods may be born in a single summer, and this species can reach extremely high densities. Introductions of mosquitofish severely threaten fish, larval amphibians, and other species in areas where *Gambusia affinis* is not native, especially the southwestern U.S.

## Blackspotted Topminnow *(Fundulus olivaceus)*

**Distinguishing Characteristics:** Length up to 7.4 cm (3"). Members of the topminnow family have upturned mouths for feeding at the surface. Dorsal fin located far back on the body. Blue-black stripe along the side with some blackish spots that are as dark as the side stripe. Whitish spot on top of the head. There are several other eastern topminnows, but most lack the black side stripe and are more colorful. The blackstripe topminnow *(F. notatus)* is very similar but has fewer spots that are not as dark as the main side stripe. The broadstripe topminnow *(F. euryzonus)* is restricted to southern Louisiana and Mississippi and has a much wider side stripe than similar topminnows.

**Habitat and Remarks:** Topminnows favor vegetated still waters, such as pools with beds of American water willow. Low-gradient coastal plain streams tend to have the most species of topminnows, and many are found in brackish waters. However, blackspotted topminnows are most often found in relatively small, clear streams. They feed largely on insects from the water's surface but also eat a variety of aquatic insect larvae and adults. Eggs are laid singly among vegetation or debris.

## Mudminnows *(Umbra spp.)*

**Distinguishing Characteristics:** Length up to 14 cm (5.5"). Resembles a topminnow or small bowfin superficially. Unlike most eastern fishes, mudminnows have a single dorsal fin located far back on the body. Topminnows and killifishes (such as the mosquitofish) also have this type of dorsal fin, but those families have upturned mouths suited for feeding from the water's surface and lack the mudminnow's black bar at the end of the caudal peduncle. There are two mudminnow species found in the eastern U.S.—the central mudminnow *(Umbra limi)* and the eastern mudminnow *(Umbra pygmaea)*. These species are easily separated by range throughout most of the eastern U.S, but the eastern mudminnow also has ten to fourteen horizontal stripes, which the central mudminnow lacks.

**Habitat and Remarks:** Mudminnows inhabit sluggish streams and swampy habitats. They favor the cover provided by vegetation and organic debris. Eggs are attached to underwater vegetation, and developing young up to about 25 millimeters have a spinal column that extends above the caudal fin. Mudminnows are capable of surviving oxygen depletion and can be found in some of the warmest, shallowest ditches. They have been observed gulping air at the surface of the water to provide needed oxygen. Mudminnows eat many microscopic crustaceans, along with amphipods, isopods, snails, and aquatic insects.

## Johnny Darter *(Etheostoma nigrum)*

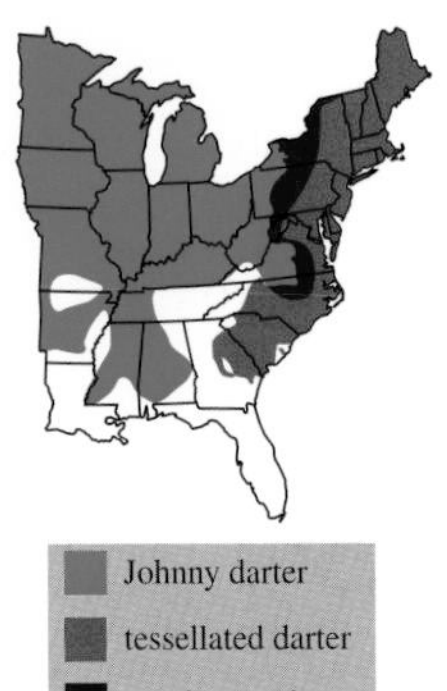


**Distinguishing Characteristics:** Length up to 7.2 cm (2.75"). Small, plain-colored darter with a single anal fin spine. Light background color with six saddles, a black teardrop, and X- and W-shaped markings along the side of the body. During breeding season, the male develops a black head and black anal and pelvic fins. The tessellated darter *(E. olmstedi)* of Atlantic slope drainages and the northeastern U.S. is very similar but is not found throughout most of the range of the Johnny darter. Other look-alikes can be distinguished by the facial striping. When viewed from the front, Johnny darters have two diagonal lines descending toward the middle of the face, while the bluntnose *(E. chlorosomum)* and Choctawatchee *(E. davisoni)* darters have a U-shaped marking.

**Habitat and Remarks:** Johnny darters inhabit small to medium rivers of various types. They are habitat generalists that may be found inhabiting areas with sandy, muddy, or rocky substrates. The male darter cleans silt and debris out from under a suitable nesting object such as a rock or log. Up to one thousand eggs may be attached to the bottom of the nesting object through spawnings with multiple females; each female contributes forty to two hundred eggs. The male guards the eggs from predators and sweeps silt away from them with his fins. Johnny darters feed on microscopic crustaceans and the larvae of aquatic insects such as mayflies, midges, and caddisflies.

## Fantail Darter *(Etheostoma flabellare)*

**Distinguishing Characteristics:** Length up to 7 cm (2.75"). Fantail darters resemble several closely related species, but fantails are the most widespread and common. Unlike similar-looking darters, fantails have gills that are connected across the throat by a transparent membrane. This is easily seen by slipping the tip of a pair of forceps under the membrane. Fantails are of relatively equal height from neck to end of tail. Males develop a dark black head and yellow balls or "egg mimics" at the tips of their dorsal fin spines during spring breeding season.

**Habitat and Remarks:** Young adults of this species can be found living in riffles and runs of extremely tiny streams, and larger adults are typically found in larger creeks. In late summer fantails may be buried deeply in the gravel of shallow riffles and covered with black parasites. Several females often contribute to a nest guarded by the same male. Each female contributes thirty or so eggs, which are usually attached to the bottom of a flat rock. Several similar darter species also guard their nests, and the egg mimics on the males' dorsal spines are thought to aid in drawing attention from the eggs. Fantail darters feed mainly on aquatic insect larvae and crustaceans such as midges, caddisflies, mayflies, copepods, amphipods, and isopods.

## Orangethroat Darter *(Etheostoma spectabile)*

**Distinguishing Characteristics:** Length up to 7.2 cm (2.75"). This species is a deep-bodied darter with several vertical bars along its side and shows quite a bit of geographic variation in color. Bars along the side are blue in males (with orange between bars) and brown in females (tan between bars), and the throats of males are orange. Both sexes have a blue bar at the outer edge of the first dorsal fin, although in the female it can be extremely drab and mottled. Orangethroats lack the red coloration present in the anal fins of rainbow darters *(E. caeruleum)*.

**Habitat and Remarks:** This is the brightly colored darter that you are most likely to encounter in small gravel riffles of headwater streams; however, this species can also be present in small rivers. They often inhabit the same streams as rainbow darters, although the latter species tends to prefer deeper riffles. Orangethroat darters usually lay their eggs in gravel substrate. They feed on fish eggs, isopods, amphipods, and the larvae of aquatic insects such as caddisflies and midges.

## Rainbow Darter *(Etheostoma caeruleum)*

**Distinguishing Characteristics:** Length up to 7.7 cm (3"). A deep-bodied darter that has red fins with blue edges. Bars along the side are blue in males (with orange between bars) and brown in females (tan between bars).

The very similar orangethroat darter lacks red in the anal fin; there are also other, less obvious characteristics.

**Habitat and Remarks:** Rainbow darters are typically found in fast-flowing riffles of small to medium-sized streams. They are typically found in streams with rocky substrate. The female partially buries herself in gravel to lay the eggs in this substrate during spawning. Young rainbow darters eat microscopic crustaceans and midge larvae while adults feed on fish eggs and the larvae of midges, caddisflies, and mayflies.

## Greenside Darter *(Etheostoma blennioides)*

**Distinguishing Characteristics:** Length up to 16.6 cm (6.5"). This is the largest darter in the genus *Etheostoma* (which includes most of the colorful darters), and is one of the most easily identified. A yellow or green darter with six or seven dark green saddles and W- or U-shaped markings along the sides. These are green in males and brown, gray, or green in females. There are also red or brown spots along the upper sides. The dorsal fin has a red base, and the rest of the fin is green in males and clear in females. The skin along the rear part of the upper lip is fused to the snout, creating a face that is distinctive among the darters. Like other darters, the breeding male can become very dark.

**Habitat and Remarks:** Found primarily in riffles of small to medium-sized streams with cobble- or boulder-size substrate. Juveniles may be found in shallow pools near riffles, and adults tend to retreat to deeper pools in winter. Greensides are also attracted to beds of aquatic plants such as water willow. Eggs are laid under aquatic vegetation or among rocks in a riffle. Juveniles eat microscopic crustaceans and midge larvae, while adults tend to eat snails and aquatic larvae of insects such as black flies, midges, mayflies, and caddisflies.

## Logperch *(Percina caprodes)*

**Distinguishing Characteristics:** Length up to 18 cm (7.25"). The largest darter species found in most streams. The end of the face is pointed into a distinct snout, and the sides have alternating long and short vertical bars that resemble tiger stripes. Black caudal spot. In some regions, the dorsal fin has an orange band. There are usually no scales on top of the head or on the area in front of the pectoral fins. There are several other species of logperch (such as the Roanoke logperch, *P. rex*), but this is the most widespread and the only one that is simply called the "logperch." This species may be distinguished from other eastern logperch by the following characteristics: vertical bars extend over top of back to join, no scales on top of head, lack of a black breast, and lack of a black spot at the pectoral fin origin. Range can also be used to identify logperch species.

**Habitat and Remarks:** This darter is more of a habitat generalist than many other darter species. It is most often found in rocky, medium-sized rivers but also occurs in large rivers and reservoirs. In spring, spawning logperch often move into smaller streams, especially ones that flow into reservoirs. They aggregate in gravel-bottomed runs where they partially bury their eggs in gravel. Males are not territorial. Young logperch eat microscopic crustaceans, and adults use their characteristically elongated snouts to flip rocks in search of snails, fish eggs, riffle beetles, and the larvae of mayflies, caddisflies, midges, and stoneflies. Unlike other darters, logperch may occasionally be captured with hook and line by those using fairly small hooks near the bottom.

## Mottled Sculpin *(Cottus bairdii)*

**Distinguishing Characteristics:** Length up to 15 cm (6"). Superficially resemble darters, but have very large heads, wide mouths, and dorsal-facing eyes. Light background color with five or six dark brown dorsal saddles (a few usually darker than the others) and a dark head. Two large black spots in the first dorsal fin. Incomplete lateral line (not all lateral line scales have pores). Adult males have an orange band at the tip of the first dorsal fin. Difficult to distinguish from several other sculpins without a microscope or dissection, but this is one of the most common and widespread eastern species.

**Habitat and Remarks:** Usually found in small- to medium-sized streams with boulder or cobble substrate. This species may be found under rocks in some of the tiniest creeks, which are often barely flowing in summer condition. Like many of the darters, sculpins lack a swim bladder, which aids them in living on the bottoms of swift streams. The male cleans out a nesting cavity, which is usually under a rock or ledge. He mates with one to several females who contribute to a clutch of eggs that the male defends and cleans until hatching. Having large mouths, sculpins are capable of ambushing fairly large prey such as crayfish and fish, but they also feed on fish eggs and the larvae of midges, caddisflies, mayflies, and stoneflies.

## Brook Silverside *(Labidesthes sicculus)*

**Distinguishing Characteristics:** Length up to 13 cm (5"). Very slender silver or transparent minnowlike fish. Silversides have beaklike upturned mouths and a long, sickle-shaped anal fin. Superficially similar to minnows and topminnows (which have single dorsal fins), but silversides have two widely separated dorsal fins. Origin of anal fin is right under the origin of the dorsal. The similar inland silverside *(Menida beryllina)* has a shorter nose, and the origin of the anal fin is behind that of the dorsal.

**Habitat and Remarks:** Brook silversides are not found in brooks. They typically inhabit the open water of pools in medium-sized and large rivers. Silversides are typically seen in large schools near the water's surface. Scientists believe that they spawn in open water, and the eggs drift until attaching to various substrates. Silversides eat zooplankton, microscopic crustaceans, and midge larvae. These minnowlike fish are not a great choice for live bait or aquariums because they die immediately if confined.

## Silverjaw Minnow *(Notropis buccatus)*

**Distinguishing Characteristics:** Length up to 9.8 cm (3.75"). Relatively small silver minnow. The "pearl organs," which are silver-white chambers most prominently seen on this minnow's jaw, give it its name. The silverjaw might be mistaken for a few other minnows with subterminal mouths, such as blacknose dace or central stonerollers, but no other minnow has the distinctive pearl organs.

**Habitat and Remarks:** A fairly common inhabitant of tiny headwater streams of reasonably high gradient. This minnow may be found in riffles from small streams to medium-sized rivers and often prefers sandy substrate. Little has been published about the actual spawning behavior of this species. Young and adults eat microscopic crustaceans, and adults also feed on midge larvae. Silverjaw minnows are declining in some areas due to pollution from mining.

## Southern Redbelly Dace *(Phoxinus erythrogaster)*

**Distinguishing Characteristics:** Length up to 9.1 cm (3.5"). Minnow with tiny, almost nonexistent scales that give the skin a very smooth appearance. Has two black stripes on the upper side, with the upper one breaking up into spots toward the rear. The mouth is slightly subterminal and the snout is longer than the diameter of the eye. Males are very brightly colored, with red bellies. Might be mistaken for a *Rhinichthys,* but those species have much more ventral mouths and larger scales. There are several similar dace *(Phoxinus),* but in the others the bottom stripe is broken, the entire length of the top stripe is broken into spots, or the stripes are fused into a broad black stripe. The northern redbelly dace *(P. eos)* is similar but has a blunt snout that is shorter than the diameter of the eye.

**Habitat and Remarks:** Redbelly dace inhabit the clear, cool waters of small, rocky streams. These creeks are often spring fed. They spend much of their time in shallow pools and spawn in gravel or over the nests of other minnows, such as stonerollers. Dace feed largely by grazing algae that grows on rocks, logs, and roots. Diatoms, roothairs, and bacteria are also eaten during grazing, and aquatic insects are eaten fairly often. The similar blackside dace *(P. cumberlandensis),* of the upper Cumberland River drainage, is federally listed as threatened due to habitat degradation largely caused by mining.

## Blacknose Dace *(Rhinichthys atratulus)*

**Distinguishing Characteristics:** Length up to 12.4 cm (4.9"). Minnow with a ventral mouth and a snout that overhangs in front of it. Body is flat on the bottom. Has fairly small scales and many black specks. There is often a single, black horizontal stripe, and the sides of males may be washed with a rusty red color. Young may be mistaken for creek chubs but have a strongly ventral mouth. Unlike stonerollers, blacknose dace have no groove separating the snout from the front of the mouth. The similar longnose dace *(R. cataractae)* has a longer, fleshier snout and upturned eyes.

**Habitat and Remarks:** Found from tiny headwater streams to medium-sized rivers, especially with rocky substrate. This species, along with creek chubs, may be the only fish encountered in some tiny creeks. During spawning, females bury their snouts in the gravel and deposit eggs in or on the substrate. Blacknose dace feed on oligochaetes, isopods, and larvae of insects such as midges and blackflies.

## Central Stoneroller *(Campostoma anomalum)*

**Distinguishing Characteristics:** Length up to 28.7 cm (11.3"). Elongate minnow with a strongly ventral mouth. The lower lip has a distinctive ridge of cartilage used for scraping. Unlike *Rhinichthys*, stonerollers have a groove separating the snout from the upper lip. Usually thirty-six to forty-six scales around the body at the dorsal fin origin. Breeding male has many tubercles (including a crescent of three or four tubercles along the inside edge of each nostril), a red eye, and orange dorsal and anal fins with black bands. This is the most widespread of the *Campostoma*. Largescale stonerollers (*C. oligolepis*) have thirty-one to thirty-six scales around the body at the dorsal fin origin, and breeding males lack the crescents of tubercles. Bluefin stonerollers (*C. pauciradii*) have bluish-green dorsal and anal fins.

**Habitat and Remarks:** Found in headwater streams to small rivers with rocky substrate. This is one of the most commonly captured minnows in small streams and is often associated with riffles and swift runs. Males excavate a depression in gravel for spawning. Many other species spawn in nests built by stonerollers, which can lead to hybridization. Stonerollers are commonly seen grazing biofilm from rocky substrate. They also feed on rotifers (tiny, sometimes microscopic, animals in the phylum Rotifera), aquatic insects, and microscopic crustaceans.

## Bluntnose Minnow *(Pimephales notatus)*

**Distinguishing Characteristics:** Length up to 11 cm (4.3"). Small silver minnow with a subterminal mouth and a blunt snout that protrudes slightly beyond the mouth. Body is square or circular in cross section. There is a black, horizontal stripe along the side of the body that extends through the eye onto the snout. Strong black spot at the base of the caudal fin. Scales before the dorsal fin are more crowded than rear scales and have black edges that give them a diamond-shaped pattern. Breeding male becomes very dark, with a black head and many tubercles on the snout. Coloration also may vary with water clarity. The similar bullhead minnow (*P. vigilax*) has only a black spot at the upper rear corner of the mouth rather than a black band.

**Habitat and Remarks:** Bluntnose minnows are found from small streams to large rivers in pools and other relatively slow water. They are often associated with beds of semi-aquatic vegetation, such as American water willow. During spawning, the male excavates an area under a rock, log, or other surface. He uses his snout to push large material away and fans away silt with his fins. The eggs are attached to the underside of the nest chamber's roof, and the male fans fresh water over them in order to remove silt and provide oxygen. Bluntnose minnows feed on detritus, algae, small crustaceans, and aquatic insects.

## Rosyside Dace *(Clinostomous funduloides)*

**Distinguishing Characteristics:** Length up to 11 cm (4.5"). This species has a very large mouth for a shiner. The sides of the breeding male are brick red. The redside dace *(C. elongates)* of more northern areas is very similar but has a longer, pointed snout and is relatively slender.

**Habitat and Remarks:** This species, and the very similar redside dace, is found most often in crystal-clear pools of small, spring-fed streams. These dace are easily seined but are also easily observed by snorkeling the clear pools they so often frequent.

## Redfin Shiner *(Lythrurus umbratilis)*

**Distinguishing Characteristics:** Length up to 8.8 cm (3.5"). Similar to many other types of silver, relatively deep-bodied shiners. *Lythrurus* species have much smaller scales on the nape than further back on the body. Dorsal fin origin is behind the pelvic fin origin, and mouth is terminal. Also has a black spot at the front base of the dorsal fin. Mature male is iridescent blue and has red fins with black membranes. Redfin shiner lacks irregular dark bars on the upper sides, which are present in adult male rosefin *(L. ardens)* and scarlet shiners *(L. fasciolaris)*.

**Habitat and Remarks:** Found in small, low-gradient creeks to medium-sized rivers. Usually swims in schools in the middle of pools or other slow water. Spawning occurs over sand or gravel substrate in sluggish pools, often over active sunfish nests. The similar rosefin shiner has been observed spawning in swift water in the same stream where the redfin occupies slow water. Redfin shiners feed on algae and insects, which are largely captured from the water surface.

## Striped Shiner *(Luxilus chrysocephalus)*

**Distinguishing Characteristics:** Length up to 24 cm (9.3"). Deep-bodied, silver-colored shiner with a brown or black bar behind the operculum. Large, terminal mouth. Scales on sides of the front of the body are much deeper than wide. Three dark, horizontal stripes on each upper side parallel to the mid-dorsal stripe. When viewed from the top, the stripes meet to form a V on the tail. Adults develop vertical black crescents along the sides. Males and some females develop a pink wash along the sides and fins. Very similar to the widespread common shiner *(L. cornutus)*, but that species has only one or two horizontal stripes on each side of the mid-dorsal stripe, which do not meet to form a V when viewed from the top.

**Habitat and Remarks:** Found in small creeks to medium-sized rivers with clear or slightly turbid waters and usually rocky or sandy substrates. Large schools of striped shiners often inhabit pools near riffles. They spawn mostly over gravel substrate. Males sometimes dig shallow depression nests, although spawning also occurs over the nests of other minnow species. Striped shiners eat algae, terrestrial insects gleaned from the water surface, and many types of aquatic invertebrates up to the size of small crayfish. They are large enough to be occasionally captured using small hooks and are often seined to be used as live bait. However, they don't do well in aquariums or bait buckets.

## Golden Shiner *(Notemigonus chrysoleucas)*

**Distinguishing Characteristics:** Length up to 36.7 cm (14.5"). A very deep-bodied shiner, but thin when viewed from the top. The mouth is very small and slightly upturned. The color is silver in clear water but becomes golden in water stained with tannins. The dorsal fin origin is behind the pelvic fin origin. Lateral line curves strongly downward. There is an unscaled keel along the belly from the pelvic fins to the anal fin.

**Habitat and Remarks:** Found mostly in sluggish streams or pools of larger creeks and rivers, but also in reservoirs, swamps, and other still water. Quite tolerant of warm, low-oxygen water, which helps make them a popular bait minnow. The eggs stick to aquatic vegetation or sunfish nests over which they are dispersed. This minnow can live up to eight years. Golden shiners eat zooplankton, aquatic and terrestrial insects, algae, and snails. They are occasionally caught on a hook, but most often by seining or cast-netting.

## Creek Chub *(Semotilus atromaculatus)*

**Distinguishing Characteristics:** Length up to 30 cm (12"). Somewhat cylindrical minnow with a black spot at the front base of the dorsal fin, a black spot at the caudal fin origin, and a large terminal mouth that extends backward past the front of the eye. There are tiny triangular flaps above the rear corners of the mouth in *Semotilus* minnows. A black stripe along the sides and continuing around the snout is especially prominent in young creek chubs. Breeding male takes on a rosy coloration, especially along the belly and fins.

**Habitat and Remarks:** This is probably the most common fish in many types of eastern creeks. It can be found in a huge number of habitats but is most prolific in streams ranging from headwater pools to small rivers, mostly with rocky or sandy substrates. This species is able to withstand the high temperatures and low dissolved oxygen content of intermittent stream pools and is a popular bait fish. The spawning behavior is surprisingly extensive. The male digs a depression by picking up gravel in his mouth and moving it. He stands guard over the nest, attracting females and sometimes other species of spawning minnows. As eggs are laid, the male covers them with gravel and digs a new nest immediately downstream. In this way he may form a long ridge of nests. Creek chubs can become the dominant fish species in headwater pools. Their large mouths allow them to eat a huge variety of prey, including worms, fish, crayfish, and both aquatic and terrestrial insects. They bite ferociously on small hooks and can be seined by the hundreds very easily.

## Fallfish *(Semotilus corporalis)*

**Distinguishing Characteristics:** Length up to 51 cm (20.25"). The largest native minnow in the eastern U.S. There are tiny triangular flaps above the rear corners of the mouth in *Semotilus* minnows. Large scales and large eye. Scales on back and upper sides are darkly outlined in adults, and these minnows may have a purple or blue sheen. Breeding male has face tubercles and pinkish coloration. The superficially similar large minnows of the genus *Nocomis* (river chubs) have much smaller eyes and larger barbels in the corners of the mouth. Creek chub has smaller scales and eyes.

**Habitat and Remarks:** Fallfish inhabit rocky pools and runs of small to medium-sized streams. They build large nests by carrying small stones into a large pile that may add up to hundreds (or thousands, according to some accounts) of pounds of stone. After spawning, the male covers eggs deposited in the nest. Fallfish may be caught on hook and line and are often seined to be used as a bait fish.

## Common Carp *(Cyprinus carpio)*

**Distinguishing Characteristics:** Length up to 122 cm (48"). Weight up to 36.3 kg (80 lbs). Often gold-colored fish with huge, thick scales and a fleshy ventral mouth modified for sucking. More than fifteen dorsal fin rays. The first dorsal and anal fin elements are spiny and serrated. Members of the sucker family lack these serrated spines. Native minnows have less than thirteen dorsal fin rays. Goldfish lack barbels. The "mirror carp," a variety of common carp, has enlarged, silver scales. In addition, new species of Asian carp seem to be continually introduced to our streams and cause endless detriment.

**Habitat and Remarks:** Introduced invasive fish from Eurasia. Inhabits virtually all types of medium-sized to large eastern streams but perhaps most common in muddy pools of low-gradient rivers. Carp are very tolerant of low oxygen and warm water. Spawning is usually stimulated by heavy rains, and eggs are deposited on submerged vegetation. Carp eat aquatic plants, various invertebrates, and even small fish. Much of their food is obtained by rooting through sediment and detritus at the stream bottom. This activity reduces growth of native aquatic plants and contributes significantly to turbidity of the water. The resultant increased siltation essentially suffocates many native species and their eggs. Carp are often caught on hooks baited with worms, corn kernels, or dough balls. They have a tendency to feed in the shallows with half of their backs exposed, which makes them excellent targets for bowfishing. The flesh has an undeserved bad reputation for taste. For some of the best cooking results, remove the red tissue below the lateral line, soak the meat in cold salt water for several hours, and then smoke it. It is also quite good fried in a tasty batter and then squirted liberally with lime juice.

## Creek Chubsucker *(Erimyzon oblongus)*

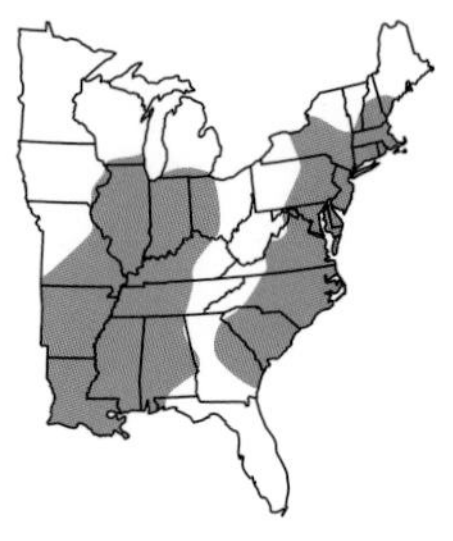

**Distinguishing Characteristics:** Length up to 39.4 cm (15.5"). A small member of the sucker family that can very easily be mistaken for a minnow; however, it usually has ten to twelve dorsal rays, while most native minnows (which excludes carp) have ten or fewer dorsal fin rays. Members of the sucker family also have a protrusible mouth that is lacking in most minnows, and the anal fin in suckers is farther back on the body. Mouth is slightly ventral but closer to being terminal than those of most suckers. Young creek chubsuckers have a dark lateral stripe that extends through the eye onto the snout. No lateral line, no dark spot in the center of each scale, and dorsal fin has rounded (usually convex) edge. Upper sides of adults are marked with slightly darkened blotches. Breeding male has pink or orange underparts, yellow or orange fins, and an anal fin with two lobes. Lake chubsucker *(E. succata)* is deeper-bodied and lacks side blotches. Sharpfin chubsucker *(E. tenuis)* has a sharp-tipped dorsal fin.

**Habitat and Remarks:** Found from headwater streams to medium-sized rivers. Usually found in pools with rocky or sandy substrate. Males congregate over gravel in still water and wait to spawn with approaching females. They sometimes use the nests of minnows. Creek chubsuckers are often seen at the bottoms of clear pools, with their face down to the gravel, searching for microscopic crustaceans, aquatic insects, and algae.

## Northern Hogsucker *(Hypentelium nigricans)*

**Disinguishing Characteristics:** Length up to 61 cm (24"). Weight up to 1.93 kg (4.25 lbs). Strongly camouflaged sucker with a distinctive shape. Flattened on the ventral side, with a large, rectangular head and a protruding ventral mouth. Tan/gold background color with three to six darker brown saddles. Lips with a beaded surface. Usually has eleven dorsal fin rays. Alabama hogsucker *(H. etowanum)* is almost identical but has ten dorsal rays. Roanoke hogsucker *(H. roanokense)* has lips with folds of skin and a beaded surface on the outer edges.

**Habitat and Remarks:** Usually found in clear, rocky riffles of small streams to large rivers. Hogsuckers spawn over gravel, and although they do not build a nest, spawning action may result in areas of clean gravel and small depressions. The protruding mouths of hogsuckers are used to flip small rocks in search of benthic insect larvae and snails. Other fishes sometimes follow hogsuckers and feed on stray organisms dislodged by their feeding. Few people fish specifically for this species, but hogsuckers are occasionally seined and deep-fried or canned for later use.

## White Sucker *(Catostomus commersonii)*

**Distinguishing Characteristics:** Length up to 64 cm (25"). Weight up to 3.3 kg (7.25 lb). White or gray with a ventral mouth. Scales on front of body are much smaller than those on the rear. Ten to thirteen dorsal fin rays.

Young may have four dark blotches along the side. Males may develop reddish coloration along the side during spawning. Unlike white suckers, most native minnows lack protrusible mouths and have ten or fewer dorsal fin rays, carp have barbels, and redhorses have scales of uniform size on front and rear of body. White sucker lacks rows of obvious dark spots on scales, which are characteristic of the spotted sucker *(Minytrema melanops)*. Mouth characteristics, such as shape and texture, are very important for identification of catostomids, so it can be helpful to take a picture of the mouth of a fish you are trying to identify.

**Habitat and Remarks:** There are many more species in the genus *Catostomous* in the western U.S. White suckers inhabit streams ranging from small creeks to large rivers. They may be found in riffles or pools with various substrates. White suckers ascend smaller streams in the spring to spawn and can be seen at times swimming up riffles with their backs half exposed. This species spawns over gravel, and some individuals return to the same stream to spawn every year. Juveniles eat zooplankton, while adults eat benthic invertebrates such as midge larvae, snails, and amphipods. Much detritus is also digested, most likely as a result of their benthic feeding behavior and not because they are actively trying to eat it. White suckers are quite edible, although disdain for any bottom-feeding fish prevents many anglers from trying them. They can be captured with hook and line using bait such as corn kernels or worms left on the bottom.

## Golden Redhorse *(Moxostoma erythrurm)*

**Distinguishing Characteristics:** Length up to 78 cm (30.5"). Weight up to 2.04 kg (4.5 lbs). Golden or silver-colored sucker with orange fins. Dorsal and caudal fins are gray in adults. Mouth is separated from snout by a groove. Unlike with white sucker, the scales on front and back of body are the same size in golden redhorse. Dorsal fin is usually concave. There are nearly a dozen redhorse species in the eastern U.S., and they can be extremely challenging to tell apart. Description of every redhorse is beyond the scope of this book, but the golden redhorse is one of the most common and wide-ranging species. Lateral-line scale counts, fin shape, head length, mouth texture, and mouth shape are important characteristics for redhorse identification.

**Habitat and Remarks:** Inhabits large creeks and small rivers. May be found in habitat ranging from mud-bottomed pools to rocky riffles. This redhorse species is not known to build a nest. Instead, males tend to congregate in gravelly shoals, and females join them there to spawn. The diet includes mollusks, such as pea clams, and larvae of insects such as mayflies, caddisflies, and midges.

## Yellow Bullhead *(Ameiurus natalis)*

**Distinguishing Characteristics:** Length up to 47 cm (18.3"). Weight up to 1.65 kg (3.6 lbs). Tan or yellow upper sides with light-colored belly. Unlike in madtoms (*Noturus* spp.), the rear end of the adipose fin is free from the body. Unlike many of the larger catfish species, most bullheads have a rounded caudal fin. Flathead catfish *(Pylodictis olivaris)* have a white spot along the upper edge of the caudal fin, which bullheads lack. Yellow bullhead has yellow or white chin barbels, unlike black *(A. melas)*, and brown *(A. nebulosus)* bullheads which both have brown or black chin barbels. Three other bullhead species have a dark blotch at dorsal fin base, which is lacking in yellow bullheads.

**Habitat and Remarks:** Occurs from creeks to large rivers. Often found over soft substrates in pools and other slow-water habitats. *Spines located in the pectoral and dorsal fins can cause a painful sting.* Venom is produced in the membranes covering the spines and in glandular cells located at the bases of the spines. Both the male and female may participate in hollowing out a nest cavity, but the male guards the eggs and the school of youngsters until they reach about 50 mm (2") in size. Catfish are notorious bottom-feeders and tend to eat benthic invertebrates such as snails, pea clams, crustaceans, midge larvae, and oligochaetes. Yellow bullheads, in particular, eat quite a bit of vegetation and sediment (probably in search of benthic invertebrates). Catfish are very keyed-in to olfactory cues. They use their barbels and taste buds to find food, which comes in handy as bottom feeders that are often very active at night. Bullheads are most readily caught using hook and line with the bait at, or near, the bottom. A variety of baits will work, including worms, dough balls, chicken livers, and "stink" baits designed to appeal to catfishes' dominant sense, smell. Because of their bottom-feeding lifestyle, many catfish accumulate toxins in their flesh from consuming chemical-laden sediments and organisms. Limit consumption where you suspect pollution.

## Channel Catfish *(Ictalurus punctatus)*

**Distinguishing Characteristics:** Length up to 127 cm (50"). Weight up to 28.2 kg (62 lbs), although larger ones have been reported. Body may be light shades of white, blue, gray, or yellow, with a sprinkling of darker spots. Adipose fin is free from body at its rear end. Unlike in bullheads, the caudal fin is relatively deeply forked. Unlike the blue catfish *(I. furcatus)*, which has a straight-edged anal fin (with thirty or more rays), channel catfish has a rounded anal fin (with fewer than thirty rays). A deeply forked caudal fin and spots separate this species from the superficially similar white catfish *(Ameiurus catus)*.

**Habitat and Remarks:** Typically a species of larger creeks and rivers. The channel catfish spends most of its time in the sluggish water of pools but also forages in swifter water, primarily at night. The nest is built and guarded by the male and may consist of a crater or a cavity under some type of structure, such as a log, rock, or tire. Juveniles eat small invertebrates, such as midge larvae, caddisfly larvae, and various worms. Adults feed heavily on fish but also eat mollusks, crayfish, and various other invertebrates. Catfish use their barbels and taste buds to locate food, which helps them feed in the darkness of the stream bottom at night. Catfish are readily caught using hook and line with the bait near the bottom. A variety of baits will work, including worms, dough balls, chicken livers, and "stink" baits designed to appeal to catfishes' dominant sense, smell. Night fishing, jug lines, and trot lines left out overnight are usually the most effective methods.

## Pirate Perch *(Aphredoderus sayanus)*

**Distinguishing Characteristics:** Length up to 14 cm (5.5"). Small, gray fish with a large head. One of the most distinguishing characteristics is that the anus is located under the throat. However, when pirate perch are juveniles the anus is located normally; it moves forward as the fish approach maturity. Pirate perch are most easily confused with small sunfish (Centrarchidae), but unlike pirate perch, sunfish have more than three dorsal spines.

**Habitat and Remarks:** Pirate perch live in sluggish streams and swampy habitats where they stick to cover provided by undercut banks and organic debris. They are fairly common in coastal plain streams and can also be found throughout much of the Midwest and Great Lakes region. Pirate perch eat small invertebrates that inhabit their sluggish water environment such as microcrustaceans (e.g., Cladocera), isopods, amphipods, and fly larvae.

## Blue-spotted Sunfish *(Enneacanthus gloriosus)*

**Distinguishing Characteristics:** Length up to 9.5 cm (3.75"). Horizontal lines of silver or blue spots on sides. Black teardrop. Unlike most other sunfishes, this species has a rounded caudal fin. Unlike the pygmy sunfishes (family Elassomatidae), they have eight or more dorsal spines. Black-banded *(Enneacanthus chaetodon)* and banded sunfish *(Enneacanthus obesus)*

both have prominent vertical bands along the sides of the body. Blackbanded sunfish also have black at the front of the first dorsal fin. Blue-spotted sunfish lack all these markings.

**Habitat and Remarks:** All three *Enneacanthus* are fishes of mud- or sand-bottomed, sluggish streams and wetlands, where they prefer beds of vegetation. They are often encountered in brackish creeks. Like other sunfish, blue-spotted males build a saucer-shaped nest in the substrate for spawning. Blue-spotted sunfish of all ages feed on microscopic crustaceans, midge larvae, and aquatic oligochaetes, while more mature fish also eat things like amphipods and gastropods. The small size of these fish brings them little attention in hook-and-line fishing, but they may be easily caught in a seine. Blue-spotted sunfish have become a fairly popular aquarium species.

## Bluegill *(Lepomis macrochirus)*

**Distinguishing Characteristics:** Length up to 41 cm (16.2"). Like most members of the sunfish family (also called "panfish"), this species is deep-bodied, with spines in the first dorsal fin and anal fin. Unlike rock bass and crappie (which have five anal spines), members of the genus *Lepomis* have three anal spines. Bluegill have very long, pointed pectoral fins that extend past the eye when bent forward. Unlike other sunfish with this characteristic, bluegill usually have a dark spot in the second dorsal fin and paired vertical bars along the side of the body. *Lepomis* species occasionally hybridize.

**Habitat and Remarks:** Bluegill are found in a huge variety of habitats. In streams, they tend to be associated with pools of small creeks to large rivers. These fish love beds of vegetation and tree roots. Like other sunfish, male bluegill excavate dish-shaped nests in shallow, still water. The male defends the eggs until they hatch. Bluegill are one of the sunfish most likely to be encountered in pools of intermittent streams. In the absence of predators, such as largemouth bass, bluegill tend to become overpopulated and stunted. They feed on a wide variety of invertebrates, such as midge larvae, crustaceans, and insects slurped from the water surface. These sunfish are readily caught with live bait suspended on a hook and bobber but may also be captured on lures, such as spinners and jigs or top-water bugs and flies.

## Redear Sunfish *(Lepomis microlophus)*

**Distinguishing Characteristics:** Length up to 25 cm (10"). Weight up to 2.5 kg (5.5 lbs). Like most members of the sunfish family (also called "panfish"), this species is deep-bodied, with spines in the first dorsal fin and anal fin. Usually silver or gold above and white or yellow below. Similar to bluegill, pumpkinseed, and orangespotted sunfish *(L. humilis)* in having long, pointed pectoral fins that reach at least to the front rim of the eye when extended forward. Unlike the other species with long pectorals, however, the redear lacks a dark spot or bold spots in the second dorsal fin; has a red, orange, or light-colored rear edge on the ear flap; has pectoral fins that extend at least to base of the dorsal fin; and lacks silvery green sides with well-spaced orange or brown spots. *Lepomis* species occasionally hybridize.

**Habitat and Remarks:** Inhabits soft-bottomed pools and backwaters of small to medium rivers. Also found in many reservoirs. Like other sunfish, male redears excavate dish-shaped nests in shallow, still water. Nests are often excavated in small colonies, and the male defends the eggs until hatching. The redear sunfish goes by the nickname "shell cracker" because of its propensity for eating snails and small bivalves such as Asian clams. They also feed on many benthic invertebrates, such as midge larvae and mayfly larvae. Redears are often caught on hook and line using live bait near the bottom.

## Pumpkinseed *(Lepomis gibbosus)*

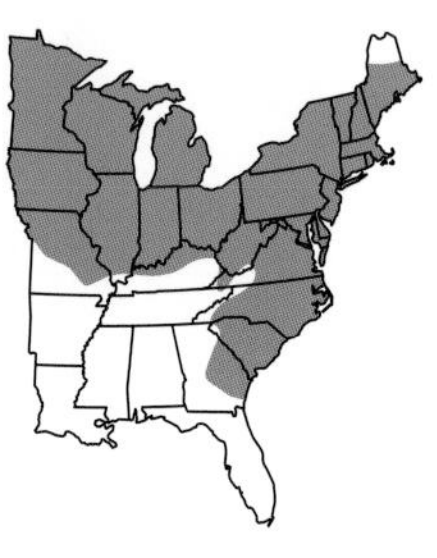

**Distinguishing Characteristics:** Length up to 40 cm (16"). Weight up to 0.62 kg (1.4 lbs). Like most members of the sunfish family (also called "panfish"), this species is deep-bodied with spines in the first dorsal fin and anal fin. Adult pumpkinseeds are blue with orange spots and an orange breast, but the young may be much paler. Similar to bluegill and orangespotted sunfish *(L. humilis)* in having long, pointed pectoral fins that reach at least to the front rim of the eye when extended forward. Unlike those species, the pumpkinseed lacks a single black spot or bold spots in the second dorsal fin; has a red, orange, or light-colored rear edge on the ear flap; has pectoral fins that don't extend to base of the dorsal fin; and lacks silvery green sides with well-spaced orange or brown spots. *Lepomis* species occasionally hybridize.

**Habitat and Remarks:** This sunfish is primarily found in low-gradient streams of the glaciated northern U.S. and Atlantic coastal plain. Often found in the upper reaches of tidal creeks. Like many sunfish, pumpkinseed like beds of aquatic vegetation and other underwater structure. Males build dish-shaped nests in shallow, still water. This species feeds largely on microscopic crustaceans, snails, midge larvae, and burrowing mayflies. Like many sunfish, they are relatively easy to catch with live bait on a small hook suspended from a bobber, or on tiny lures such as jigs, popping bugs, or flies.

## Longear Sunfish *(Lepomis megalotis)*

**Distinguishing Characteristics:** Length up to 24 cm (9.5"). Weight up to 0.79 kg (1.75 lbs). This species is deep-bodied, and has spines in the first dorsal fin and anal fin, like most members of the sunfish family. Mature males, with bright orange and blue coloration, are among the most stunning of freshwater fishes. It usually has wavy blue lines on the face. Superficially similar to pumpkinseed, but with short rounded pectoral fins that don't extend to the front edge of the eye. Distinguished from other short-pectoral sunfish by the following characteristics: small mouth does not extend backward past front edge of eye, ear flap is entirely black except for a thin white band around outer edge, and second dorsal and caudal fins lack reddish tips. *Lepomis* species occasionally hybridize.

**Habitat and Remarks:** Inhabits pools and backwaters of small creeks to medium-sized rivers. This is one of the species most likely to be encountered in pools of small streams. This species prefers to spend much of its time near beds of aquatic vegetation, logjams, and undercut banks. Like other centrarchids, male longear sunfish excavate dish-shaped nests in shallow, still water. The male defends the eggs during early development. Longear sunfish are readily caught using live bait on small hooks or small lures.

## Redbreast Sunfish *(Lepomis auritis)*

**Distinguishing Characteristics:** Length up to 24 cm (9.5"). Weight up to 0.77 kg (1.75 lbs). This species is deep-bodied, and has spines in the first dorsal fin and anal fin, like most members of the sunfish family. It usually has wavy blue lines on the face. Superficially similar to pumpkinseed, but with short rounded pectoral fins that don't extend to the front edge of the eye. Distinguished from other short-pectoral sunfish by the following characteristics: small mouth does not extend backward past front edge of eye, very long ear flap is entirely black (lacking a white band around outer edge), and it has rows of orange-brown spots along the upper sides. *Lepomis* species occasionally hybridize.

**Habitat and Remarks:** Inhabits pools and backwaters of small creeks, rivers, and lake margins. This species was originally native to Atlantic and Gulf drainages but has been widely introduced elsewhere. Like other centrarchids, male redbreast sunfish excavate dish-shaped nests in shallow, still water. The male defends the eggs during early development. Redbreast sunfish are readily caught using live bait on small hooks or small lures.

## Green Sunfish *(Lepomis cyanellus)*

**Distinguishing Characteristics:** Length up to 31 cm (12.2"). Weight up to 1 kg (2.1 lbs). This species is less deep-bodied than most members of the sunfish family, but like other centrarchids, the green sunfish has spines in the first dorsal fin and anal fin. Unlike rock bass and crappie (which have five anal spines), members of the genus *Lepomis* have three anal spines. Dark back with yellowish belly. Usually has irregular blue or green lines on the face. Unlike most other *Lepomis,* it has a large mouth that extends backward to the rear edge of the eye. Unlike the warmouth, this species lacks black bars on the cheeks and lacks a patch of teeth on the tongue. Might be mistaken for a smallmouth bass, but that species has separate dorsal fins while the green sunfish has joined fins. *Lepomis* species occasionally hybridize.

**Habitat and Remarks:** Inhabits pools and backwaters of small creeks to medium-sized rivers. This is one of the species most likely to be encountered in pools of intermittent streams. Like other centrarchids, male green sunfish excavate dish-shaped nests in shallow, still water. The male defends the eggs during early development. This species is smaller than many other sunfish, but its large mouth allows it to feed on relatively huge prey items, including aquatic insects, small crustaceans, crayfish, and other fish. Green sunfish are readily caught using live bait or small lures. Green sunfish can be fairly detrimental to native fish where they are introduced.

## Warmouth *(Lepomis gulosus)*

**Distinguishing Characteristics:** Length up to 31 cm (12"). Weight up to 1.1 kg (2.5 lbs). The warmouth is deep-bodied, and has spines in the first dorsal fin and anal fin like most members of the sunfish family. Unlike rock bass and crappie (which have five anal spines), members of the genus *Lepomis* have three anal spines. Body is heavily mottled with dark pigment, and eye may be reddish, especially in breeding males. Unlike most other *Lepomis,* the warmouth has a large mouth that extends backward to the rear edge of the eye. Unlike the green sunfish, warmouth have black bars on the cheeks behind the eye and a patch of teeth on the tongue. *Lepomis* species occasionally hybridize.

**Habitat and Remarks:** The warmouth prefers pools and sluggish streams with logjams or beds of vegetation. It is often found over muddy substrates or hidden beneath undercut banks. Young warmouth feed on small crustaceans and aquatic insects, while more mature individuals use their large mouths to engulf fish, crayfish, and freshwater shrimp. The nest is made in siltier areas than would be used by most other sunfish. Warmouth can be taken on hook and line with live bait, but they are not as commonly caught as other sunfish. People sometimes capture them while seining root wads and undercut banks.

## Rock Bass *(Ambloplites rupestris)*

**Distinguishing Characteristics:** Length up to 43 cm (17"). Weight up to 1.7 kg (3.7 lbs). Often called "redeye" because of their red-pigmented eyes. This species is deep-bodied, and has spines in the first dorsal fin and anal fin, like most members of the sunfish family. Has five anal spines (unlike *Micropterus* and *Lepomis*) and fewer than eleven soft rays in the anal fin (unlike *Pomoxis* and *Centrarchus*). There are four species of *Ambloplites,* but *A. rupestris* is the most widespread. The shadow bass *(A. ariommus)* is the rock bass' southern counterpart, and the two other *Ambloplites* have restricted ranges—one is found in the Ozarks and the other in Virginia and North Carolina.

**Habitat and Remarks:** Typically found in clear, rock-bottomed streams, often in sheltered pools, near undercut banks, and in water willow beds. The male fans out a nest, which is typically located in the sand or gravel of a moderately flowing pool. Rock bass feed mostly on small fish, crayfish, and various other aquatic invertebrates. These "redeyes" are often caught while pursuing smallmouth bass with spinners or crayfish-shaped lures along sheltered pools.

## Black Crappie *(Pomoxis nigromaculatus)*

**Distinguishing Characteristics:** Length up to 49 cm (19.5"). Weight up to 2.7 kg (6 lbs). This species is deep-bodied, and has spines in the first dorsal fin and anal fin, like most members of the sunfish family. Black crappie are whitish silver with black mottling evenly covering the sides of the body. Unlike members of the genus *Lepomis,* this species has five to seven anal fin spines, and unlike the flier *(Centrarchus macropterus)* it has only seven or eight dorsal spines. The white crappie *(P. annularis)* is very similar but not quite as widespread. White crappie usually have five or six dorsal fin spines and dark spots organized into vertical bars on the side.

**Habitat and Remarks:** Inhabits sluggish streams and pools of more high-gradient systems. Often found near aquatic vegetation. A shallow nest is constructed and defended by the male near underwater brush or undercut banks. The diet includes insects, crustaceans, and many small fish as crappie get larger. Crappie can be caught using minnows, jigs, and other lures. It is often productive to fish at night under a lantern.

## Smallmouth Bass *(Micropterus dolomieu)*

**Disinguishing Characteristics:** Length up to 69 cm (27.3"). Weight up to 5.2 kg (11.9 lbs). Has spines in the first dorsal fin and anal fin like most members of the sunfish family. Much less deep-bodied than members of the genus *Lepomis,* except the green sunfish; the green sunfish usually has some iridescent, irregular blue-green lines on the face, however, which smallmouth bass lack. Juvenile smallmouth bass and the spotted bass *(M. punctatus)* have a distinctly tricolored caudal fin (yellow, black, and white). May be separated from other similar fishes by the following characteristics: large mouth that extends backward to under the eye (not past the eye), three anal spines, reddish eye, shallow notch between first and second dorsal fins that does not completely separate the two, bronze or brown coloring with three darker bars radiating from rear side of the eye, darker vertical bars along the sides, and lack of rows of dark spots along lower sides.

**Habitat and Remarks:** Found mostly in clear, high-gradient streams. Smallmouth bass spend a lot of their time hanging out near rock outcrops or under logs. The male excavates and defends a nest in gravel substrate of shallow, still water. Several females may spawn with the male, who will defend the eggs until they hatch. As juveniles, smallmouth bass eat microscopic crustaceans and insect larvae. They continue to eat insect larvae as adults, but the adult diet is dominated by fish and crayfish. This is one of the most pursued game fish around. They can be caught using a variety of spinners, jigs, rubber worms, flies, poppers, and other artificial lures. Live bait, such as minnows, soft crayfish, and hellgrammites, can also be used.

## Largemouth Bass *(Micropterus salmoides)*

**Disinguishing Characteristics:** Length up to 97 cm (38"). Weight up to 10 kg (22.3 lbs). Has spines in the first dorsal fin and anal fin, like most members of the sunfish family. Much less deep-bodied than members of the genus *Lepomis,* except the green sunfish, which usually has some iridescent, irregular blue-green lines on the face that the largemouth bass lacks. May be separated from other similar fishes by the following characteristics: large mouth that extends backward past the eye, three anal spines, deep notch between first and second dorsal fins that almost completely separates the two fins, silver or green coloring with a thick horizontal bar along the lateral line.

**Habitat and Remarks:** Largemouth bass can be found in a huge variety of stream types. They are fairly tolerant of warm water, turbidity, and even brackish water. The male builds a shallow nest on firm substrate in shallow water. He then seeks out a female, and the pair spawns over the nest. The male guards the eggs until they hatch. Young largemouths eat zooplankton and small aquatic insects. Larger individuals feed mostly on fish and crayfish but will take frogs, mice, birds, and virtually any other moving thing that they can catch. There has probably been more written about catching largemouth bass than any other fish, but in summary, they can be taken on a wide variety of top-water lures, jigs, rubber worms, spinners, and live baits, such as nightcrawlers, minnows, and crayfish.

## Brook Trout *(Salvelinus fontinalis)*

**Distinguishing Characteristics:** Length up to 87 cm (34.3"). Weight up to 7.5 kg (16.5 lbs). Salmonids have an adipose fin and also a small axillary process at the base of the pelvic fin. Unlike brown and rainbow trout, brook trout have a dark upper back with light spots, green or cream-colored wavy lines on the back and dorsal fin, and red or pink spots surrounded by blue halos on the sides of their bodies.

**Habitat and Remarks:** This is the only native trout species in most of our Appalachian streams. Brook trout inhabit only the cleanest, coolest mountain streams. However, there are some anadromous populations. They feed on a variety of aquatic invertebrates and smaller fish. Brook trout are very sensitive to siltation, fishing pressure, water temperature over 16 degrees C (61 degrees F), and competition with introduced trout species. Brown trout and rainbow trout, which are not native to the eastern U.S., tend to outcompete brook trout for available food resources. Brook trout are voracious feeders and can be very easy to catch using flies, spinners, and a variety of other bait.

## Brown Trout *(Salmo trutta)*

**Disinguishing Characteristics:** Length up to 109 cm (43"). Weight up to 18.8 kg (41.4 lbs). Salmonids have an adipose fin and also a small axillary process at the base of the pelvic fin. Unlike brook trout, browns tend to have black spots covering the sides and gill cover. They also have some red spots, often surrounded by light-colored (but usually not blue) halos. Brown trout lack extensive amounts of spotting in the caudal fin, which is present in adult rainbow trout's caudal fin. Hybrids of brown and brook trout are stocked in some areas.

**Habitat and Remarks:** The brown trout is native to Europe but has been introduced throughout the world. It has been stocked extensively in U.S. streams even though it competes with native species. There are some anadromous populations. It has been stocked so widely because it is more tolerant of warm water temperatures, grows larger in streams, and is less sensitive to heavy fishing pressure than brook and rainbow trout. Brown trout tend to be nocturnal feeders, which probably contributes to the consensus that they are more difficult to catch than other trout. They eat aquatic invertebrates and are known to feed fairly extensively on fish such as minnows, sculpins, and darters. Small browns may be caught using dry flies or small live bait, but larger ones are more likely to go after lures, spoons, and streamer flies.

## Rainbow Trout *(Oncorhynchus mykiss)*

**Distinguishing Characteristics:** Length up to 120 cm (47"). Weight up to 22 kg (48 lbs). Salmonids have an adipose fin and also a small axillary process at the base of the pelvic fin. Rainbow trout have a pink or red stripe along the side of the body. They also have irregular black spots in the fins and rows of black spots in the caudal fin. Young rainbows may lack the caudal spots but tend to have a black-edged adipose fin, unlike brook and brown trout.

**Habitat and Remarks:** Rainbow trout are native to streams of the northwestern U.S., but they have been raised extensively in hatcheries and stocked almost anywhere that the water is cool enough to support them (and in some cases, they have been stocked in streams that are only cool enough to support them in winter). Rainbows are most likely to be encountered in mountain streams, spring-fed rivers, and below dams where cold water is released from the bottom of a reservoir. There are some anadromous populations (which are called "steelhead"). Rainbow trout eat the aquatic and terrestrial forms of many insects, such as mayflies, caddisflies, stoneflies, and beetles. They also eat some small fish and can be captured using a variety of flies, spinners, spoons, and live bait such as hellgrammites. Rainbow trout are more tolerant of warm water than native brook trout and cause problems for many native species where they have been introduced.

## Chain Pickerel *(Esox niger)*

**Distinguishing Characteristics:** Length up to 99 cm (39"). Weight up to 4.26 kg (9.4 lbs). A cylindrical fish with a green body and yellow eyes. The snout is shaped like a duck bill. This species is smaller than the widely sought northern pike *(E. lucius)* and muskellunge *(E. masquinongy)* and is more often found in smaller streams. Unlike in those species, the chain pickerel's black teardrop extends straight down to the bottom of the chin. The grass pickerel *(E. americanus)* is quite similar but lacks the chainlike pattern on the side, and the black teardrop under its eye slants backward.

**Habitat and Remarks:** Chain and grass pickerel are found fairly often in low-gradient creeks and the slow parts of other streams. They are often associated with beds of vegetation, logjams, and undercut banks. These species have a mouth full of sharp teeth that they use to feed on other fishes. They are often seined from slow water, and larger ones may be caught using minnows or various types of lures.

## Bowfin *(Amia calva)*

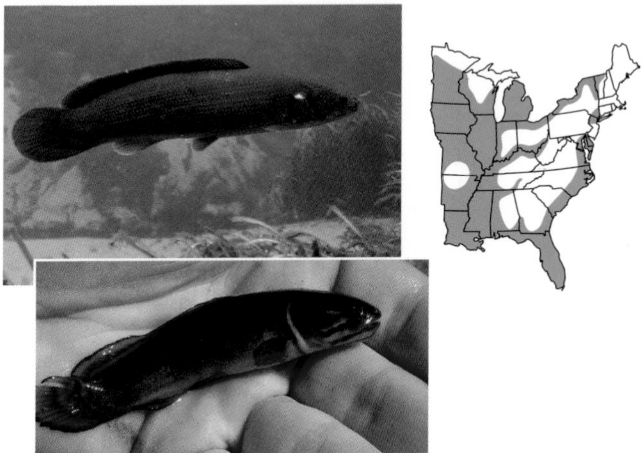

**Distinguishing Characteristics:** Length up to 109 cm (43"). Weight up to 9.74 kg (21.5 lbs). This is a long, cylindrical fish with a mouth full of teeth. The dorsal fin extends along the length of most of the body and tail and is moved using a rippling motion like that of an eel. Adult males usually have a yellow spot with a black center at the top end of the tail, and juveniles are strikingly colored with orange, brown, and black. The bowfin is most likely to be confused with one native fish—burbot *(Lota lota)*—and a group of recently introduced exotic pest species—snakeheads (*Channa* spp.). Unlike bowfin, burbot have two dorsal fins and a single barbel (whisker) in the center of the chin. The pelvic fins of snakeheads are located almost directly under their pectoral fins, while bowfins have pelvic fins located near the middle of the body.

**Habitat and Remarks:** The bowfin is the only species still living from this prehistoric family. It has characteristics of primitive fish, including a bony "gular plate" covering its throat and a lunglike swim bladder that allows it to breathe air gulped at the water's surface. This adaptation allows the bowfin to inhabit swamps and backwaters where decomposition often removes much of the oxygen from the water. Bowfin are most often encountered in low-gradient streams and sloughs and may be found in the upper reaches of brackish creeks. The male excavates and guards a nest in shallow water, and when the young hatch, they follow him around in a tight school until they are about 10 cm (3.9") long. Young bowfin eat insects and crustaceans, and adults feed mostly on fish and crayfish, but they will also eat amphibians such as amphiumas (*Amphiuma* spp.) and sirens (*Siren* spp. and *Pseudobranchus* spp.). Bowfin may be caught with lures, minnows, crayfish, or cut bait. They are often caught on trot lines—but watch out for their teeth.

## Long-nose Gar *(Lepisosteus osseus)*

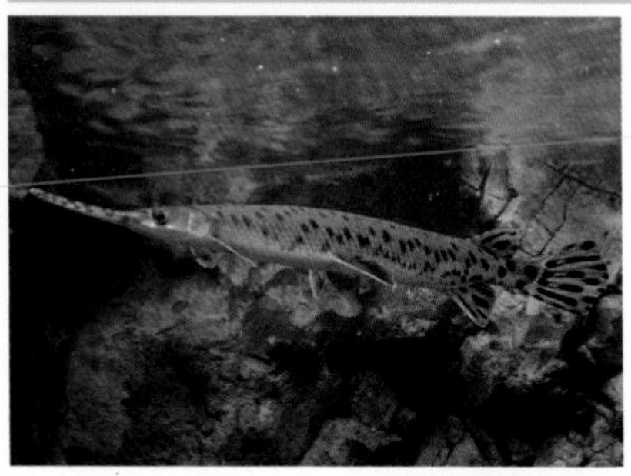

**Distinguishing Characteristics:** Length up to 183 cm (72"). Weight up to 22.8 kg (50.3 lbs). Very cylindrical, long fish with an exceptionally long nose (more than twice as long as the rest of the head). All gar species have jaws lined with sharp teeth and thick diamond-shaped scales that don't overlap. The dorsal and anal fins are located extremely far back on the body (near the caudal fin). There are four other gar species in the eastern U.S., but this is the most widespread. The other species have much shorter noses.

**Habitat and Remarks:** Long-nose gar may be found in a variety of stream types, from highland rivers to the brackish waters of estuarine streams. Gar are typically found in larger rivers, reservoirs, and backwaters, but they are also commonly seen in pools of smaller streams—especially during the spring spawning season. Eggs are laid in gravel, cobble, and vegetation beds, but the eggs may also be found in smallmouth bass nests, which are protected by the male smallmouth. Gars are fierce predators of smaller fish such as minnows, sunfish, and shad. They are primitive fishes and have a lunglike swim bladder that allows them to breathe air gulped at the water's surface. This allows them to live in many low-oxygen waters such as swamp streams. Gar can be captured using live bait or minnows that attract their attention, but they are hard to hook.

# Herpetofauna

Identification of reptiles and amphibians can be a very difficult task. Herpetofauna (the collective term for these animals) display a bewildering amount of variation in the color and size within species. Also, many reptiles and amphibians breed with other species or subspecies to create hybrids and intergrades (mixed animals that exhibit intermediate characteristics). Range maps are often extremely important for identifying which subspecies you may be dealing with. For simplicity's sake, we have not included extensive discussion of subspecies.

Reptiles and amphibians are often variable in appearance. Color and pattern can vary between geographic regions, and can even change with the animal's mood in some cases. For many of the taxa covered here, there are many similar-looking species, and we have covered them together. In some cases we were able to cover all the species in a group on a single range map (e.g., leopard frogs), but in other cases there are just too many species with overlapping ranges (e.g., true toads).

## Amphibians

*Above: Film of eggs from a true frog or cricket frog. Left: Two-lined salamander eggs on the bottom of a stone in a small stream.*

## Signs of Amphibians

Tracks and scat of amphibians are not normally as obvious of those of mammals and other large animals. However, frogs often leave tracks in soft mud, and egg masses of various amphibians may found in still backwaters and wetlands. These egg masses vary widely: Toads leave strings of eggs, cricket frogs and true frogs usually produce a floating film of eggs, tree frogs and chorus frogs often attach a small packet of eggs to underwater structures, and salamanders may produce various types of egg masses or attach eggs singly to underwater surfaces.

## Two-lined Salamanders (*Eurycea* spp.)

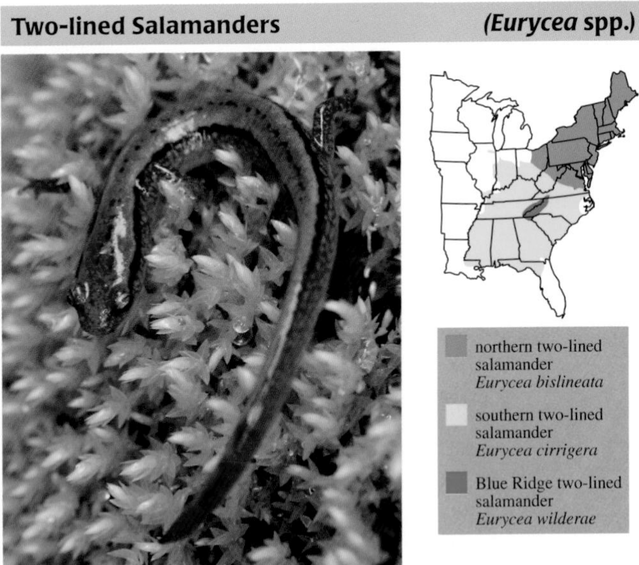


**Distinguishing Characteristics:** Length up to 12 cm (4.75"). Small, slender, yellow salamander with a black stripe down each side of the back. Between the stripes, the back is often covered with black dots. There are three species, which are most easily identified by range. The larvae are one of the most commonly encountered salamander larvae in eastern streams. They typically have short red-brown gills and a grayish-brown back marked with several light-colored round spots.

**Habitat and Remarks:** Two-lined salamanders are especially fond of tiny creeks and may also be found along the fringes of larger streams, wherever they can find refuge from fish. They are more tolerant of poor water quality than most dusky salamanders. Adult two-lineds may venture fairly far into adjacent uplands but can usually be found in streams during the spring. Larvae may be found in streams virtually year-round. Breeding males have cirri (small, fleshy lores) on the sides of their nose, which give the appearance of a little Fu Manchu mustache. Female two-lineds attach one to several dozen eggs to hard substrate, such as a flat rock in a riffle. Larvae and adults both eat various types of invertebrates, including mosquito larvae, midge larvae, small mollusks, beetles, and caddisfly larvae.

## Dusky Salamanders *(Desmognathus spp.)*

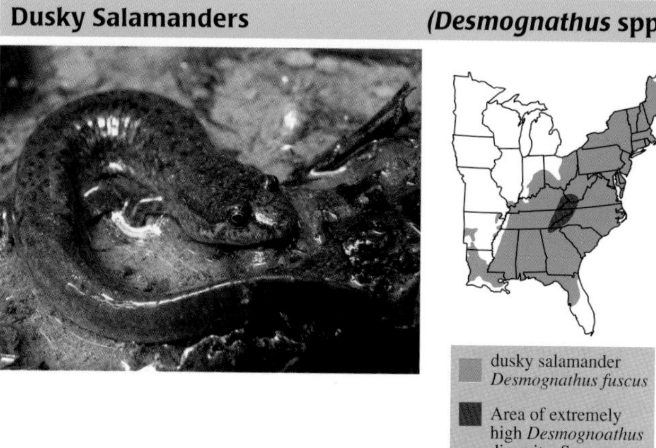


**Distinguishing Characteristics:** Length up to 15 cm (5.9"). Salamanders in the genus *Desmognathus* are collectively called dusky salamanders. Species and subspecies are extremely variable in coloration, but all usually have a light-colored diagonal line that extends from the corner of the eye to the angle of the jaw. Duskies are often brilliantly patterned with a broad, rough-edged stripe down the back, but young ones may have paired spots instead of a stripe. As they get older, duskies tend to become darker in color, and evidence of patterning and the diagonal jaw line may disappear.

**Habitat and Remarks:** There are about a dozen species of dusky salamander, but some are virtually impossible to tell apart, and some "species" may actually contain several undescribed species. The southern Appalachian mountains are the area of maximum diversity for this group. The majority of duskies live in or near small, cool streams and springs, but some species can be found in stagnant swampy pools of the coastal plain. Eggs are usually deposited under logs, rocks, or moss near water. Both larvae and adults feed on aquatic insects, worms, sowbugs, and other small aquatic animals.

## Red and Mud Salamanders *(Pseudotriton spp.)*

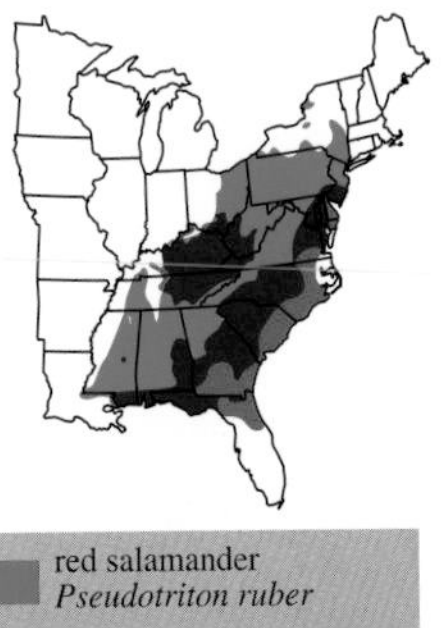


**Distinguishing Characteristics:** Length up to 20 cm (8"). Bright red or purple, medium-sized salamanders with black spots. Red salamanders *(P. ruber)* typically have yellow eyes and more spots. Mud salamanders *(P. montanus)* are more sparsely spotted and have brown eyes. Both species tend to get darker with age, often taking on a brownish, blackish, or purple color. The coloration of both species varies over their range, and both are divided into multiple subspecies.

**Habitat and Remarks:** The mud salamander typically inhabits low-gradient streams, muddy seeps, and nearby wetlands. This makes sense because much of its range is in the southeastern coastal plain, where low-gradient streams are common. The red salamander tends to inhabit streams with clear water. In both species, eggs are attached to the substrate by a single stalk. Less is known about the mud salamander because it spends much of the time buried in mud at the bottom of murky waters. In contrast, red salamanders may often be seen walking along the bottoms of small, clear streams on summer nights. Both species are thought to feed primarily on aquatic invertebrates and on smaller salamander larvae to some degree.

## Spring Salamander (*Gyrinophilus porphyriticus*)

**Distinguishing Characteristics:** Length up to 22.6 cm (8.5"). These salamanders are typically salmon-colored with small dark spots. They may look very similar to red or mud salamanders; however, spring salamanders have a whitish line that extends from each eye to each nostril. This line is bordered below by a black or gray line. The nose ends rather abruptly. The combination of these characteristics gives the snout a squarish appearance.

**Habitat and Remarks:** Spring salamanders stay true to their name, inhabiting springs, caves, and cool streams. Unlike many salamanders, this species breeds in the fall and winter months. Eggs (one to several dozen) are usually attached singly to the bottom of a rock. This species may stay in the aquatic larval stage for two or three years. Adults tend to stay near water, but they also venture out to forage in nearby forest litter or in underground burrows. Spring salamanders eat many kinds of aquatic insects, snails, and crustaceans, but they also feed on terrestrial millipedes, centipedes, earthworms, and spiders. They will occasionally eat frogs and salamanders, including members of their own species.

## Hellbender (*Cryptobranchus alleganiensis*)

**Distinguishing Characteristics:** Length up to 74 cm (29"). Large, wrinkly, totally aquatic salamander. Mudpuppies (*Necturus* spp.) are also large, aquatic salamanders, but unlike hellbenders, they have external gills as adults. Instead of external gills, hellbenders breathe through two small, circular openings and, like many amphibians, through their skin. Amphiumas are another kind of large, totally aquatic salamander lacking external gills, but they are eel-like, and their limbs have been reduced to four tiny, virtually useless appendages. Also, amphiumas are found in swampy streams where hellbenders would not occur.

**Habitat and Remarks:** Hellbenders only live in the cleanest streams we have left. They prefer the swift currents of riffles and runs containing large stones. They require high levels of oxygen and do not tolerate siltation and pollution, which has lead to their demise in many streams. Breeding occurs in late summer or fall in a nest cavity that the male excavates and defends until the young hatch. Unlike those of most non-fish vertebrates, hellbender eggs are fertilized externally in the nest cavity. One male may fertilize the eggs of more than one female. Hellbenders, also called "devil dogs" and "Allegheny alligators," are the subject of quite a bit of modern-day mythology. Some people think that they have venomous bites, and fisherman have often killed them on sight. In reality, they are completely harmless and are very much imperiled by humans. Hellbenders eat aquatic animals such as fish, worms, mollusks, and especially crayfish.

## Cricket Frogs *(Acris spp.)*

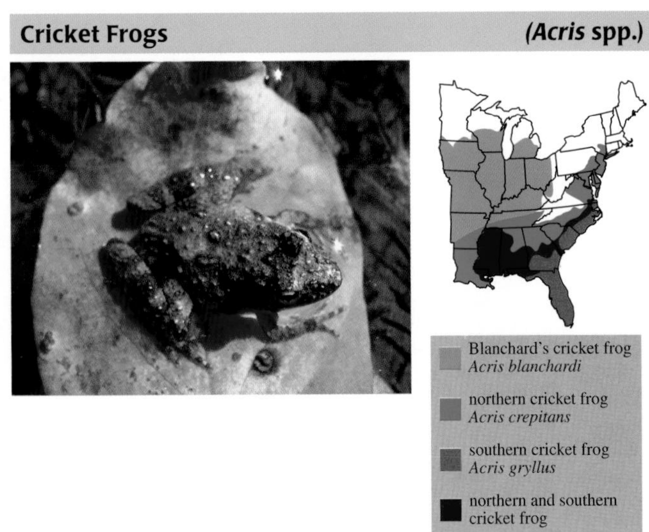


**Distinguishing Characteristics:** Length up to 3.2 cm (1.25"). Small frogs with pointed snouts. Their skin is moist but usually has some warts. The southern cricket frog *(A. gryllus)*, Blanchard's cricket frog *(A. blan-*

*chardi),* and northern cricket frog *(A. crepitans)* are all variable in coloration. All three species often (but not always) have a dark triangle between the eyes and a dark stripe on the rear side of the thigh. Some chorus frogs can also have the dark triangle, but those species lack the thigh stripe. Coloration varies greatly, even within a single species or subspecies. The body is often gray, tan, or blackish with a wash of orange-tan or neon green on the back. Tadpoles of these species have distinctive, black-tipped tails. The *click-click-click . . .* call of a cricket frog is often the first indicator of its presence. The call sounds like pebbles or marbles being smacked together.

**Habitat and Remarks:** Cricket frogs are often the only frogs calling during the hottest days of summer. They can be found in various types of streams, ditches, and wetlands. Their eggs are typically attached singly or in small groups to vegetation or to the bottom of still, fish-free stream backwaters or wetlands. As tadpoles, cricket frogs feed on algae and other organic matter scraped from underwater surfaces. They are insectivores as adults.

## Chorus Frogs *(Pseudacris spp.)*

**Distinguishing Characteristics:** Length up to 3.8 cm (1.5"). Small frogs with poorly developed discs on the toes and little webbing between toes. These frogs seldom climb very high into the trees. Most species have a white line along the upper lip. Some have distinctive markings, such as the X-shaped marking found on the back of the spring peeper *(P. crucifer)*. Many of the other species and subspecies have dark lines or lines of dark spots, and there is often a broad, dark band running through the eye.

**Habitat and Remarks:** The most common, widespread group of chorus frog species were once considered to be a single species—the western chorus frog *(P. triseriata)*. Several species have since been separated from *P. triseriata*. In some areas, it is virtually impossible to tell the different species apart, so we will discuss them generally. Spring peepers, however, are easily distinguished from most other chorus frogs, both visually and by call. Chorus frogs and spring peepers are the first frogs to begin calling in winter or early spring, often calling from the same pool. Spring peepers give loud, repetitive *peep!* sounds, while many chorus frog calls sound like a fingernail being run up the teeth of a comb *(crreeeeeeeek)*. The sound coming from shallow forested wetlands and very temporary grassy pools can be deafening. These temporary pools are often found in the floodplains of large streams or in the grassy swales that make up the upper headwaters of many creeks. Eggs are laid in loose gelatinous clumps, usually attached to underwater vegetation. Tadpoles feed on algae and adults eat spiders, flies, beetles, moths, and many other kinds of insects.

## Gray Treefrog *(Hyla spp.)*

**Distinguishing Characteristics:** Length up to 6.1 cm (2.4"). There are two species *(H. versicolor* and *H. chrysoscelis)* of gray treefrog; however, they can be differentiated only by their calls and the number of chromosomes they possess. They are medium-sized gray frogs with suction disks on the toes that allow these species to climb high into the treetops. The body is often covered with a mottled camouflage pattern made up of various shades of gray. However, coloration varies between individuals and often includes green, white, and black. Like many treefrogs, color can also change with temperature and stress level. This species can be separated from similar treefrogs, such as the squirrel treefrog *(H. squirella)* and the bird-voiced treefrog *(H. avivoca)*, by the presence of both a distinct light-colored spot under the eye and a bright orange or yellow wash on the inner surface of the thigh. Call is a high-pitched trill usually coming from the treetops.

**Habitat and Remarks:** These frogs may be heard in most types of forested habitats from upland forests near headwater streams to bottomlands near our largest rivers. Often, the only way to know that this species is around is by sound. On spring and summer evenings, especially after recent rain, gray treefrogs call from lower and lower heights as they come down to shallow wetlands to breed. Gray treefrogs range further north than other true treefrogs, at least partly because they are able to withstand being partially frozen during hibernation. Eggs are attached to underwater structures in clusters of up to a few dozen. Tadpoles eat underwater algae, while adults feed on insects, spiders, snails, and even smaller frogs.

## Green Treefrog *(Hyla cinerea)*

**Distinguishing Characteristics:** Length up to 6.4 cm (2.5"). Normally bright green, although this species can change to a yellowish color after changes in temperature or activity level. There is usually a sharply defined white stripe that begins as a white upper lip and may extend to the hind leg. There are often flecks of gold on the back. The similar squirrel treefrog *(H. squirella)* usually lacks the white stripe, but when a stripe is present, the lower edge is undefined. Also, squirrel treefrogs are typically brown and only turn green temporarily. The green treefrog's call is a loud nasal *wank!*

**Habitat and Remarks:** This is a frog of southeastern bottomlands. It may be heard calling loudly from forested wetlands or the fringes of sluggish streams on spring and summer nights. On average, several hundred eggs are laid in a gelatinous mass attached to underwater structure. Tadpoles scrape underwater vegetation to feed on, and adults eat insects such as flies.

## Leopard Frogs *(Lithobates spp.)*

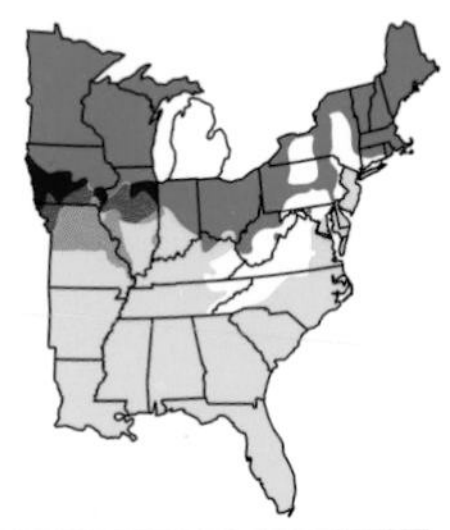

northern leopard frog *Lithobates pipieus*

southern leopard frog *Lithobates spenocephalus*

plains leopard frog *Lithobates blairi*

northern leopard frog and plains leopard frog

southern leopard frog and plains leopard frog

**Distinguishing Characteristics:** Length up to 12.7 cm (5"). Tan or green frogs with dark spots like those of a leopard. There are four species, although they were all once considered to be members of the same species. The two most widespread species are the northern *(L. pipiens)* and the southern *(L. utricularia)* leopard frogs. Northern leopards often have a dark spot on the tip of the nose and lack the distinct, light-colored spot that is usually present in the center of the tympanic membrane (circular ear membrane) of the southern leopard. Southern leopards are more slender in appearance and have few spots along the side of the body. Plains leopards *(L. blairi)* have dorsolateral ridges that are broken and pinched inward toward the rear of their bodies. The similar pickerel frog has squarish spots and a yellow wash on the inner thigh. Calls vary, from those of southern leopard frogs, which sound like a flock of laughing ducks, to those of northern leopards, which make a low snore followed by several clucking sounds.

**Habitat and Remarks:** Leopard frogs are often found far from water in damp meadows. They occur near a variety of stream types within their range. Northern leopard frogs are thought to be in decline. Southern leopard frogs are extremely common near southeastern coastal plain streams and even breed in brackish waters. Eggs are laid in globular clusters of several hundred that are attached to underwater structure. Tadpoles graze on algae, but large tadpoles occasionally eat small invertebrates. Adults eat mostly insects.

## Pickerel Frog *(Lithobates palustris)*

**Distinguishing Characteristics:** Length up to 8.9 cm (3.5"). A slender frog that is similar to leopard frogs except that its dark spots are squarish and arranged in two parallel rows going down the back. The inner surfaces of the thighs are bright yellow or orange. Call is a low, quiet snore.

**Habitat and Remarks:** Throughout much of its range the pickerel frog is found in cool, clear streams, near springs, or in the entrances of caves. However, in the Southeast, it also inhabits more low-gradient streams. Like leopard frogs, this species wanders far out into grassy areas. Spherical egg masses of up to several thousand eggs are attached to underwater vegetation or branches. Eggs are usually laid in small temporary wetlands. The pickerel frog has poisonous skin secretions that predators probably find distasteful. These secretions will kill other frogs if they are kept in the same terrarium with a pickerel frog.

## Green Frog *(Lithobates clamitans)*

**Distinguishing Characteristics:** Length up to 8.9 cm (3.5"). Fairly large, green frog with a small ridge extending down each side of the back (called a dorsolateral ridge). This species is often dark green with a few inconspicuous dark spots. The body color can vary from tan to almost black, but there is usually a bright green upper lip. This species is most likely to be confused with the bullfrog *(R. catesbeiana)*, but the bullfrog lacks dorsolateral ridges. The call is a loud, abrupt *BOw!* that sounds like a single pluck of a banjo string.

**Habitat and Remarks:** Green frogs are very common stream residents and may be found in some of the tiniest headwaters. Breeding usually takes place in late spring, and several thousand eggs are laid by each mating pair. The eggs may float at the surface or cling to underwater structure. Tadpoles eat algae, plant matter, and other contents of biofilms that accumulate on underwater surfaces. Adults are carnivores and eat virtually anything that will fit in their mouth, including insects, crustaceans, spiders, small snakes, and other frogs.

## Bullfrog *(Lithobates catesbeiana)*

**Distinguishing Characteristics:** Length up to 20.3 cm (8"), but much longer with the legs extended. The largest true frog found in North America. The bullfrog is a large green frog that lacks dorsolateral ridges (distinguishing it from the green frog). The call is a loud, low *jug-o-rum* repeated over and over on warm summer nights.

**Habitat and Remarks:** The bullfrog is larger and more aggressive than most other native frogs. This species will often try to eat anything moving that gets near its face, including insects, crustaceans, worms, salamanders, fish, snakes, small mammals, tadpoles, and other frogs (including its own kind). Several thousand eggs are laid in a film that floats on the water surface. This species breeds in still backwaters, ponds, and wetlands. Unlike many frogs, the bullfrog is likely to be found in warm, sun-exposed waters where fish are present. The very large tadpoles feed on algae and plant matter and may take two to three years to develop into adults. This species is highly sought after for frog legs and has been introduced to the western U.S. and other continents. The aggressive bullfrog is pushing out native species in those areas.

## True Toads (*Anaxyrus* spp.)

**Distinguishing Characteristics:** Length up to 11.4 cm (4 .5"). Rough-skinned, warty toads with large parotid glands (warty, glandular growths that secrete toxins, which protect the toad from predators) on the back of the head. Members of this genus can be various shades of green, brown, and red, usually with splotches of darker color. American toads *(A. americanus)* tend to have one or two warts per splotch, while Fowler's toads *(A. fowleri)* have three or more warts per splotch. Throughout most of their ranges these are the only species of rough-skinned toads. However, in the deep Southeast, the southern toad *(B. terrestris)* predominates, and the Gulf coast toad *(B. valliceps)* is the major species along the western coast of the Gulf of Mexico. There are also several more localized species. To complicate things further, many of these species interbreed occasionally.

**Habitat and Remarks:** True toads are found in all kinds of habitats, including many types of streams. The high-pitched trill of the American toad and the short, nasal *waaaaaa* of the Fowler's toad are familiar evening sounds surrounding temporary waters in the early spring. These species prefer to breed in short-lived wetlands such as those left after flooding, in isolated backwaters, and abandoned stream channels. Long strings of eggs are laid in still, fishless pools, where they develop into small black tadpoles. In summer, rock and sand bars may be covered with hundreds of tiny toadlets. Tadpoles scrape algae, bacteria, and other organic matter off underwater surfaces, while adults feed on insects and other small invertebrates.

# Reptiles

## Signs of Reptiles

Reptile tracks and scats are typically not as conspicuous as those of mammals. However, with practice you may learn to identify signs such as snake trails through soft substrate and alligator slides. Turtles leave some of the most conspicuous signs. They often leave trails where they haul themselves up onto a sand bar to sun, and their nests are often seen after the eggs have hatched or been preyed upon.

*A turtle nest that has hatched from a small gravel bar.*

## Common Musk Turtle *(Sternotherus odoratus)*

**Distinguishing Characteristics:** Length up to 14 cm (5.5"). Small turtle with a high-domed, rounded shell (although shell is slightly keeled when very young). Common musk turtles are most likely to be confused with the eastern mud turtle *(Kinosternon subrubrum)* throughout much of their range, but there are several other species of mud and musk turtles that could be confused with this species. The following combination of characteristics should separate this species from the others: the plastron has one hinge, the first pair of scutes in front of hinge are rectangular, the head has two light stripes, and the chin *and throat* have barbells.

**Habitat and Remarks:** Often seen walking along the bottom of clear creeks and is likely to be mistaken for a round stone. Capable of producing a malodorous musk when threatened, which has earned this turtle the nickname "stinkpot." Musk turtles often sun on rocks and logs and are known for their tendency to ascend fairly high into small, leaning trees. This species eats a variety of foods, including plants, fish, carrion, mollusks, and various other invertebrates.

## Mud Turtle *(Kinosternon subrubrum)*

**Distinguishing Characteristics:** Length up to 12.2 cm (4.8"). Small turtle with a high-domed, rounded shell. Unlike the very similar common musk turtle, the mud turtle's plastron is double-hinged and lacks lines on its face. The two scutes in front of the front hinge on the plastron are obviously triangular.

**Habitat and Remarks:** The eastern mud turtle appears to be declining throughout much of its range due to wetland drainage and habitat loss. Mud turtles prefer sluggish streams and wetlands but will also venture far from permanent water to forage in vernal pools. They often move relatively far from water to lay eggs and hibernate, making conservation of uplands next to streams and wetlands a priority for management of this species. Eastern mud turtles are also very commonly captured in brackish tidal creeks. Like the musk turtle, this species forages along the bottoms of water bodies for plants, fish, crustaceans, mollusks, insects, and other invertebrates.

## Box Turtle *(Terrapene carolina)*

**Distinguishing Characteristics:** Length up to 21.6 cm (8.5"). Small turtle with a high-domed, rounded shell. Black or dark brown shell with bright orange or yellow markings. The pattern can be extremely variable between individuals. Hinges on the plastron allow for the front and rear of the shell to be closed tightly, providing an almost impenetrable protection from predators.

**Habitat and Remarks:** Eastern box turtles are a land-dwelling species, but they are often found cooling themselves in streams or foraging nearby. In fact, box turtles are more closely related to water-dwelling turtles than to the tortoises they resemble. Some box turtles have lived to be one hundred years old. Males can be distinguished from females by their red eyes and concave plastron (which makes it easier for males to stay on top of the female during mating). Females usually have brown or light orange eyes and flat plastrons. It is not uncommon to come across a female box turtle digging a hole with its rear feet to deposit eggs in. Box turtles often bury themselves in mud to avoid heat and will hibernate under logs or in mammal burrows, or burrow into loose substrate to spend the winter. This species eats vegetation, fruits, fungi, carrion, snails, earthworms, and various other invertebrates.

## Map Turtles *(Graptemys spp.)*

includes the ranges of all eastern *Graptemys* species

area where common map turtle *(Graptemys geographica)* is the only species likely to be encountered

*Above: False map turtle.*

*Left: Common map turtle head pattern.*

**Distinguishing Characteristics:** Length up to 33 cm (13"). There are ten species of map turtles in the eastern U.S. Identification of individual species relies largely on the pattern of coloration on the head and chin; however, separation of individual species is beyond the scope of this book. Unlike painted turtles, map turtles have keeled scutes (some map turtles have extremely large knobs and keels on their scutes). Unlike cooters and sliders, the roof of the mouth is smooth (it is ridged in cooters and sliders), but with a little practice, you can recognize maps turtles by coloration and shape alone. The common map turtle *(G. geographica)* is probably the most familiar species in much of the East but tends to prefer larger bodies of water. The false map turtle (*G. pseudogeographica,* with several subspecies) is also very widespread and is often found in small rivers. There are several species with ranges restricted to a single river drainage.

**Habitat and Remarks:** These turtle species inhabit our larger creeks, rivers, and lakes. Some species are well known for their ability to sun on perches too precarious for other turtles, and they can be extremely wary and difficult to capture. Like many aquatic turtles, they find sunny areas with soft soil to lay their eggs in, digging small holes with the hind legs. Map turtles are less tolerant of pollution than are some aquatic turtles, such as sliders and painted turtles. They feed mostly on crayfish, insects, aquatic snails, and other small mollusks; however, they will eat some carrion and plant material.

## Painted Turtle *(Chrysemys picta)*

**Distinguishing Characteristics:** Length up to 25.4 cm (10"). There are four recognized subspecies of this turtle, although they are all relatively similar in appearance. The shell is smooth and more highly domed than those of many aquatic turtles. There is a pattern of red and black along the margin of the carapace, which will also help to separate this species from map turtles, cooters, and sliders. The head, legs, and margins of the shell are often "painted" with a wonderful array of black, olive, yellow, and red. The shell coloration sometimes becomes obscured by algae.

**Habitat and Remarks:** Painted turtles are commonly seen basking on logs or along the banks of creeks, rivers, ponds, and wetlands. They especially prefer mud-bottomed habitats, such as the sluggish pools of low-gradient streams. In northern parts of its range, this is the only species of aquatic turtle that is commonly seen basking. Painted turtles, like pond sliders, have the habit of stacking on top each other when sunning. They have an omnivorous diet consisting largely of plants, fish, carrion, insects, and mollusks. Like many other brightly colored aquatic turtles, this species has been collected extensively for the pet trade. Many species of aquatic turtles commonly carry harmful bacteria, such as *Salmonella;* therefore, great care should be taken to sterilize your hands after handling them.

## Pond Sliders *(Trachemys scripta)*

**Distinguishing Characteristics:** Length up to 29.2 cm (11.5"). Three subspecies are found in the eastern U.S. (yellowbelly, red-eared, and Cumberland sliders). The head coloration of the red-eared subspecies (pictured) generally makes this one easy to separate from other aquatic turtles, but it sometimes lacks the characteristic red ears. Unlike painted turtles, sliders have fairly flat shells with keeled scutes. Unlike those of map turtles, the roofs of their mouths are ridged (touch them on the nose with a stick to see this). Unlike cooters, their chin is rounded on the bottom rather than flat. Intergradation of the subspecies, algal growth, and variation in the amount of dark pigment (melanin) can almost completely obscure the shell pattern at times. Some individuals are completely black.

**Habitat and Remarks:** Except in the far northern U.S., this is usually the most common species of basking turtle. They may be found in many kinds of streams and still waters within their range. Individuals sometimes stack themselves two or three high in popular sunning spots, but they are wary and will topple into the water if approached too closely—especially in areas where they are not accustomed to seeing humans. Sliders eat a variety of aquatic invertebrates as juveniles, but adults are vegetarians and feed on a variety of aquatic plants.

## River Cooter *(Pseudemys concinna)*

**Distinguishing Characteristics:** Length up to 43.2 cm (17"). This turtle resembles the pond slider but often reaches a much larger size. There are at least three subspecies of this turtle, although several races have been classified as species or subspecies in the past. A combination of the following characteristics will separate cooters from other similar-looking aquatic turtles: the shell is somewhat flattened with keeled scutes, the roof of the mouth is ridged, the chin is flat on the bottom, and the upper jaw lacks notches or cusps (which are present in the red-bellied turtle, *P. rubriventris*).

**Habitat and Remarks:** The river cooter is more closely allied with stream habitat than are pond sliders, but this species is also a prominent basking turtle. Over its range, this species can be found in a variety of habitats. In some areas, it seems to prefer rocky streams, but it can also be found in backwater sloughs and brackish water. Like pond sliders, cooters are largely vegetarian, eating plants such as eelgrass *(Vallisneria americana)* and various algae. However, they also consume small fish, crayfish, snails, and aquatic insects.

## Common Snapping Turtle *(Chelydra serpentina)*

**Distinguishing Characteristics:** Length up to 49.3 cm (19.4"). Weight up to 34 kg (75 lbs). This fierce-looking turtle has a long tail and a body that is too large for it to retreat into its shell. Snaps fiercely when molested. Young snappers have prominently keeled scutes on top of their shell, but unlike in the alligator snapping turtle *(Macrochlemys temminckii)*, these keels become rounded with age. The long tail with sawteeth on the dorsal surface will separate the common snapper from most other turtles, including the alligator snapping turtle.

**Habitat and Remarks:** Common snapping turtles can be found in almost any reasonably permanent body of fresh water and are also very common in the brackish water of coastal streams. This species and the alligator snapping turtle are both capable of snapping off human body parts, so be careful with them. Common snappers up to about 10 to 15 pounds may be handled by grabbing them at the base of the tail, but be careful, as the neck is almost long enough to reach to the back of the body! Snapping turtles eat fish, amphibians, invertebrates, carrion, a variety of other animals, and some plant matter. This species does not bask as often as most other turtles and spends a significant amount of time buried in muck or under logjams and undercut banks.

## Softshell Turtles *(Apolone* spp.)

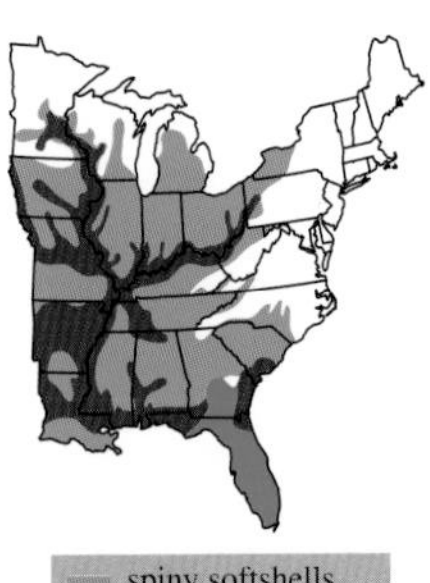

spiny softshells
*Apolone spinifera*

smooth softshells
*Apolone mutica*

Florida softshell
*Apolone ferox*

**Distinguishing Characteristics:** Length up to 43 cm (17"). The smooth softshell *(A. mutica)*, Florida softshell *(A. ferox)*, and all of the subspecies of spiny softshell *(A. spinifera)* are relatively similar in appearance. Their long necks and round shells can be recognized from a great distance while they are floating at the water's surface or sunning on a log or sandbar. With practice, you may even be able to distinguish their dragmarks in the sand of popular sunning spots from those of other turtles. However, distinguishing among species requires close examination. Spiny softshells have spines on the front edge of the carapace, a sandpapery shell, small spots on the shell, and a horizontal ridge in each nostril. Smooth softshells may have some speckling but lack all the other characteristics mentioned. The Florida softshell has an elongate shell with flattened bumps on the front of the carapace and a ridge in the nostrils.

**Habitat and Remarks:** Softshell turtles strongly prefer streams and rivers to still waters (although the Florida softshell is often found in lakes). They spend a fair amount of time buried in sand with only their heads extended, waiting to ambush prey. Their extremely long necks and tubular noses allow them to reach air at the water's surface while remaining buried. Softshells feed primarily on animals such as fish, amphibians, and aquatic insects.

## Common Watersnake *(Nerodia sipedon)*

**Distinguishing Characteristics:** Length up to 150 cm (59"). This snake is highly variable in color and pattern, and there are at least four recognized subspecies, including the northern, midland, Carolina, and Lake Erie watersnakes. When young, this species is usually strongly patterned with shades of brown and orange. As it ages, the back may darken to almost solid black. Unlike plain-bellied watersnakes, this species has a belly patterned with crescents or squares. Common watersnakes lack the black diagonal eye stripe of banded watersnakes *(N. fasciata)*. Unlike cottonmouths, they have round pupils.

**Habitat and Remarks:** This is one of the snakes most commonly seen basking on rocks and logs around virtually any aquatic habitat of the eastern U.S. below 4,500 feet in elevation. This species, like most watersnakes, has a tendency to flatten its body when agitated, giving the snake a fat appearance and making the head appear more diamond-shaped. This makes watersnakes look remarkably similar to members of the venomous pit viper family, such as copperheads and cottonmouths. Although they they are not venemous, most watersnakes bite ferociously when handled, and the saliva has anticoagulant properties that can cause quite a bit of bleeding and make the bite appear worse than it is. This species feeds primarily on frogs, fish, invertebrates, and small mammals.

## Plain-bellied Watersnake *(Nerodia erythrogaster)*

**Distinguishing Characteristics:** Length up to 158 cm (62"). As an adult, this snake has a solid brown or black back (except the blotched subspecies, which retains the juvenile pattern). The belly coloration varies by subspecies (i.e., redbelly, yellowbelly, and copperbelly subspecies) and even within a subspecies to some degree, but all plainbellies lack the checkers, stripes, crescents, or other patterns found on the undersides of other watersnakes. However, in the copperbelly subspecies (which is federally listed as threatened) dark coloration does encroach onto the belly.

**Habitat and Remarks:** This is primarily a snake of lowland swamps, shrubby wetlands, beaver ponds, and sluggish streams. All of the subspecies tend to wander farther from water than other watersnake species. It is not uncommon to come across this snake in a relatively dry bottomland forest on a hot summer day. Plainbellies are particularly fond of climbing into trees and shrubs to sun. This snake can reach fairly high population densities in good habitat. It feeds primarily on frogs, tadpoles, salamanders, crayfish, fish, and other small animals.

## Queen Snake *(Regina septemvittata)*

**Distinguishing Characteristics:** Length up to 91.4 cm (36"). The back is brown or grayish and may be solid or lined with three longitudinal (running lengthwise) stripes. There is a yellowish-white stripe along the lower sides of the body, and the belly is yellow or white with four brownish longitudinal stripes. Other, similar-looking "crayfish snakes" of the genus *Regina* occur along the coastal plain *(R. rigida)* and in the plains states *(R. grahamii)*, but those species have rows of black spots on the belly or a plain yellow belly.

**Habitat and Remarks:** This species is usually found along rocky streams, where it is often seen foraging among the rocks or peeking from a crack in the bedrock. Queen snakes are not found basking as often as other watersnakes, such as the common and plain-bellied watersnakes. This species and the other crayfish snakes are considered to be crustacaen specialists. They prefer to eat soft-shelled crayfish that have recently molted. These crayfish can often be found resting in protected little niches under rocks and seem to be waiting for their exoskeleton to harden. However, crayfish snakes are excellent at squeezing into these refuges. Although queen snakes are watersnakes, they are much less likely to inflict bites as damaging as those of the genus *Nerodia*. They are nonvenomous.

## Eastern Garter Snake *(Thamnophis sirtalis)*

**Distinguishing Characteristics:** Length up to 132.1 cm (52"). There are many species and subspecies of garter snakes, but this is the most widespread and most commonly encountered species. Coloration is highly variable, but a green and black checkered pattern is common. There is usually a light stripe along the lower sides of the body that is confined to the second and third rows of scales above the belly. The eastern ribbon snake *(T. sauritis)* is similar and also fairly common. It is very slender and has three well-defined light stripes, the lowest of which is confined to the third and fourth scale rows above the belly.

**Habitat and Remarks:** Garter snakes are closely allied with the watersnakes. Garters may be encountered anywhere, but prefer to be near water, such as a stream, ditch, pond, or wetland. They have a generalist diet, which has allowed them to become the most widespread snake in North America. They are one of the few snakes that may be found in urban developments, at high altitudes, and in far northern climates. In northern areas, this species is known for its tendency to hibernate in large groups. Garter snakes feed on frogs, salamanders, tadpoles, fish, small mammals, and invertebrates such as earthworms and leeches.

## Cottonmouth *(Agkistrodon piscivorous)*

**Distinguishing Characteristics:** Length up to 189.2 cm (74.5"). Thick-bodied semi-aquatic snake. When agitated, this species cocks its head back and displays the cottony inside of its mouth. The triangular head and vertical, catlike pupils separate this species from nonvenomous snakes. However, many snakes flatten themselves when threatened, making their bodies appear fatter and their heads more triangular. Young cottonmouths are usually strongly patterned with white-edged orange and brown bands. However, individuals usually become darker with age, and some appear to be almost pure black.

**Habitat and Remarks:** *This is an extremely dangerous snake. Do not handle it!* Cottonmouth venom is primarily hemotoxic (meaning it attacks the tissue primarily rather than the nervous system) and commonly leads to amputation of fingers and toes where bites occur. Cottonmouths, or "water moccasins," are almost exclusively found in swamps and sluggish streams of the southeast coastal plain. However, in northern parts of their range, they often migrate to nearby uplands for hibernation. Like other watersnakes and vipers, cottonmouths give birth to live young. The latin name "piscivorous" means fish-eating, but this species will feed on many animals, including fish, frogs, salamanders, lizards, mammals, birds, baby turtles, and even baby alligators.

## Alligator *(Alligator mississipiensis)*

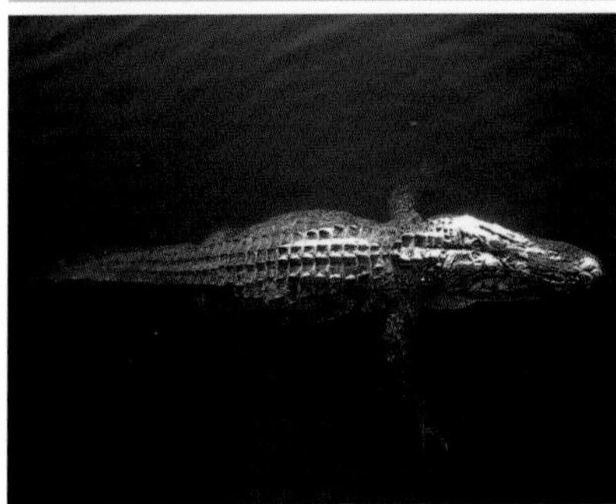

**Distinguishing Characteristics:** Length up to 5.8 m (19'). Weight up to 471.7 kg (1,040 lbs). The only large crocodilian in fresh waters of the United States. The broad, rounded snout separates this species from the American crocodile *(Crocodylus acutus)*, which is found only in southern Florida. Alligators are often seen sunning on the banks of water bodies or swimming with just their eyes and tail out of the water. Alligators make prominent slides down the banks of streams, lakes, and wetlands. Tail drags and claw marks are often evident.

**Habitat and Remarks:** Habitat loss and hunting reduced numbers of this species to the point that they were placed on the U.S. Fish and Wildlife Service's list of threatened and endangered species; however, alligators have recovered to stable population levels today. The American alligator inhabits sluggish streams of the Deep South along the coastal plain. It will feed on any animal it can get in its mouth, including turtles, fish, amphibians, mammals, birds, and invertebrates. This species lays its eggs in a nest made of decomposing vegetation, which the female protects. The alligator is an important ecosystem engineer in some areas, such as the Everglades. This large species excavates wallows that are often the only aboveground source of water left during drought summers. Adult alligators have no natural predators except for humans and perhaps introduced Burmese pythons *(Python molurus bivittatus)*.

# Mammals

## Signs of Mammals

Mammals leave some of the most easily noticed tracks and signs along our streambanks. These signs may range from the scratch marks of mouse claws running through mud to the landscape-scale changes brought on by beaver dams. In fact, for most of the mammals mentioned here it is easier to find tracks than the animals themselves, but learning to identify areas that are heavily used by a certain species can also help you to see that animal. If you find tracks, it's a good idea to take a picture or quickly sketch the print, making note of the number of toes, presence or absence of claws, length and width of the prints, shape of the heel pad, shape of the toes, presence or absence of webbing, and pattern in which multiple tracks fall. The species accounts have photos and discussions of tracks and sign for individual species.

### Short-tailed Shrew *(Blarina spp.)*

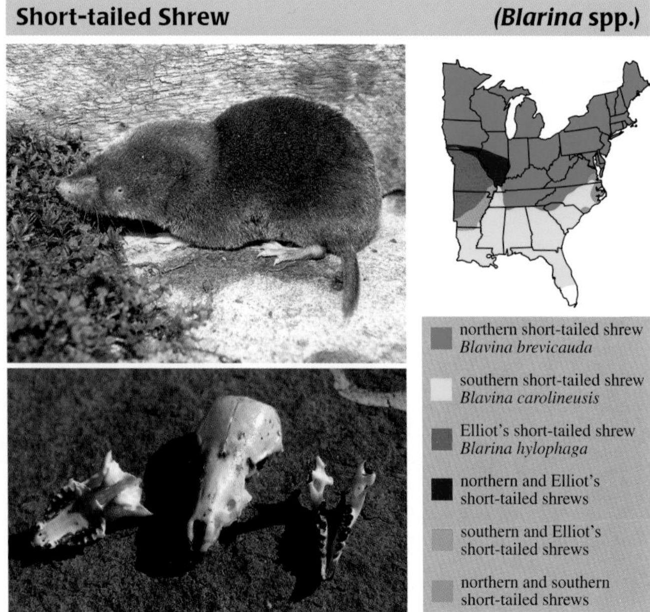


**Distinguishing Characteristics:** Length up to 14 cm (5.5"). Short-tailed shrews have velvety, gray fur very similar to that of a mole, but they lack the massively enlarged front legs of moles and are much smaller. The three short-tailed shrew species in the eastern U.S. are almost identical in appearance and are most easily differentiated by range. Short-tailed shrews have a strong, musky odor. Their skulls have a long braincase and sharp, dark-red, pigmented teeth.

**Habitat and Remarks:** Short-tailed shrews are one of very few mammals in the U.S. that are venomous. Their neurotoxin-laced saliva is capable of killing or paralyzing insects and worms but only causes swelling and pain in humans. This species is often seen when it is brought to the doorstep by house cats that refuse to eat it. Judging by the number of short-tailed shrew skulls found in barred owl pellets, this is one of the most abundant mammals in eastern forests. They forage on spiders, insects, slugs, worms, and other small animals found under forest leaf litter and in underground tunnels. Skulls and bones found in owl pellets are often the most obvious signs of the presence of these species, although the braincase is usually absent from the skulls. Bones of shrews may also be found in old, littered bottles where they often become trapped.

## *Myotis* species (*Myotis* spp.)

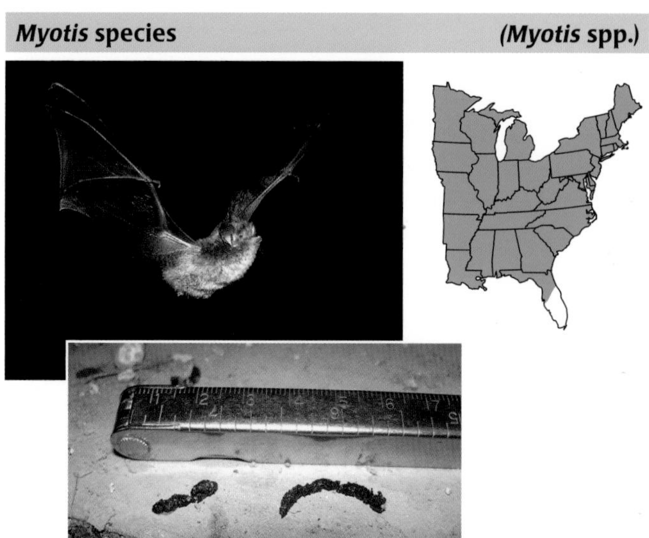

**Distinguishing Characteristics:** Length up to 8.9 cm (3.5"). This genus of bats, known as "brown bats" or "mouse-eared bats," includes several species that are extremely difficult to tell apart. They vary in color from dark gray to light brown. Their tail membranes lack fur and have sharp-tipped tragi (the small projection in the center of the ear). Caves, hollow trees, and bridges that are being used by bats will often have piles of bat guano or insect wings under prominent roosts.

**Habitat and Remarks:** Two species of eastern *Myotis,* the Indiana bat *(M. sodalis)* and the gray bat *(M. grisescens),* are on the federal list of threatened and endangered species, while others, such as the little brown bat *(M. lucifugus)* and northern long-eared bat *(M. septentrionalis),* are very common. Streams are extremely important foraging habitats and travel corridors for many *Myotis* species. In the winter, most *Myotis* hibernate in caves. In the summer, *Myotis* species have variable roosting habits. They may be found under the bark of trees such as shagbark hickory, in hollow trees, in barns, in attics, under bridges, or in caves. Diet varies by habitat and species, but they usually feed on flying insects such as moths, beetles, leafhoppers, stoneflies, caddisflies, mayflies, mosquitoes, and many other types of flies. Bats may live to be twenty-five years old. An emerging disease called white-nose syndrome has killed over one million cave-dwelling bats since its discovery in 2006. The genus *Myotis* has been hit particularly hard by this infection, which is apparently caused by a newly described fungus *(Geomyces destructans).*

## Eastern Red Bat *(Lasiurus borealis)*

**Distinguishing Characteristics:** Length up to 12.5 cm (4.9"). Males are orange-red and females rusty red. Fur of both sexes has frosted tips. This bat has white shoulder patches and black membranes. The top of the tail is fully furred.

**Habitat and Remarks:** This is one of the most common bat species found foraging over eastern streams. Red bats spend the day hanging upside down among the tree leaves. They often hang fairly low and within the south-facing edge of a forest. These bats have wings that are wide for their body size, and this, coupled with their reddish color, sometimes allows them to be identified on the wing. Red bats don't hibernate in caves like many other bat species. Instead, they usually migrate south or burrow into the leaves at the base of a tree. Red bats eat mostly flying insects, including moths, beetles, leafhoppers, and adult aquatic insects such as stoneflies, caddisflies, mayflies, mosquitoes, and many other types of flies.

## Deer Mice (*Peromyscus* spp.)

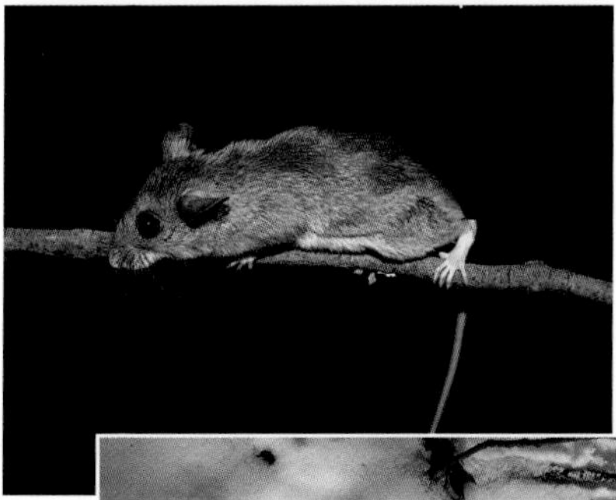

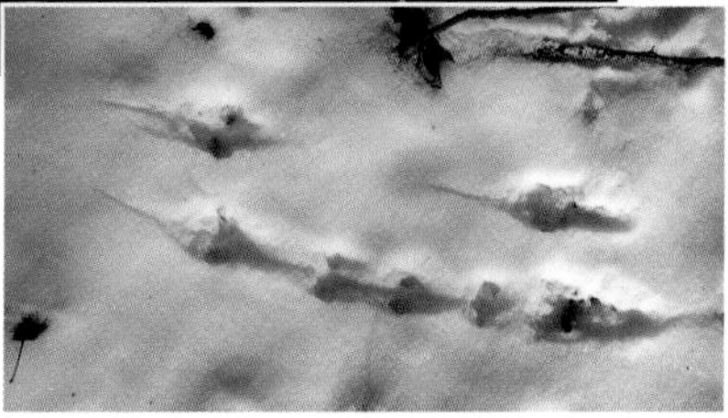

**Distinguishing Characteristics:** Length up to 17.8 cm (7"). There are several similar-looking members of the deer mouse genus, *Peromyscus.* Most eastern U.S. *Peromyscus* are brown with white underparts as adults (and gray with white underparts when young). They have large eyes and a tail covered in short fur. The white-footed mouse *(P. leucopus),* cotton mouse *(P. gossypinus),* and deer mouse *(P. maniculatus)* are the most common and widespread species found near eastern streams. The deer mouse has a tail that is more sharply bicolored than that of the white-footed mouse, and these two species are found throughout most of the East. The cotton mouse is quite large for a *Peromyscus,* has large hind feet, and is more common in the southeastern U.S.

**Habitat and Remarks:** *Peromyscus* species are the most common mice found in eastern forests. They live in hollow parts of trees, inside fallen logs, and under rocks. These species and several other types of mice often build nests by adding roofs to bird nests. During floods, deer mice, like many other small mammals, retreat to the safety of trees and shrubs. They feed on seeds, fruits, leaves, and insects. The most notable signs of their presence are gnawed seeds and nuts, nests, and tiny scats.

## Eastern Gray Squirrel *(Sciuris carolinensis)*

**Distinguishing Characteristics:** Length up to 50.8 cm (20"). Usually gray body and tail with white underparts, although populations of solid black or white animals do exist. This is the most common tree squirrel seen throughout the eastern U.S.

**Habitat and Remarks:** Gray squirrels inhabit various types of forests anywhere with mature trees. They build a nest primarily of sticks and leaves, which is usually found high up in the largest trees in the area. In northern areas they abandon the leaf nests and make their winter homes in the hollow parts of living or dead trees. Gray squirrels have a variable diet. While the majority of their diet may consist of acorns and hickory nuts, they also eat buds, the cambium layer of tree bark, fungi, fruits, bird eggs, and even carrion. They gnaw on bones and antlers for calcium, as will most rodents.

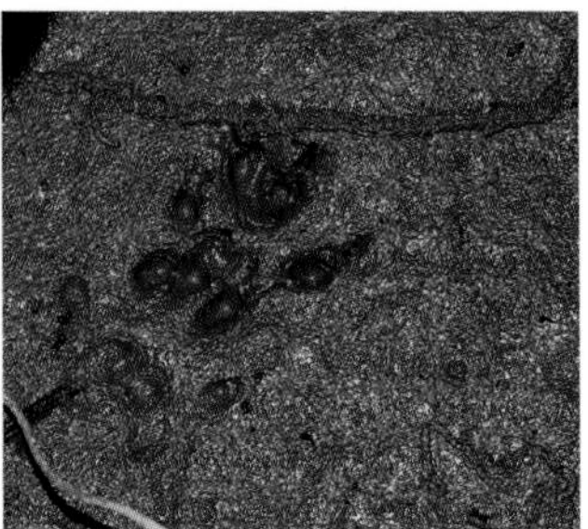

## Fox Squirrel *(Sciurus niger)*

**Distinguishing Characteristics:** Length up to 58.4 cm (23"). Noticeably larger than the gray squirrel. Throughout much of its range, this species is orange-tan with a relatively bright orange belly and very bushy tail. Southeastern U.S. populations are highly variable in color and may be various mixtures of black, gray, white, and orange.

**Habitat and Remarks:** In some parts of the Midwest, the fox squirrel is the most common tree squirrel; however, southeastern fox squirrels have been reduced to small, isolated populations in many areas. Habitat is highly variable throughout this species' range, varying from open pine forests in the south to oak and hickory forests and riparian osage orange forests of the Midwest. Like many tree squirrels, fox squirrels build large leaf and twig nests called dreys, and in the North they often abandon these nests for tree cavities in winter. Fox squirrels eat a varied diet of walnuts, hickory nuts, acorns, fruits, buds, bark, and insects. Like most rodents, they will gnaw on bones and antlers for calcium. In late summer or early fall, you may find freshly buried single nuts that have been stored in a sandy creek bank for winter by gray or fox squirrels. These single-larders usually consist of a small, circular mound with scratch marks radiating from the edges.

## Muskrat *(Ondatra zibethicas)*

**Distinguishing Characteristics:** Length up to 55.9 cm (22"). Medium-sized brown mammal with a naked, round tail.

**Habitat and Remarks:** Muskrats eat the roots and shoots of many aquatic plants, such as cattail, bulrush, and arrowhead. This species also eats a variety of animal matter, such as mussels, snails, fish, and crustaceans. There are numerous signs that indicate the presence of muskrats. Their tracks resemble a smaller version of beaver tracks, except that the much narrower tail often shows up in tail drags. Their pill-shaped scat may be found in prominent locations, such as logs or rocks that stick up out of the water. In running water, muskrats typically inhabit burrows in the streambank, but in still water, they build small lodges out of cattails and other vegetation. Feeding platforms, consisting of piles of vegetation and roots, are often found in slow-moving water. Huge "midden piles" of mussel and Asiatic clam shells sometimes accumulate at muskrat burrow entrances or near prominent feeding locations. These are some of the best places to look at native mussel shells.

## American Beaver *(Castor canadensis)*

**Distinguishing Characteristics:** Length up to 109.2 cm (43"). North America's largest rodent. Sometimes weighs more than 34 kg (75 lbs). Large, brown animal with a flat, scaly tail and protruding incisors.

**Habitat and Remarks:** Next to humans, beavers have more influence on stream ecosystems than any other North American mammal. Beavers dam small streams, which sometimes leads to the formation of large pond and wetland complexes. Beaver ponds add diversity to the landscape by providing deep water, fringe wetlands, dead timber (for insects and cavity nesters), and canopy openings. They also provide habitat for a huge number of other animals, including turtles, snakes, birds, fish, dragonflies, and many other invertebrates. The deep water of a beaver pond allows these rodents to build lodges with underwater entrances, but in swifter rivers, beavers opt to live in bank burrows. Well-worn beaver slides are used by a variety of ani-

mals, including deer and river otters. Beaver prefer to eat the inner bark of sweet, soft hardwood trees such as willow, cottonwood, and boxelder; however, they will eat a variety of other trees and vegetation such as giant ragweed and even corn where fields are too close to the streambank. Most often seen at dawn and dusk. Slaps its tail loudly on the water surface when alarmed. Beavers have five-toed rear feet that are about 15 cm (6") long, with webbing that usually shows up in the tracks. The front feet have only four toes and no webbing. The most obvious signs of beaver presence are their gnawings, dams, and lodges. Beavers also push up territorial markers made out of mud and debris that they cover with a strong-smelling musk (castoreum) secreted from their castor gland. Beaver scat resembles a ball of wood chips and sawdust.

## Virginia Opossum *(Didelphis virginiana)*

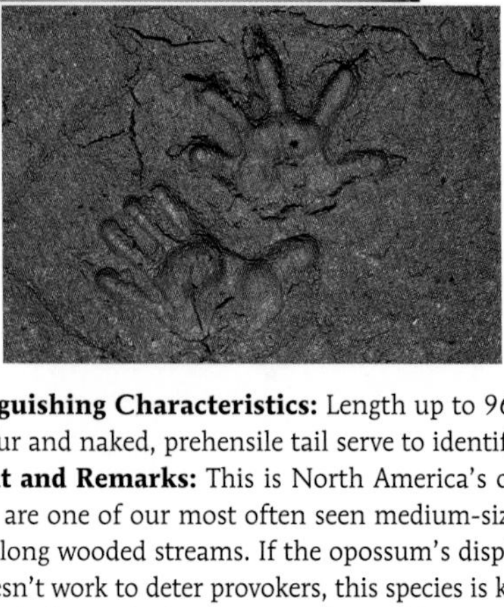

**Distinguishing Characteristics:** Length up to 96.5 cm (38"). The silvery-gray fur and naked, prehensile tail serve to identify this species.

**Habitat and Remarks:** This is North America's only native marsupial. Opossums are one of our most often seen medium-sized carnivores and are common along wooded streams. If the opossum's display of sharp teeth and hissing doesn't work to deter provokers, this species is known for its tendency to feign death, from which we get our phrase "play possum." Opossums eat a wide range of items, including fruit and invertebrates; however, they are most known for their tendency to feed on carrion such as roadkill. Opossums do not hibernate in winter, and their ears and tails often suffer damage from frostbite. Virginia opossums have an opposable "thumb" on each rear foot that extends almost straight back from the rest of the toes and shows up well in this species' tracks. Drag marks from its tail are also often evident in trails left in soft sand, mud, or snow.

## Common Raccoon *(Procyon lotor)*

**Distinguishing Characteristics:** Length up to 101.6 cm (40"). The bandit mask and ringed tail of this species make it difficult to mistake for any other animal in the eastern U.S.

**Habitat and Remarks:** Raccoons are curious, roaming animals that may be found in nearly any habitat but prefer to be near forest and water. They may even be seen in the middle of cities, where they often use storm sewers as travel corridors. This species spends most of the day sleeping, often in a tree cavity, on a large branch, or in a burrow. During prolonged cold spells raccoons hole up for several days at a time but do not go into a state of true hibernation. Raccoons are omnivorous. They eat animals such as crayfish, amphibians, small mammals, fish, insects, and mussels, and also feed heavily on fruit such as persimmons, pawpaw, and wild black cherry. The tracks resemble small human hand and footprints, except with claws. The scat is often deposited in conspicuous piles next to prominent trees or on logs that have fallen across streams. Scat is usually filled with crayfish parts, fish scales, or whatever type of fruit is in season.

## Mink (*Mustela vison*)

PHOTO BY CHRIS WILLIAMS

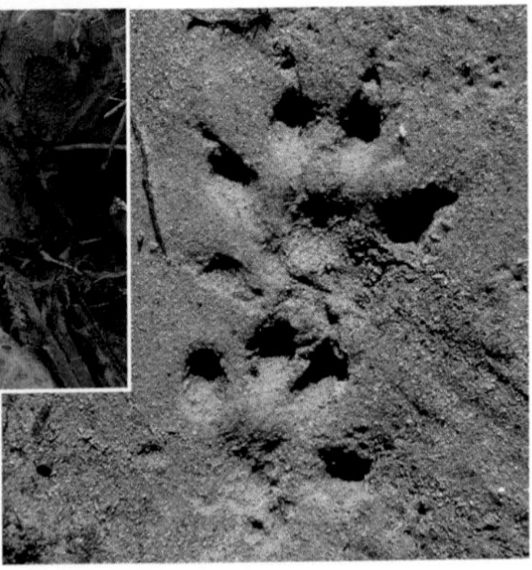

**Distinguishing Characteristics:** Length up to 68.2 cm (27"). Typically dark brown with a white patch under the chin, but coloration varies somewhat by region and between individuals. Lacks the white or yellowish underparts of smaller weasels.

**Habitat and Remarks:** Mink may be found along streams of any size. They can be almost as playful as otters at times, bounding, swimming, and sliding down snowy slopes on their bellies. Females typically stick to a small home range and only use a couple of burrows throughout the year, but males range along miles of stream and may require two weeks to complete a full trip throughout their home area. Mink feed extensively on muskrats and other small mammals. They also feed on fish, amphibians, crayfish, and other invertebrates. Mink mostly live in muskrat lodges or in bank burrows that they dig themselves or steal from muskrats after eating the inhabitants. Tracks are similar in size to those of tree squirrels but are more asymmetrical and have five toes on all feet (although the inside toe of each foot often does not register). Their bounding track pattern is similar to that of a miniature river otter. Scat is usually tight, twisted, and folded, like that of many other weasels, but the shape varies according to its contents.

## Northern River Otter *(Lontra canadensis)*

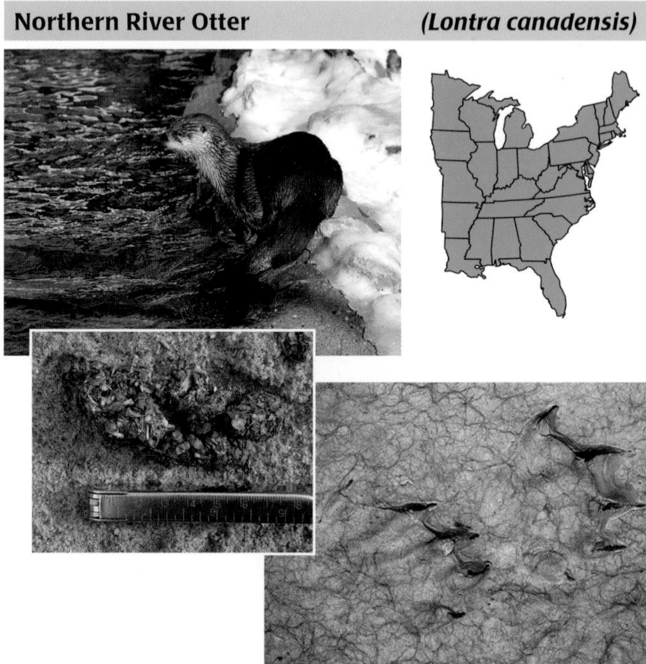

**Distinguishing Characteristics:** Length up to 111.8 cm (44"). A very skilled and playful swimmer, often found in groups. Unlike other eastern semi-aquatic mammals, river otters have a large, round, furred tail.

**Habitat and Remarks:** Otters are most often found in lakes and rivers; however, they also travel up into the headwaters of small streams and can even be found hunting in moist fields or pilfering fish from farm ponds. It is surprisingly easy today to find signs of this species in much of the eastern United States, where they had once been almost exterminated by trappers, pollution, and habitat loss. Otters feed primarily on aquatic organisms such as fish and crayfish, but also eat insects, mussels, frogs, and small mammals. They live most often in bank dens but can be found in natural cavities and beaver lodges. Good tracks show five toes in front and back, and webbing can often be seen in soft mud. Imprints of the toes are shaped like a Hershey's Kiss or a candle flame, and the tracks are quite asymmetrical compared to the similar-sized tracks of bobcats, coyotes, and beaver. Scat is often green or reddish in color and is usually made up of fish scales and crayfish parts. Piles of scat and smears of musk can often be found at prominent locations along streams, such as sand bars, prominent rocks, or at the mouth of a tributary stream.

## White-tailed Deer (*Odocoileus virginianus*)

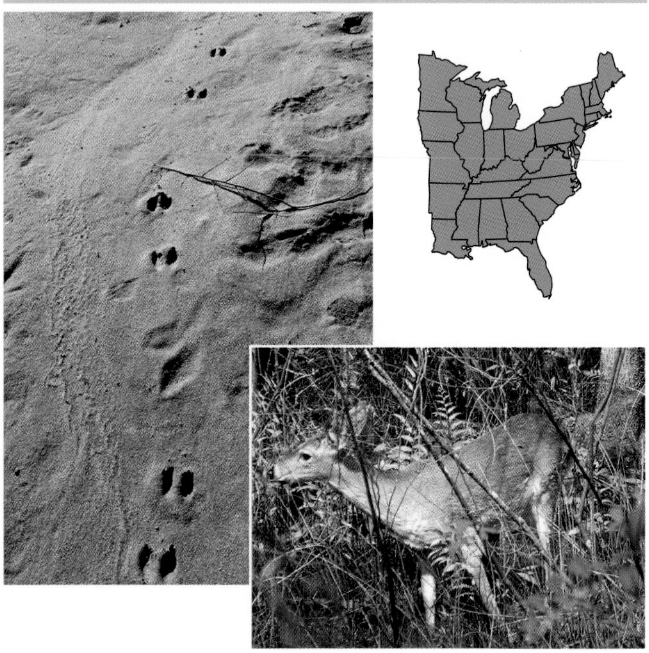

**Distinguishing Characteristics:** Length up to 244 cm (72"). Height averages 102 cm (40") at the shoulder. May weigh more than 136 kg (300 lbs). This species has white underparts and the rest of the body is brownish gray in winter and reddish brown in summer. The white underside of a bushy tail is often all that is seen as a white-tailed deer bounds into the brush with a nasal snort. This is the only native deer found throughout most of the eastern U.S., although, elk, moose, and several introduced foreign deer species can be found in certain areas.

**Habitat and Remarks:** White-tailed deer are browsers and grazers. A large part of their time is spent eating leaves, twigs, and bark from young trees, but they will also eat grasses and forbs. Where deer populations are high, one may see a "browse line" below which most trees have been stripped of their leaves. Deer slides are a prominent feature of most streams. These depressions are created when deer slide down the banks of a stream in order to cross it. Many generations of deer use the same slides and trails, so if you sit next to one of these ancestral slides at dawn or dusk, you are likely to see deer, beaver, raccoon, or many other species using the same convenient entry points into the stream. Deer tracks and scat are easily recognized through most of the year, and in the fall, "rubs" and "scrapes" are sure evidence of deer activity. A rub is an area where a buck rubbed its antlers on a tree (to remove velvet from the antlers and as method of marking territory) and removed some of the bark in the process. A scrape is an area (usually one to two feet in diameter) where the leaves have been scraped away by a deer's hooves to reveal bare dirt. Deer urinate on these spots to communicate readiness for breeding and a variety of other information during their fall rut (breeding season).

# Birds

## Signs of Birds

Birds leave quite a few distinctive signs of their presence. Some species, such as great blue herons and ducks, leave tracks that are easily recognized. Hawks and owls cough up pellets consisting of the hair, feathers, and bones of their prey. Woodpeckers excavate holes in trees for nesting or while searching for bugs, and all birds leave behind an occasional feather that may help you to detect their presence.

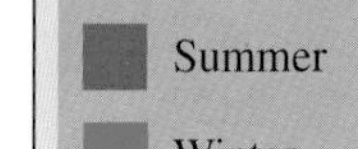

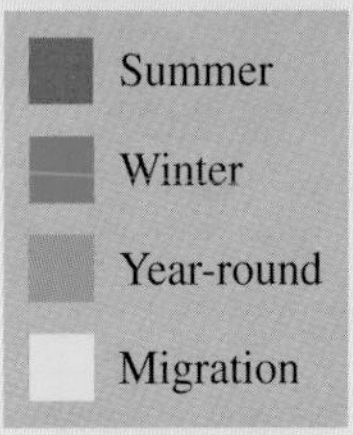

Summer
Winter
Year-round
Migration

**Key to the colors used in the bird range maps.**

*Top: Great blue heron tracks.*

*Above: An owl pellet.*

*Left: Pileated woodpeckers create distinctive rectangular holes in trees.*

## Prothonotary Warbler *(Protonotaria citrea)*

**Distinguishing Characteristics:** Up to 14 cm (5.5") tall. Large for a warbler, but still a rather small bird. This is a striking bird with a deep yellow-orange head and breast. They have greenish backs and steely blue wings without wing bars. The belly and undertail are white and there are some white spots in the tail. The song is a loud *tweet, tweet, tweet,* all on one pitch.

**Habitat and Remarks:** Can be found in wooded areas near water such as flooded bottomland forest, swamps, and the edges of large rivers and lakes. Their diet consists mostly of insects that they forage for on the bark of trees. They are one of only two species of warbler that nest in cavities. They are named for the clerks in the Roman Catholic Church whose robes were bright yellow.

## Louisiana Waterthrush *(Seiurus motacilla)*

© BRIAN SMALL/VIREO

**Distinguishing Characteristics:** Up to 15.2 cm (6") tall. Small brown member of the warbler family with a bicolored eye stripe (white behind the eye and buffy in front of it). Buffy wash on the belly and flanks. This species constantly bobs and wags its tail while feeding at the stream edge. It almost looks as though it is dancing to an inaudible rhythm. The call begins with a descending *chick weer weer* followed by a warbled jumble of notes. The very similar northern waterthrush *(S. noveboracensis)* lacks the buffy wash on the belly.

**Habitat and Remarks:** The Louisiana waterthrush, along with other members of the warbler family, returns early in the spring from wintering grounds in Central and South America. It can be found along the edges of lakes and even some of our smallest streams, often in dense woodlands. The nest is usually located at ground level in crevices or brush. Feeds mostly on invertebrates such as aquatic insects but also takes some small fish.

## Bank Swallow *(Riparia riparia)*

**Distinguishing Characteristics:** Up to 13 cm (5") tall. A small, slender swallow. They are brown on top and white underneath with a distinct dark band across the chest. They have long wings and a wedge-shaped tail. The voice is a trilling rattle.

**Habitat and Remarks:** As the scientific name suggests, this bird is almost always found near water. Bank swallows nest in colonies in the banks of streams, lakes, and ponds. The colony can consist of as few as ten nests or as many as a couple thousand. They dig long burrows into streambanks and line them with plant matter to make nests. Their diet consists primarily of insects that they catch in flight.

## Tree Swallow *(Tachycineta bicolor)*

**Distinguishing Characteristics:** Up to 14.6 cm (5.7") tall. A small, slender bird with a small bill and long wings. Males are white underneath with iridescent blue-green on the back and head. Tails and wing tips are blackish. Young females are more drab, with only a faint greenish sheen and perhaps only a few iridescent feathers. They are also white underneath, sometimes with a faint brown stripe across the chest. Older females are closer to the male in appearance. The song is a series of clear, repeated whistles: *twit-tweet . . . liliweet* and also *tsuwi tsuw*. The call is a high pitched-twitter.

**Habitat and Remarks:** This species is usually found where there are many dead standing trees with cavities, which it uses for nesting. This kind of habitat can often be found in areas with timber killed by beaver ponds. Tree swallows forage by catching insects in flight but will also eat some berries and plant matter to help make it through hard times. When they are not nesting, they form groups, sometimes containing hundreds of thousands of birds. They gather together just before dusk over their roosting site, forming a large, dark, swirling cloud. As the flock passes back and forth over the roost, large numbers of birds drop down until the cloud disappears.

## Cliff Swallow *(Petrochelidon pyrrhonota)*

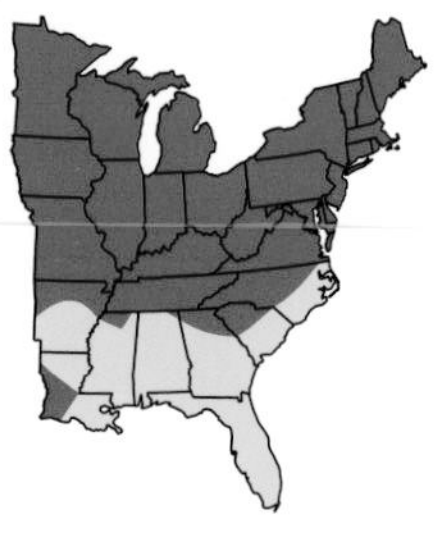

**Distinguishing Characteristics:** Up to 15 cm (6") tall. A small multicolored swallow. Cliff swallows have long pointy wings and square tails. The wings are dark bluish black and the belly is gray. They have brown faces with black caps and black throat patches. There is also a white patch in the middle of the forehead above the bill. They have a pale, buffy rump and a dark tail. The song is a squeaky twitter, and the call is a low *chur.*

**Habitat and Remarks:** Cliff swallows are often found near lakes, ponds, and rivers, where they nest in colonies on the cliffs that border these areas. They will also nest under bridges and on buildings. Their nests are built out of mud and placed on a vertical wall. Sometimes they will lay eggs in the nests of others in the colony, or they will move an egg from their own nest to another one. They consume insects that they catch in flight. When food is scarce, they will watch other birds in the colony and follow them to food. Away from the nest site, they call to each other to signal that food has been found.

## Indigo Bunting *(Passerina cyanea)*

**Distinguishing Characteristics:** Up to 14 cm (5.5") tall. Breeding males are bright, deep blue all over with black in front of the eyes. Females are plain brown with paler bellies and very faint buff wing bars. Occasionally they have some blue tinged feathers on the wings or tail. Non-breeding males become more brown, like the females, but usually retain some blue in the wings and tail. Their song is lively and high pitched, consisting of paired notes. Their songs are unique to specific areas. Birds living far apart have different songs, while those in neighboring territories often have nearly the same one.

**Habitat and Remarks:** Indigo buntings inhabit early successional habitat (brushy habitat that usually occurs when a cleared area begins to grow back into a forest) made up of shrubs and herbaceous plants, which often occurs where forests and fields meet. The thin riparian corridor of trees and shrubs left near streams in many agricultural areas provides extensive lengths of this brushy edge habitat; also, some streams are wide enough to let in sunlight and create their own forest edge habitat. Females place their nests close to the ground in a shrub or plant. Nests are constructed of leaves, stems, and bark formed into a cup and held together with spiderweb. Indigo buntings' diet consists of insects, seeds, and berries. They migrate at night and use the stars to find their way.

## Song Sparrow *(Melospiza melodia)*

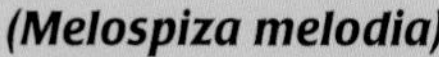

**Distinguishing Characteristics:** Up to 17 cm (6.5"). A medium-sized sparrow with a long rounded tail, broad wings, a short bill, and round head. They are streaky russet brown and gray, with bold streaks on their white chests and bellies that come together to form a central spot. The voice is musical, and the song usually starts with three or four repeated notes: *sweet, sweet, sweet*. There are many note variations.

**Habitat and Remarks:** Song sparrows inhabit a huge variety of open, brushy, and wet areas. They can be found at forest and lake edges, in marshes and fields, and in mixed woodlands and suburbs. Their diet consists mostly of seeds and fruit but is also supplemented with invertebrates such as beetles, caterpillars, and grasshoppers. Song sparrows nest in shrubs and pairs usually search for nest sites together. Males attract females with their song, and females are more attracted to males that show a greater ability to learn songs.

## Swamp Sparrow *(Melospiza georgiana)*

**Distinguishing Characteristics:** Up to 13 cm (5") tall. A small songbird with a gray chest, white throat, and unstreaked whitish belly. The wings and back are dark, rusty, and streaked with gray. They have a reddish cap and a gray face. The voice is a trill, sometimes simultaneously using two or more pitches. The call is a hard *chip*.

**Habitat and Remarks:** As the name suggests, swamp sparrows are often found in swamps, but they can also be found in a variety of other wetland habitats, such as marshes and bogs. Their diet consists of seeds, fruit, and aquatic invertebrates. Occasionally they will stick their heads underwater to catch prey. This species also has longer legs than other sparrows, allowing them to wade for food. They nest in dense grass, shrubs, or cattails.

## Eastern Phoebe *(Sayornis phoebe)*

**Distinguishing Characteristics:** Up to 18 cm (7") tall. A small flycatcher. It is dark grayish brown above with lighter underparts. They have no eye ring, and no conspicuous wing bars. The call is a very familiar *phee-bee*. They are also easily recognizable by their nearly constant tail wagging.

**Habitat and Remarks:** Eastern phoebes are found in open woodland and at forest edges, often near water. Their moss-covered nests are often found on cliff faces, bridges, and buildings near streams. Their diet consists mostly of flying insects and occasionally fruit. Phoebes are very solitary birds and are rarely seen with others of their own species. Mated pairs may roost together for a short period of time early in mating season but afterward do not spend much time together. This was the first bird banded in North America.

## Gray Catbird *(Dumetella carolinensis)*

**Distinguishing Characteristics:** Up to 22.9 cm (9") tall. A slender slate gray bird with a small black cap, black tail, and rusty coloration under the tail. They have broad rounded wings and rounded tails that they flip often. The song is very distinctive, sounding very much like a cat's meow. They are members of the mockingbird family, so they too copy sounds of other birds and put them together to create their own song; however, the catbird does not repeat each sound multiple times, as do mockingbirds and thrashers.

**Habitat and Remarks:** *Dumetella* means "small thicket," and that is where these birds are typically found. They nest in places with thick underbrush and vines. They are energetic and hop around in the brush but prefer not to come out into open spaces. They take short flights, low to the ground. Their diet consists mostly of ants, beetles, grasshoppers, and moths but they will also eat berries when they are in season.

## Red-winged Blackbird *(Agelaius phoeniceus)*

**Distinguishing Characteristics:** Up to 24.1 cm (9.5") tall. Males are glossy jet black with red and yellow shoulder patches. Females are brownish overall with dark, well-defined streaking and often a whitish eyebrow. Females look like very large sparrows but have the sharp, pointed bill typical of blackbirds. Males stay more visible on high perches while females tend to stay hidden in lower vegetation. Their song is a loud *konk-la-ree*.

**Habitat and Remarks:** Red-winged blackbirds are found most often in marshes, where they breed, but may be seen in virtually any wet or grassy habitat. Females build elaborate nests by wrapping wet vegetation around several upright plant stems, filling the inside with mud to make a cup, and then lining it with dry grass. They are ground foragers whose diet is made up mostly of insects in the summer and seeds in the winter. Red-winged blackbirds will sometimes use their long, sharp beaks to pry apart wetland plants at the base and eat whatever insects they might find inside. In winter they gather into huge flocks with other blackbirds and starlings to roost and search for food. This is perhaps the most abundant native bird in North America.

## Killdeer *(Charadrius vociferous)*

**Distinguishing Characteristics:** Up to 25 cm (10") tall. A lanky bird with long tail and wings. Killdeer are brown on top with a white belly and a white chest that has two black bands. The face is brown with black and white patches, and they have a buffy orange rump that is most visible in flight. The call is a loud *kill-deer!*

**Habitat and Remarks:** A type of shorebird, killdeer can be found on river banks, mudflats, and sand bars, but they are found in dry places too. They are a very vocal species and will call insistently when startled or when they fear their nest is in danger. Killdeer are ground nesters and will pretend to be injured to lead predators away from their nests. They feed mostly on invertebrates, such as worms, crayfish, and aquatic insect larvae, but will also eat seeds from agricultural fields and sometimes frogs and minnows.

## Spotted Sandpiper *(Actitis macularius)*

**Distinguishing Characteristics:** Up to 19 cm (7.5") tall. A medium-sized shorebird with a fairly long neck and legs. The back is olive-brown and the underparts are white with distinct dark spots in summer. The voice is clear and either *peet, peet-weet* or *peet weet weet weet weet.* They constantly bob their tails up and down as they walk. They also walk with a distinct teeter.

**Habitat and Remarks:** Spotted sandpipers inhabit almost any water edge. They are most commonly found on the shores of ponds, lakes, and streams in the summer and can be seen on ocean shores in the winter. They are the most widespread sandpiper in North America, and one of the two species most commonly seen along inland streams (solitary sandpiper is the other). The spotted sandpiper's diet consists of aquatic and terrestrial insects, and they are ground nesters, often nesting on large sand and gravel bars.

## Solitary Sandpiper *(Tringa solitaria)*

**Distinguishing Characteristics:** Up to 23 cm (9") tall. A medium-sized bird with moderately long neck and legs. The back and wings are dark with scattered white spots. Underparts are white, and the tail edges are white with thick, dark bars. They have a white eye ring. The voice is similar to a spotted sandpiper but higher in pitch: *peet* or *peet weet weet.*

**Habitat and Remarks:** The solitary sandpiper is found near water, at stream edges, by freshwater ponds, and in wooded swamps. They are most often found near forested areas but are sometimes seen in open freshwater marshes as well. They consume insects they find by probing into the ground or water. Although they are not truly solitary, they do migrate in much smaller flocks than other species of sandpipers. This species nests in trees, in nests that have been abandoned by other birds.

## Yellow-bellied Sapsucker *(Sphyrapicus varius)*

**Distinguishing Characteristics:** Up to 23 cm (9") tall. A medium-sized woodpecker. They are mostly black and white with barring on the back, a black wing with a long white patch, and a red patch on the forehead. The male also has a red patch on the throat, while the female's throat is white. Might be mistaken for a downy *(Picoides pubescens)* or hairy woodpecker *(P. villosus)*, but those species lack the large, solid white wing patch. The voice is a nasal squeal. Sapsuckers also drum distinctively at nesting sites with several quick thumps, followed by slower ones.

**Habitat and Remarks:** Breeding occurs in young forests and at forest edges near streams. Sapsuckers prefer to spend winter in semi-open woodland but will use multiple forest types. As the name suggests, a large part of their diet is tree sap, but they also consume fruit and insects. Their drilling for sap creates distinctive rings of small holes around the trunks of live trees. This is the only truly migratory species of woodpecker in eastern North America.

## Red-bellied Woodpecker *(Melanerpes carolinus)*

**Distinguishing Characteristics:** Up to 23.5 cm (9.25"). A medium-sized woodpecker with a long bill and short wings. They have black and white barring on the back, a bright red cap on the head and nape of the neck, and pale underparts with a very slight reddish tint. The rump is white, and there are white patches near the wing tips. The central tailfeathers are barred black. The most common call is a shrill, rolling, slightly rising *quirr.*

**Habitat and Remarks:** Can be found in forests and wooded suburban areas but are slightly more commonly found in areas near water. They nest in cavities in dead trees, or in dead limbs of live trees. The diet consists mostly of insects, but they will also consume nuts, seeds, fruits, and sometimes even lizards and fish. They forage by scaling the tree, usually staying on the trunk and main branches. They sometimes use cracks in trees and fence posts to store food for use later in the year, and to hold food while they use their beaks to crack it into pieces they can consume. They are capable of sticking out their tongue two inches beyond the tip of the beak. The saliva is sticky and the tongue is barbed, which helps them to catch prey deep within crevices in a tree. In some areas, up to half of all red-belly nests are invaded by the European starling.

## Pileated Woodpecker *(Dryocopus pileatus)*

**Distinguishing Characteristics:** Up to 50 cm (19.5") tall. A very large woodpecker. They are predominantly black with bright red crests. They have black and white striping on the face and a white stripe that runs down the side of the neck and under the wings. Males also have a red stripe on the face. The voice is loud and ringing, *kik-kikkik.*

**Habitat and Remarks:** Found in forests with large trees, often in bottomland hardwood forests. They eat ants and beetle larvae, as well as other insects, fruit, and nuts. Pileated woodpeckers make very large, deep rectangular holes in trees. Sometimes these holes can be so deep that they make small trees break and fall over. Other birds often follow them to feed at their excavation spots. Pileated woodpeckers nest in tree cavities, usually in dead trees. Pairs stay together all year long.

## Belted Kingfisher *(Megaceryle alcyon)*

**Distinguishing Characteristics:** Up to 33 cm (13"). A medium-sized bird with a large head, bushy crest, and large, thick bill. They have a white throat, collar, and belly, and are blue-gray above with a blue-gray band across the chest. The female has a reddish band across the chest below the blue one. In males, there can be some red in the bluish chest band, or on the flanks. The call is a loud, harsh rattle.

**Habitat and Remarks:** A common resident along streams, the belted kingfisher can often be seen hovering over the water and then diving head-first to catch a meal. They nest in burrows that they dig into the walls of streambanks. Often they will share these burrows with swallows, which dig rooms out within the tunnel walls to nest in. Their diet consists mostly of fish, but they will also eat aquatic invertebrates, insects, and small vertebrates. They fly the meal back to their perch, where they pound it to kill it. Kingfishers will also dive into water to escape being eaten by predators.

## Wood Duck *(Aix sponsa)*

**Distinguishing Characteristics:** Up to 47 cm (18.5") tall. The male is one of the most brilliantly colored ducks in the U.S. The orange bill and green head coloration remain even during the drab non-breeding plumage. The female's crested gray head and white teardrop are distinctive. Call is a nasal, ascending *oo-eeek,* and the wings whistle in flight.

**Habitat and Remarks:** Wood ducks require fairly large trees with cavities for nesting. They nearly went extinct because of unregulated hunting and loss of many bottomland forests to logging and agriculture. However, wood ducks have recovered and become the waterfowl species most often seen on our eastern woodland streams. This recovery is thanks to widespread nesting box installation, hunting regulation, and preservation of forested wetlands in conservation lands such as our National Wildlife Refuge system. Wood ducks are known to "parasitize" the nests of other females by laying eggs in them, which causes some nests to end up with forty or more eggs. Wood ducks feed on a variety of seeds, fruits, and invertebrates.

## Hooded Merganser *(Lophodytes cucullatus)*

**Distinguishing Characteristics:** Up to 48 cm (19") tall. A small duck with a long, sharp bill and a fan-shaped crest. The male's head, neck, and back are black. The crest has a large white patch within it that is bordered by black. The breast is white and is bordered on each side by two black stripes. The wings have a white patch, and the belly is brown. In the female, the crest is shaggy and brown. Both sexes have yellow eyes. The voice is a low grunt or croak.

**Habitat and Remarks:** Can be found in wooded streams and wetlands where they breed, but also in other types of wetlands during migration and wintering. This species typically nests in tree cavities. Mergansers are divers that look for their food underwater. They are even capable of adjusting their vision underwater to see more clearly and have a transparent third eyelid that helps them swim with their eyes open. Their diet consists of fish, aquatic insects, and crayfish.

## American Black Duck *(Anas rubripes)*

**Distinguishing Characteristics:** Up to 63.5 cm (25") tall. A large dark brown duck that looks superficially similar to a female mallard. The black duck's head and neck are paler than the body, and the wing has a bluish iridescent patch. In flight, they are very dark with the exception of heavily contrasting white wing linings. Their bills are olive green or yellow, and the feet and legs are reddish or brown. Unlike female mallards, black ducks lack the relatively broad white bars at the front and rear of their blue wing patch (though they may have a thin white trailing edge). Males produce a low croak, and females quack like mallards.

**Habitat and Remarks:** American black ducks inhabit a variety of wetland habitats such as salt marshes, bogs, and beaver ponds. They filter feed at the top of the water and tip up in shallow water to reach food beneath the surface. Occasionally they will dive in deeper water. Their diet consists primarily of insects, but they also consume seeds, roots, plant stems, crustaceans, some fish, and mollusks.

## Mallard *(Anas platyrhyncos)*

**Distinguishing Characteristics:** Up to 71.1 cm (28") tall. The male (drake) mallard is easily distinguishable thanks to a shiny green head with no crest and a white ring around the base of the neck. The body is grayish with a rusty brown chest, a white tail, and a yellowish bill with a black tip. Female mallards are mottled brown all over with white tails and yellowish orange bills patched with black. Both sexes have orange feet and iridescent bluish wing patches. On the flying female, this patch is lined on both sides with a white stripe. Male voice is a low *kwek,* while females quack rambunctiously.

**Habitat and Remarks:** The mallard is one of the most common ducks. It is found in all kinds of wetland habitats, including city park ponds. Like many other ducks, they filter feed at the surface, tip up to reach food below them in shallow water, and occasionally dive in deeper water. Their diet consists of aquatic plants, invertebrates, insects and larvae, seeds, and even acorns.

## Red-shouldered Hawk *(Buteo lineatus)*

**Distinguishing Characteristics:** Up to 61 cm (24") tall. A medium-sized, fairly robust hawk. They are brownish above, and adults have red patches on the shoulders, reddish barred bellies, and distinct black and white barred tails. The call is a screaming *kee-yer;* this is one of the most vocal species of hawk.

**Habitat and Remarks:** Red-shouldered hawks are found in open-canopied forests, usually near rivers, streams, and swamps. Their diet consists of small birds, reptiles, mammals, and crayfish. Often they can be seen in flight with crows. American crows regularly mob and try to steal food from red-shouldered hawks, but the reverse also happens. Sometimes the two species band together to chase larger predators, such as owls, from the hawk's territory.

## Osprey *(Pandion haliaetus)*

**Distinguishing Characteristics:** Up to 62 cm (24.5") tall. Ospreys have a wingspread between 1.4 and 1.8 m (4.5 to 6'). They are dark brown or blackish on the back, wings, and tail and have a white chest and belly. The head is also mostly white, but they do have a dark stripe across the cheek and down the back of the neck. Ospreys are very vocal and speak in sharp whistles: *cheep, cheep.*

**Habitat and Remarks:** Fish make up 99 percent of an osprey's diet, therefore they are almost always found near water, including ponds, lakes, rivers, and streams. They nest in large trees or on a variety of man-made structures such as telephone poles. The osprey is the only species of raptor in North America that will dive into the water for a meal. They will fly above the water, sometimes hovering over it looking for a meal, and then dive in feet first to catch it. They have rough pads on the bottoms of their feet to help them grip slippery fish.

## Bald Eagle *(Haliaeetus leucocephalus)*

**Distinguishing Characteristics:** Up to 109.2 cm (43") tall. The adult has a black body and bright white head and tail, with a huge yellow bill and yellow feet and legs. The voice is a loud scream during flight and a series of chirps while resting.

**Habitat and Remarks:** Bald eagles are found near mid-size and large rivers, wetlands, and lakes, where they breed and nest in nearby forested areas. Their nests are large, constructed of sticks, and placed in a large tree, often a pine. They use the same nests for many years, and nests can eventually consist of thousands of pounds of material. Bald eagles prefer fish but will also eat birds and mammals and scavenge for roadkill. They are soaring birds but will engage in dramatic flight displays when courting. A mated pair will fly to a great height, lock talons, and tumble nearly to the ground before releasing each other.

## Barred Owl *(Strix varia)*

**Distinguishing Characteristics:** Up to 61 cm (24") tall. Barred owls are grayish brown with large brown eyes and round heads. They are very fluffy in appearance. The chest is white with dark bars, and the belly is white with dark streaking. They have yellowish beaks and feet. The call is a series of eight hoots, usually in two groups of four followed by a very characteristic *aw* at the end of the second group: *hoohoo-hoohoo, hoohoo-hoohooaw* or "who cooks for you . . . who cooks for you all?"

**Habitat and Remarks:** Barred owls inhabit all types of forest, from wetlands and marshes to upland forest habitats. They prefer large, uninterrupted wooded areas. They consume small mammals, birds, reptiles, and invertebrates. One food of choice is crayfish, and they can be seen wading in water to catch them. Occasionally the belly feathers can appear pink as a result of eating large amounts of crayfish. As in all owls, the edges of their feathers are frayed to make them silent fliers. They are able to stalk and catch prey without being heard.

## Green Heron *(Butorides virescens)*

**Distinguishing Characteristics:** Up to 56 cm (22") tall. A short, squat heron with a long neck that it often keeps drawn back close to its body, a long dark beak, long greenish yellow or orange legs, and a shaggy crest that is most visible when the neck is extended. The back is dark with a blue-green tint, and the neck is dark chestnut. The voice is either a series of *kucks* or a loud squawking.

**Habitat and Remarks:** The green heron is a wading bird that can be found in marshes, ponds, creeks, streams, and swamps. It stands motionless over the water waiting for small fish, invertebrates, or frogs to come close enough to grab out of the water. Green herons also frequently use bait, such as worms or feathers, to lure their prey to within striking distance. They nest in trees, usually over water.

## Great Egret *(Ardea alba)*

**Distinguishing Characteristics:** Up to 97 cm (38") tall. A large, slender white heron. They have a long, straight yellow bill and long black legs and feet. The voice is a low-pitched croak or a *cuk, cuk, cuk*. The snowy egret *(Egretta thula)* is similar, except it is smaller and has black legs with yellow feet.

**Habitat and Remarks:** Great egrets nest in large groups with other species in trees over water and on islands. They can be found in swamps, tidal streams, lakes, marshes, rivers, ponds, and even flooded fields. They feed on fish, reptiles, amphibians, birds, invertebrates, and small mammals. Like other herons, they wade through shallow water to stalk their prey. They stand, leaning forward with their neck extended, and quickly stab prey with their long sharp beaks.

## Great Blue Heron *(Ardea herodias)*

**Distinguishing Characteristics:** Up to 121.9 cm (48") tall. Large gray-blue bird with a long neck and usually a white crest or white face. One variety found in the Florida Everglades area has white plumage, but it has yellow legs, which separate it from the great egret, which has black legs. Voice is a rough croak usually repeated several times, especially when alarmed.

**Habitat and Remarks:** Great blue herons spend their time stalking frogs, fish, snakes, and other aquatic creatures on the edges of streams and other water bodies. They sometimes venture into uplands in search of small mammals. This species is known for its tendency to nest in large colonies, called rookeries, which are usually found in large sycamores or other trees near streams or lakes. On the coast, they may be found in large mixed rookeries with other wading birds.

CHAPTER 6

# Stream Stewardship

The importance of our streams cannot be overstated. After all, our very lives depend on having clean water to drink. Yet we have a long history of misusing and abusing our creeks and rivers. We dump raw sewage and chemicals into them, turn them into ditches, and choke them with dams. Some of those problems have been partially rectified, but we still have a long way to go. Now we are also beginning to recognize more subtle, but equally serious problems, such as nonpoint source pollution and pavement-induced flash flooding. There are laws and agencies in place to protect streams, but in many cases, the efforts of volunteers and nonprofit groups who love a stream go much further to preserve our waterways and improve watersheds. It is everyone's responsibility to be a watchdog, an advocate, and, at times, a strong-voiced activist for our streams and rivers. Here's a little bit about how to do that.

## WHAT DOES A HEALTHY STREAM LOOK LIKE?

If you want to know what a natural stream ecosystem is supposed to look like, it can help to visit areas that are relatively undisturbed. It is exceedingly difficult to find a pristine stream with no evidence of impairment by human activities, but there are some areas that come close. Your best bet is to go to a large block of wilderness where the majority of a stream's watershed has been left intact, vegetated, unpaved, unmined, and unditched.

The state and federal agencies charged with managing water quality use intact watersheds as reference streams, to learn what types of plant and animal communities should inhabit a healthy stream of similar type. Usually, healthy streams have a stable channel, stable banks, and a variety of habitats that can be colonized by various organisms. In fact, the Environmental Protection Agency (EPA) and many other state and non-governmental groups have developed protocols for assessing stream stability and habitat quality. The characteristics of a healthy stream will vary according to what part of the country you are located in, so it is wise to seek out materials that are specific to your region and stream type. This is most easily done by typing your state name and "water quality," "stream monitoring," or a similar phrase into an internet search engine. Citizen monitoring groups, such as "Riverwatch" and "Waterwatch" groups, often have excellent training materials and may offer watershed-monitoring workshops.

*A small stream carrying sediment from a plowed field.*

While specific qualities of streams are naturally different depending on what part of the country you are in, there are some broad-reaching indicators that your stream is healthy, such as the following:

- Native vegetation is growing on the streambanks.
- A wide riparian corridor is present (the wider, the better).
- The banks are not highly eroded.
- If the stream holds water most of the year, there should be quite a bit of aquatic life (at least during the spring).
- The community of organisms that is present should be similar to that of a reference stream with a similar watershed.
- There is no evidence of channelization, gravel mining, or other highly destructive alterations.

Stream managers use a variety of organisms as indicators of stream health, including algae, diatoms, fish, salamanders, and aquatic invertebrate animals. Of these groups, invertebrates are probably the most widely used indicators of stream health. Some organisms, such as certain fly larvae and some snails, are very tolerant of pollution, while others, such as many kinds of stonefly and mayfly larvae, can't live in a degraded stream. Pollution tolerance values have been produced for many species that indicate how tolerant they are of poor water quality or pollution. Some species may be tolerant of low-oxygen conditions caused by sewage but intolerant of other types of pollution, so the best way to get an idea of the condition of a stream is to take the whole invertebrate community into account.

*This clubshell mussel is just one example of a species that was once widespread but now occupies only a few streams.*

The relative abundances of different types of invertebrates can tell us more about the health of a stream than the abundance of any one species. However, it is important to remember that different types of streams naturally have different invertebrate communities. For instance, a mountain riffle will naturally have many stoneflies and mayflies, while a low-gradient coastal plain river is home to more creatures like midge larvae and water boatmen. State and federal agencies have developed complex equations (usually called "macroinvertebrate biotic indices") that allow us to determine how similar the invertebrate community in a given stream is to the community that should be present in a natural stream of the same type and in the same region. These indices usually show whether water quality in a stream is poor, moderate, or high.

The usefulness of certain indices will vary by stream type, so it's a great idea to check out the tools and resources available from your state division of water, department of natural resources, or other agency in charge of monitoring stream health.

## HOW CAN I TELL IF MY STREAM IS DEGRADED?

Stream organisms are accustomed to living in a changing environment. They are able to withstand the changes brought on by floods, freezing, and beaver dams—yet humans have managed to negatively affect most streams in the eastern U.S. In some cases the changes are obvious. For instance, through the mid-1900s many streams were channelized into deep, straight ditches in the name of flood control and to drain large wetlands for agriculture. These streams usually still have berms of soil sitting next to their arrow-straight channels, even if a forest has grown up in what was once surrounding farmland. Channelization destabilized these channels, destroyed in-stream habitat for fish and invertebrates, prevented the stream from dropping sediment onto its floodplain, increased flooding downstream, and created an endless number of other detriments to the landscape. Yet it still occurs today!

In other cases, the impairments to stream health may not be nearly so obvious. For instance, nonpoint source pollution is contributing many different types of pollutants to the environment. Fertilizers, herbicides, pesticides, and automobile fluids (such as oil, gas, and antifreeze) are carried overland by storm water and deposited in our waterways. This problem is intensified where increasing amounts of pavement and channelized streams carry water quickly to our streams instead of allowing it to soak into the ground or into wetland areas.

There are many different types of challenges to stream ecosystem health, but here are a few indicators that your stream may be in trouble:

- The banks lack trees or other native vegetation and are slumping into the water.
- Areas of bare soil are washing sediment into the stream.
- Thick mats of algae grow in the channel during summer, indicating possible nutrient enrichment from fertilizers or non-functioning septic systems.

*Streams without a riparian buffer of trees are highly susceptible to bank erosion.*

- Your municipality has a combined sewer, many of which overflow during storm events, allowing sewage to escape untreated.
- Many dead fish float to the surface in the middle of summer due to low-oxygen conditions.
- The invertebrate community lacks taxa that are intolerant of pollution.

## WHAT CAN I DO?

Taking care of the tiny stream in your backyard may be just as important as participating in a trash cleanup in a big river. A lot of attention is focused on saving larger rivers—we can canoe in them and fish them, and we tend to notice when something wrong is being done to them. It's easy to forget that the water in our rivers was in dozens or even hundreds of smaller creeks before ending up in that river. The water in the river may have picked up eroded bank sediment from tributaries whose riparian vegetation has been clearcut, or it may have been filled with fertilizer from fields too close to small streams. Even if your local fifth-order stream hasn't been channelized, it may be receiving water from small channelized streams, ditches, and tiles. Therefore, the fifth-order stream may still end up with flash floods of high-velocity water that destabilize the channel. It is extremely important to work toward restoring the places where we can fish and swim, but health of the entire watershed is essential, and it can start in the rivulet in your backyard or local park.

*Above: An unvegetated section of stream has been seeded with native grasses, covered with erosion-control fabric, and staked with live willow stakes.*

*Left: A willow stake leafing out.*

You may choose to get involved with a citizen watershed watch group, or to volunteer with a state agency or nonprofit conservancy. There are too many streams out there for government agencies to protect by themselves!

Watershed restoration can begin in your own yard. A good first step is to avoid putting pesticides and excessive fertilizer on your yard. At least some of those chemicals will eventually end up being washed into a stream. A manicured yard produces no food for anyone, so pouring chemicals onto it equates to poisoning your water supply for no reason. Rain barrels, pervious pavement, and rain gardens can all help to slow down storm-water runoff.

*It is our responsibility to protect streams for future generations.*

Restoring a riparian corridor is one of the most important things you can do for our streams. Strips of riparian vegetation help to keep sediment from eroding into our water and sequester some chemicals and fertilizers before they make it into the stream channel. It is important to use native forbs, grasses, shrubs, and trees. Most states can provide you with a list of suitable species for your area, or you can just take a look to see what is growing next to a healthy local stream. One of the quickest ways to establish some streambank vegetation is with willow staking. All you have to do is cut a section of willow branch (in winter or spring, before the leaves are out) and drive it into the stream bank until several inches of the stake are below the level of the water table. In areas with harder soils, you can make a starter hole by driving a piece of rebar into the ground, wiggling it around, and removing it. Good stakes are typically one to two feet long, and at least a few buds should be sticking out above water or ground level. These stakes quickly develop roots that will stabilize streambanks, although in cases of severe erosion, more drastic measures are needed. Your local U.S. Department of Agriculture

Soil and Water Conservation District office may be able to provide you with some help pursuing large scale restorations. There are companies and books that are totally devoted to various types of stream restoration, and various institutions have funds available for stream and wetland stewardship.

The past stewardship of people who love streams has given us water to drink and some truly amazing places to swim, fish, revel, and contemplate. It is our responsibility to leave our creeks and rivers at least as nice as we found them for future generations. It is also our responsibility to inspire others to enjoy and learn from the natural world. There are few better places to show someone an interest-sparking wonder of nature than on the banks of a creek. By showing a friend, family member, or student the glorious colors of a rainbow darter or explaining that "bugs" can tell us how clean the water is, you may be starting someone down a path of lifelong love for the natural world. May you explore many streams, and may this book be a good companion on many creek-walking expeditions.

# Glossary

**Acuminate.** In plants, usually refers to a leaf tip that is distinctly pinched at the tip into a small point or "drip tip."

**Adipose Fin.** Small, fleshy fin located on the back of fish between the dorsal fin and the caudal fin.

**Alternate Leaf Pattern.** Leaf pattern in which a leaf occurrs singly at each node along the main stem (not paired with another leaf).

**Anadromous.** Refers to fish that return from the sea to breed in the rivers where they hatched.

**Astringent.** A substance that constricts body tissue, usually after being applied topically.

**Benthic.** Bottom-dwelling.

**Biofilm.** A film of algae, diatoms, bacteria, and other matter that often adheres to hard underwater surfaces.

**Bipinnate.** A leaf with leaflets arranged along side stems that grow opposite each other on a main rachis.

**Bract.** A modified leaf, often reduced in size, that is often associated with a flower.

**Carapace.** A bony covering on the back of an animal, such as the shell on a turtle's back.

**Catadromous.** Refers to fish that live in fresh water but travel to marine environments to breed.

**Catkin.** A cylindrical flower cluster, often drooping, with very small or no petals, made up of many usually unisexual flowers.

**Compound Leaf.** A leaf that is made up of several smaller leaflets.

**Cone.** A usually woody fruit with overlapping scales.

**Cordate.** Heart-shaped.

**Corymb.** A flower cluster in which the individual flower stalks grow upward from different points on the main stem to nearly the same height, giving the cluster a flat-topped appearance.

**Crest.** A tuft of feathers on the head of a bird.

**Deciduous.** A tree or shrub that loses its leaves seasonally.

**Dorsal.** Toward the top of the body.

**Dorsolateral Ridge.** A ridge located toward the sides of the back of an animal.

**Doubly Serrate.** A leaf in which the margins are doubly toothed, with small teeth upon larger ones.

**Elliptical.** Shaped like an oval.

**Ephemeral Stream.** A stream that flows only after precipitation, remaining dry most of the year.

**Evergreen.** A tree or shrub whose leaves remain attached through all four seasons.

**Forb.** An herbaceous plant that is not grasslike.

**Glabrous.** Smooth, free of hair.

**Gland.** In plants, a small dotlike protuberance on a leaf that usually secretes liquid.

**Glide.** The portion of a stream that begins at the downstream end of a pool and ends at the upstream end of a riffle.

**Herbaceous.** A plant with little or no woody tissue, whose leaves and stems die back to ground level over the winter.

**Hirsute.** Covered with coarse, stiff hairs.

**Inflorescence.** A cluster of flowers arranged on a branch.

**Intermittent Stream.** A stream that flows for only part of the year.

**Interstice.** A very small space or opening between two objects, such as between pieces of gravel in a streambed.

**Interstitial.** Situated in or related to an interstice. In streams this usually refers to the zone where water flows under the streambed through spaces between pieces of gravel or other substrate.

**Keeled.** Having a central ridge, like that on the keel of a boat.

**Key.** As it is used here, a winged, one-seeded fruit.

**Lanceolate.** Shaped like a spear point—rounded at the base, broadest toward the middle, and tapering to a point at the tip.

**Lateral.** Toward the sides of the body.

**Lateral Line.** An organ in aquatic organisms used to detect movement and vibration in surrounding water.

**Leaf scar.** The mark left behind when a leaf falls off a twig.

**Leaflet.** One of the small blades that make up a compound leaf.

**Lenticel.** A corky growth on bark that serves as a pore allowing air to reach inside a twig or branch.

**Ligule.** A small protrusion extending from the top of the leaf base where the leaf meets the stem. This is a useful structure in identification of grasses.

**Lobe.** A clear anatomical division, somewhat rounded, of a leaf.

**Margin.** As it is used here, the edge of a leaf.

**Monospecific.** Composed of one species.

**Obovate.** Egg-shaped, with the broader end toward the tip (refers to leaves).

**Operculum.** A lidlike structure, such as that found over the shell openings of some snails and covering the gills of fishes.

**Opposite.** Occurring in pairs at each node along the stem.

**Orbicular.** Flat and circular.

**Ovate.** Shaped like a longitudinal section of an egg, being broader at the base and tapering toward the end.

**Palmate.** Refers to a leaf with lobes or leaflets radiating from one central point; shaped like an open hand.

**Panicle.** A compound inflorescence made up of many racemes of flowers.

**Pedicel.** In plants, a small stalk that attaches flowers to the main stem of the inflorescence.

**Peduncle.** A narrow part by which some larger part of the body is attached, such as a stalk that supports a flower or the caudal peduncle that supports the caudal fin in fishes.

**Peritoneum.** Connective tissue that forms the lining of the abdominal cavity.

**Pinnae.** A leaflet or deeply cleft lobe of a compound or pinnatifid leaf.

**Pinnate.** Refers to a leaf with leaflets arranged along both sides of a main axis.

**Pinnatifid.** A leaf with pinnate lobes that remain attached to each other so that they are not actually separate leaflets.

**Plastron.** A hard plate covering the ventral surface of an animal, such as a turtle's breast plate.

**Pool.** A stretch of water where the depth is above average and the velocity of water movement is well below average.

**Pubescent.** Covered in small hairs, often having a velvety or fuzzy texture.

**Race.** Often used as a synonym for *subspecies*. However, *race* usually implies a less formally separated subgroup within a species, similar to the way the word *variety* is applied to plants.

**Raceme.** An unbranched inflorescence made up of a main stalk with flowers attached to it by a pedicel.

**Rachis.** As it is used here, the main stem of a compound leaf.

**Rhizome.** A horizontal plant stalk usually found underground that sends out shoots and roots from nodes.

**Riffle.** A part of a stream where the water is shallowest and flows at a faster velocity than the rest of the stream, creating small, rippled waves.

**Rostrum.** A nose or noselike protrusion located on the face.

**Run.** A part of a stream where the water is fast moving but deeper and slower than a riffle.

**Samara.** A winged tree fruit.

**Scute.** A hard external plate, such as the plates that make up a turtle shell.

**Serrate.** Having a toothed margin.

**Shrub.** A woody plant with multiple stems, less than 20 feet tall.

**Simple Leaf.** A leaf that is made up of a single blade.

**Sinus.** As it is used here, the space between two lobes of a leaf.

**Snag.** A dead, standing tree or piece of wood that sticks up from where it is partially embedded in a stream's substrate.

**Sp.** A single species (abbreviation).

**Spike.** A type of inflorescence in which a group of flowers is attached directly to a central stem (unlike racemes, in which flowers are attached via a pedicel).

**Spp.** More than one species (abbreviation).

**Subterminal.** Located not quite at the end.

**Swim Bladder.** A gas-filled organ that helps a fish control its buoyancy and stay at a specific water depth without wasting energy swimming.

**Terminal.** Located at the end of something.

**Tree.** A woody perennial plant with many branches supported off the ground by a single or forked trunk that is clearly dominant over other branches and is at least 15 feet tall and 2 inches in diameter.

**Tubercles.** Small, rounded, sometimes warty growths.

**Turbidity.** A measure of the cloudiness of a liquid. In streams, this is usually a measurement of the amount of suspended sediment and/or algae in the water.

**Two-ranked.** Existing in two planes when viewed from the end (like an X or + shape).

**Umbel.** Inflorescence that has flower stalks that arise from the stem at the same point (like an umbrella).

**Vein.** Threads of tissue in a leaf through which food and water pass.

**Venation.** The arrangement of veins in a leaf.

**Ventral.** Toward the bottom side of the body.

**Whorled.** Refers to a leaf arrangement in which three or more leaves occur at each node along the stem.

# References


## PLANTS

Brown, Lauren. *Grasses: An Identification Guide.* New York: Houghton Mifflin, 1979.

Duncan, Wilbur H., and Marion B. Duncan. *The Smithsonian Guide to Seaside Plants of the Gulf and Atlantic Coasts.* Washington, DC: Smithsonian Institution Press, 1987.

"Flora of the Southeast." University of North Carolina Herbarium. 2010. http://www.herbarium.unc.edu/seflora/firstviewer.htm

Foster, Steven, and James A. Duke. *Peterson Field Guides: A Field Guide to Medicinal Plants.* New York: Houghton Mifflin, 1990.

Little, Elbert L. *The Audubon Society Field Guide to North American Trees: Eastern Region.* New York: Alfred A. Knopf, 1980.

Martin, Alexander C., Herbert S. Zim, and Arnold L. Nelson. *American Wildlife & Plants: A Guide to Wildlife Food Habits.* New York: Dover Publications, 1951.

"Native Plant Information Network." Lady Bird Johnson Wildflower Center, The University of Texas at Austin. 2010. http://www.wildflower.org/

Newcomb, Lawrence, with Gordon Morrison. *Newcomb's Wildflower Guide.* Boston: Little, Brown and Company, 1977.

Peterson, Lee Allen. *Peterson Field Guides: Edible Wild Plants.* Boston: Houghton Mifflin, 1977.

"Plants Database." U.S. Department of Agriculture. 2010. http://plants.usda.gov/index.html

Preston, Richard J., Jr. *North American Trees,* 4th Edition. Ames, IA: Iowa State University Press, 1989.

Sibley, David Allen. *The Sibley Guide to Trees.* New York: Alfred A. Knopf, 2009.

"U.S. County-Level Atlas of the Vascular Flora of North America." 2010. Chapel Hill, N.C: The Biota of North America Program (BONAP). http://www.bonap.org/MapSwitchboard.html

## INVERTEBRATES

Evans, Arthur A. *National Wildlife Federation Field Guide to Insects and Spiders of North America.* New York: Sterling, 2008.

Dunkle, Sidney W. *Dragonflies through Binoculars: A Field Guide to Dragonflies of North America.* New York: Oxford University Press, 2000.

Merritt, R. W., K. W. Cummins, and M. B. Berg. *An Introduction to the Aquatic Insects of North America,* 4th Edition. Dubuque, IA: Kendall/Hunt Publishing Co., 2008.

Nikula, Blair, and Jackie Sones, with Donald and Lillian Stokes. *Stokes: Beginner's Guide to Dragonflies and Damselflies.* Boston: Little, Brown and Company, 2002.

Smith, Douglas Grant. *Pennak's Freshwater Invertebrates of the United States: Porifera to Crustacea,* 4th Edition. New York: John Wiley and Sons, Inc., 2001.

Taylor, Christopher A., and Guenter A. Schuster. *The Crayfishes of Kentucky.* Special Publication No. 28. Champaign, IL: Illinois Natural History Survey, 2004.

Thorp, James H., and Alan P. Covich, eds. *Ecology and Classification of North American Freshwater Invertebrates,* 2nd Edition. San Diego: Academic Press, 2001.

Voshell, J. Reese, Jr., with Amy Bartlett Wright. *A Guide to Common Freshwater Invertebrates of North America.* Blacksburg, VA: McDonald and Woodward, 2002.

## FISH

Breining, Greg, and Dick Sternberg. *Fishing Tips & Tricks.* Minnetonka, MN: Cy DeCosse, 1990.

Etnier, David A., and Wayne C. Starnes. *The Fishes of Tennessee.* Knoxville, TN: University of Tennessee Press, 1993.

Froese, Rainer, and Daniel Pauly, eds. "Fishbase." 2010. www.fishbase.org.

Hauptman, Cliff. *Basic Freshwater Fishing.* Mechanicsburg, PA: Stackpole Books, 1988.

Machacek, Heinz. "World Records Freshwater Fishing." 2010. http://www.fishing-worldrecords.com/

Page, Lawrence M., and Brooks M. Burr. *Peterson Field Guides: Freshwater Fishes.* Boston: Houghton Mifflin, 1991.

## REPTILES AND AMPHIBIANS

Behler, John L., and F. Wayne King. *National Audubon Society Field Guide to North American Reptiles and Amphibians.* New York: Alfred A. Knopf, 1995.

Conant, Roger, and Joseph T. Collins. *Peterson Field Guides: Reptiles and Amphibians: Eastern/Central North America.* New York: Houghton Mifflin, 1998.

Martof, Bernard S., William M. Palmer, Joseph R. Bailey, Julian R. Harrison III. *Amphibians and Reptiles of the Carolinas and Virginia.* Chapel Hill, NC: University of North Carolina Press, 1980.

## MAMMALS


Bowers, Nora, Rick Bowers, and Kenn Kaufman. *Kaufman Field Guide to Mammals of North America.* New York: Houghton Mifflin, 2004.

Reid, Fiona A. *Peterson Field Guides: A Field Guide to Mammals of North America,* 4th Edition. New York: Houghton Mifflin, 2006.


## BIRDS


"All About Birds." The Cornell Lab of Ornithology. 2010. http://www.allaboutbirds.org/guide/search

"Field Guide to Birds of North America." Whatbird.com. 2010. http://identify.whatbird.com/mwg/_/0/attrs.aspx

Dunn, Jon L., and Jonathan Alderfer. *National Geographic Field Guide to the Birds of North America,* 5th Edition. Washington, D.C.: National Geographic Society, 2006.

Peterson, Roger T. *Peterson Field Guide to Birds of Eastern and Central North America,* 6th Edition. New York: Houghton Mifflin Harcourt, 2010.

Sibley, David Allen. *National Audubon Society: The Sibley Guide to Birds.* New York: Alfred A. Knopf, 2000.


## ANIMAL TRACKS AND SIGN


Elbroch, Mark. *Mammal Tracks & Sign: A Guide to North American Species.* Mechanicsburg, PA: Stackpole Books, 2003.

Elbroch, Mark, with Eleanor Marks. *Bird Tracks & Sign: A Guide to North American Species.* Mechanicsburg, PA: Stackpole Books, 2001.

Murie, Olaus J., and Mark Elbroch. *The Peterson Field Guide to Animal Tracks,* 3rd Edition. New York: Houghton Mifflin, 2005.

Young, Jon, and Tiffany Morgan. *Animal Tracking Basics.* Mechanicsburg, PA: Stackpole Books, 2007.


## STREAM ECOLOGY, MONITORING, AND RESTORATION


Barbour, M. T., J. Gerritsen, B. D. Snyder, and J. B. Stribling. *Rapid Bioassessment Protocols for Use in Streams and Wadeable Rivers: Periphyton, Benthic Macroinvertebrates and Fish,* 2nd Edition. Washington, D.C.: U.S. Environmental Protection Agency; Office of Water, EPA 841-B-99-002, 1990.

Benke, Arthur C., and Colbert E. Cushing, eds. *Field Guide to Rivers of North America.* Burlington, MA: Academic Press, 2010.

Brookes, A. *Channelized Rivers: Perspectives for Environmental Management.* Great Britain: John Wiley and Sons, 1988.

Brown, T. Travis. "Tidal Creek Nursery Schools." *Wildlife in North Carolina* (September 2008): 14-19.

Brown, T. T., T. L. Derting, and K. Fairbanks. "The Effects of Stream Channelization and Restoration on Mammal Species and Habitat in Riparian Corridors." *Journal of the Kentucky Academy of Science* 69, no. 1 (2008): 37-49.

Giller, Paul S., and Björn Malmqvist. *The Biology of Streams and Rivers.* New York: Oxford University Press, 1998.

Harding, J. S., E. F. Benfield, P. V. Bolstad, G.S. Helfman, and E. B. D. Jones III. "Stream Biodiversity: The Ghost of Land Use Past." *Proceedings of the National Academy of Science* 95, no. 25 (1998): 14843-14847.

Lampert, Winfried, and Ulrich Sommer. *Limnoecology: The Ecology of Lakes and Streams.* New York: Oxford University Press, 1997.

Leopold, Luna B. *A View of the River.* Cambridge, MA: Harvard University Press, 1994.

Murdoch, Tom, and Marth Cheo, with Kate O'Laughlin. *Streamkeeper's Field Guide: Watershed Inventory and Stream Monitoring Methods.* Everett, WA: The Adopt-A-Stream Foundation, 2001.

Palmer, Tim. *America by Rivers.* Washington, DC: Island Press, 1996.

Rosgen, Dave. *Applied River Morphology.* Pagosa Springs, CO: Wildland Hydrology, 1996.

Simpson, P. W., J. R. Newman, M. A. Keirn, R. M. Matter, and P. A. Guthrie. *Manual of Stream Channelization Impacts on Fish and Wildlife.* Washington, D.C.: U.S. Fish and Wildlife Service, Office of Biological Services, 1982.

Vannote, R. L., G. W. Minshall, K. W. Cummins, J. R. Sedell, and C. E. Cushing. "The River Continuum Concept." *Canadian Journal of Fisheries and Aquatic Science* 37 (1980): 130–137.

Wessels, Tom. *Reading the Forested Landscape: A Natural History of New England.* Woodstock, VT: Countryman Press, 1998.

## GENERAL RESOURCES

Animal Diversity Web. University of Michigan Museum of Zoology. http://animaldiversity.ummz.umich.edu/site/index.html

Integrated Taxonomic Information System. http://www.itis.gov/

U.S. Geological Survey National Hydrography Dataset. http://nhd.usgs.gov/

U.S. Geological Survey Real-Time Water Data for the Nation. http://waterdata.usgs.gov/nwis/rt

# Acknowledgments

First and foremost we would like to thank our parents: Tim and Jayne Brown and Royce and Kaye Delk. We are so thankful to have had the opportunity to grow up in the country and spend our childhoods playing in and learning to respect the natural world. We also thank them tremendously for the help they provided watching our girls so we could finish this book.

Thank you to all of the teachers and family members who inspired both of us along the way. Thank you to Elaine Wilson (Shanda's aunt) for being my very first wildlife "educator." The summers spent as a child, combing creek beds for "pretty rocks," fishing, swimming, and hiking will forever be some of my most treasured memories. Thank you to Frances Carter (Shanda's high school biology teacher) for nurturing the love of nature that was already in me, and encouraging me to follow that path. Also, for providing me with the most amazing and relevant experience thus far in my life to really make a difference as far as the environmental world is concerned.

Thank you to Mrs. Smiley, who helped to start me (Travis) down the natural path at an early age. Thank you to Scott Eldridge and the whole Eldridge clan, who taught me (Travis) a lot about a lot of things. Thank you to many of the professors at Murray State University, especially Dr. Terry Derting, Dr. Claire Fuller, Dr. Steve White, Dr. Edmund Zimmerer, Dr. David White, Dr. Tom Timmons, Dr. Howard Whiteman, Dr. Ralph Thompson, Dr. Tom Kind, and Dr. Haluk Cetin. This book holds influences from all of you. We thank all of the biologists with whom we've spent time sampling streams and rivers, and especially Lee Droppelman, Scott Slankard, and Robert Oney for reviewing this book. A special thanks to Mark Allison and Kathryn Fulton at Stackpole Books for making this possible.

# Index